Teaching Mathematics in Rudolf Steiner Schools

How to become holistic
and imaginative

Volume 1
Up to age 14

Ron Jarman

Teaching Mathematics © 1998 Ron Jarman

Published by Hawthorn Press, Hawthorn House, 1 Lansdown Lane, Stroud, Gloucestershire, GL5 1BJ Tel. (01453) 757040 Fax. (01453) 751138
www.hawthornpress.com

Ron Jarman is hereby identified as author of this work in accordance with Section 77 of the Copyright, Designs and Patent Act, 1988. He asserts and gives notice of his moral right under this Act.

Copyright All rights reserved. No part of this publication may be reproduced, stored in a retrieval system, or transmitted, in any form or by any means (electronic or mechanical, through reprography, digital transmission, recording, or otherwise) without the prior permission of the copyright holders. Material not for resale.

Edited by Matthew Barton
Typeset at Hawthorn Press by Frances Fineran
Cover image by Abigail Large
Cover design by Bill Hicks

First edition 1998
Reprinted in 2001 by the Bath Press, Bath

Acknowledgements
The author would like to thank Barbara Low and Jonathan Swann for reading through the script and making suggestions and the latter for checking answers to examples – but for any remaining errors the author is to blame. The author would also particularly like to thank Elisa Wannert for her cartoons.

A catalogue record of this book is available from the British Library Cataloguing in Publication Data

ISBN 1 869 890 92 2

Contents

Foreword by Chris Clarke vii

Author's Preface xi

Introduction: Mathematics and the Mystery Schools

    1. Greek teachings xvii
    2. Mathesis xxiv
    3. A holistic overview xxvi
    4. Mathematics and paths into the spiritual xxviii

Chapter 1: Mathematics and Education

    1. Its invisible nature 1
    2. School mathematics today 4

Chapter 2: What Stimulates the Child

    1. The child up to the age of 6 or 7 9
    2. Early arithmetic (especially Class 1) 11
    3. Stimulation of mathematical activity up to the age
       of 8 or 9 (going on from Class 1 towards Class 3) 22
    4. Working with Class 3 30

Chapter 3: Suitable examples for children's written arithmetic in Classes 1 to 3 (6 to 9 years old)

    1. Class 1 37
    2. Class 2 44
    3. Class 3 46
    4. Practice periods 49

Chapter 4: The Heart of Childhood

1. Child development 51
2. Arithmetic 53
3. Freehand geometry 54
4. The 4 kinds of integers (whole numbers) 56
5. Curricular aims for mathematics in Classes 4 and 5
   (ages 9-14) 57
6. Developmental summary 59

Chapter 5: Suitable examples in Classes 4 and 5 (9-11 year olds)

1. Class 4 Fractions 63
2. Class 4 Decimals 72
3. Class 4 Drawing 74
4. Class 4 Arithmetic 76
5. Discovery situations 80
6. Class 5 Geometry 81

Chapter 6: Class 6 Mathematics (ages 11-12)

1. The approach to puberty 87
2. Money problems and the approach to algebra 89
3. Examples for Class 6 (numerical and algebraic) ..93
4. Practical constructions and exact Deduction Geometry 95

**Chapter 7: Arithmetic and Algebra in Classes 7 and 8
(children of 12 to 14)**

1. Becoming a teenager 115
2. Teaching algebra 117
3. Equations and the problems they solve 126
4. Identities 128
5. Areas and volumes 131
6. Other arithmetical work including powers and
   square roots for Class 7 142
7. Simultaneous equations; also the dissolution of brackets
   (Class 8 topics) 146
8. A further possible topic in Class 8 150

Chapter 8: Geometry in Classes 7 and 8 (ages 12 to 14)

1. Dimensional development 153
2. Class 7 geometry 157
3. Geometrical examples for Class 7 .163
4. Class 8 geometry (i) loci 169
5. Class 8 geometry (ii) solids 173
6. Geometrical examples for Class 8 .182
7. Perspective drawing 186

Chapter 9: Statistics and Graphs

1. Their value and place in the world 193
2. Statistics and statistical graphs in education 198
3. Algebraic graphs 203

Chapter 10: A Summary of a modern Waldorf Curriculum in Mathematics

1. The original curriculum 1919-1925 and subsequent development 209
2. The main ingredients, class by class, of the curriculum in mathematics 213
3. How much time needs to be allocated to mathematics in school and in homework? 220

Chapter 11: Looking forward – to the Upper School and beyond

1. Upper school work 225
2. Mathematics and initiation 232
3. Astronomy 235

Appendix: More on mathematics and initiation 247

Chapter Notes and References 253

Foreword
by Chris Clarke

Mathematics is a tricky subject to teach. Children can switch off so easily from the subject that it becomes an ogre to be feared. Why should this be when Mathematics can also portray great beauty, be such fun with its puzzles and brain-teasers as well as being an essential 'language' and lifeskill?

Recently, British Government ministers expressed great concern again that children were falling short of the standards required for Mental Arithmetic. As if to prove the point, an education minister said '7 x 8 = 54' in a recent television interview!

'The aim of every teacher,' says Ron Jarman, 'is to bring about a confident capacity in those he is teaching...' So much of the mathematics teaching I observed began with the 'cold abstraction' little related to the world of the child. For example a group of 4 year olds was asked by their Reception class teacher to draw and stick pictures onto a frieze to indicate preferences for food – hopefully to illustrate the terms 'more than' and 'less than'.

Should children be taken into this area of abstraction so soon? What differences do *they* see, in their private worlds, perhaps relating to colour, movement and texture – important precursors of a later numerical understanding? How do *they* feel? What would a Mathematics education taking into account the feelings of young children really amount to?

We must begin with where the children are. By contrast, my own Class I (Waldorf seven year olds) are currently comparing the strides of Gnomes, Elves, Dwarves and Giants as they cross a stream by way of twelve stepping stones. The 'longer-legged' step on every other, or every third or fourth stone (12 = 6 x 2, 4 x 3 or 3 x 4). The humble short-legged Gnome has to step on every one (12 = 12 x 1) but the Giant can get across in two great strides crossing six stones with each one (12 = 2 x 6). The experience of trying this ourselves using sawn logs on the classroom floor makes a useful follow-up in movement to a colourful fairy story.

If we offer our children a 'pile of stones', what can they do with such abstractions? What children need is 'loaves of bread', real food for thought. Stones in Mathematics represent pure abstraction, such as 12 = 4 x 3. The images created by the story and involving fairy folk as they struggle to outdo the other by the length of their stride together with the colourful pictures lovingly created in Main Lesson Maths books are 'bread' – one of the most palatable foods. Children in their early years work best with images. Images can be 'held' in the child's imagination, relating thought and feeling. Like the dough in bread they can 'rise' or expand as the image is developed in the imagination of the child.

The importance of *imitation* is stressed at the pre-school stage. This continues into the school years where we also find *story, picture* and *image* as well as *gesture* playing an important part. A focus on these properly precedes *abstraction*. The three 'pillars' of *thinking, feeling* and *willing* however are central to all Waldorf practice. Maths is properly a subject of the *will*. Ron Jarman writes 'The will has to be brought into the thinking'.

The world of children is alive and the most essential aspect of children is 'spirit'. Children should meet the life in Maths and not cold, hard abstractions. Ron Jarman breathes life into this subject in line with good Waldorf school practice: Arithmetic arises out of the rhythmic system of the body, geometry out of the limbs and bones. So we sing, clap and dance to the rhythm inherent in number. Thus, potentially dull tables come alive.

Here then, is an holistic approach to Maths teaching. The author gives a spiritual context for the origins of the subject. Numerical relationships, like so many things in life, have their birth in the soul. The author begins with this, and, as with the Waldorf curriculum as a whole, also illustrates the development of Mathematical ideas in their historical context.

The graphic overview of the origins and development of mathematics offers inspiration. This, in turn, helps the teacher reach a deeper understanding in their pupils. Mathematics as presented here is a subject to be worked at by teacher and pupil alike: to read, practise, reflect on, assimilate and so to understand.

In essence, Mathematics is about relationships, numerical relationships and the making of connections. As a child beholds the universe it looks for connection with the elements of that universe as well as with the contents of his or her own mind and soul: a connection with the innermost Self. This was graphically illustrated by six year olds who walked into and out of a spiral and discovered not only something about spirals and reversals but also about the need to work together as a group in order to have that experience repeated. Here the spiral can be said to be a development of the circle: the circle is broken as one member ventures ever closer to the centre while others follow on, only to return to the circle once the centre has been reached and experienced.

By contrast, there are times when children's discoveries need the wise counsel of an adult, such as when a group of ten year olds were asked to explain the delay between a lightning flash and the associated clap of thunder. One 'bright spark' suggested that the eyes saw the flash before the ears got the message as they were set further forward on the head!

As mind takes over the digestion of mathematical facts and the experience of the individual, abstractions begin to emerge. These are necessary for the sharing and communication of ideas. If abstraction is required or encouraged too early however, children lose the connection with themselves leading to a loss of meaning. Disenchantment with Mathematics and the resulting poor standards of achievement may stem from early abstraction encouraged by a fairly rigid syllabus such as the National Curriculum Programmes of Study.

The use of textbooks and television may also encourage this abstraction because they ignore the social dimension of learning. Every teacher knows in his or her heart that children learn best in conversation with others, especially with an enthusiastic teacher.

During the time I re-trained as a Waldorf teacher and before I took over my class of six and seven year olds at Wynstones School, I warmed to the skill, insight and humanity of Ron Jarman. His understanding struck chords in me as his words connected with the many experiences of my own, now lying like so many 'skeletons in cupboards'. These had accumulated during thirty years as primary class teacher and headteacher in the state system. My preference now is to follow my intuition when deciding material, – 'reading' the children's needs and avoiding text books wherever possible, whilst teaching instead from my own life experience. For example, 'I needed to cut a stick into smaller pieces for firewood. The "one" became two and the "two" became "four"'. The 'whole' is primary in our experience: 'work from the whole to the parts' says the author.

'The best games to play with children are those made up on the spot out of the child's and parents' imagination, utilizing the things and events around them'. Freed from the constraints of a rigid syllabus I can cultivate my own insight into what the children need to know and how to address this. Here I recall a favourite game of Class I that involves each child bouncing and catching and clap-catching and pat-bouncing 'Golden' (tennis) balls ten, twenty and thirty times or more in various ways. This 'brings magical energy' into the hands to give them the power to climb up imaginary steps to escape from the garden of the 'Enchantress'. Counting the catches or bounces in tens to reckon up our credit for the escape from the garden is both great fun and great mathematical experience.

An overview of the way in which children develop is given. Throughout his book another principle is championed: 'To anticipate with a light touch in a younger class something which will be developed in an older one is the stuff of which real education is made.' 'Sowing seeds' for a 'later harvest' plays an essential part in the 'four rules' of arithmetic as, for example, when the teacher encourages children to put numbers in their correct 'home', so anticipating 'place value'. Or offers them something to think about for a later lesson on 'long multiplication'.

There is so much the teacher can learn from this book that I for one will spend many happy hours poring over its contents. Both mainstream and Steiner school teachers will be enthused by this holistic approach to Mathematics.

Ron Jarman's jaunty style makes for easy reading and assimilation. Indeed the book is rare among teachers' books: it is compulsive reading and conveys the magic of good Maths teaching.

March 1998

Preface

Alive to what radiates into them through all their senses, young children approach their school life with expectancy. The world is full of interest to them: activities in which they want to participate, all sorts of things to learn about, adults and other children to meet and share with, the vitality and beauty of the world of nature and often its stillness too. Instinctively they feel that gifts from the world's wisdom await them. That their source is something of a mystery and will reveal as yet hidden joys and dangers, enhances their expectant mood. Children have an inner sense that life is a challenge, and a desire to meet it creatively. To help them gain quiet faith in themselves and in what lies deep within them is the task which parents and teachers, acting out of love in the true sense of the word, have before them.

The surrounding world, stimulating in every way though it is, cannot by itself bring knowledge to children. Only their own inner activity, responding to and uniting with what the world presents, can do that. What is it that exists within? An earlier age spoke of the human psyche. Today we can justifiably speak of the soul provided that we can clearly describe its activities – and it has three of them. First we have the impulses to act and to determine the course of our actions, so the soul can affect, indeed change the world about us. Secondly, the world affects us, and to it the soul responds with manifold *feelings* – of wonder, distaste, joy, fear, curiosity, affection, boredom, enthusiasm, envy, gratitude, etc. Thirdly, to whatever we perceive through our physical senses or in inward contemplation of ourselves, the soul responds in *thinking*. This is no automatic reaction. At every moment, in fact, the soul can engender or repress these three activities.

If we pass by a mountain in our travels, for example, our soul can choose to ignore it as a mere lump, or fill itself with wonder at its beautiful shape, its colours, its forested slopes and streams, and feel joy in following the flight of its birds or the clouds drifting past its peak. Whether we also think about the mountain's origin – the weathered result of the slow upward buckling of ancient sedimentary rocks, themselves created through age-long deposits of the bodies of small sea creatures, or ancient plant forms perhaps – is again up to us. The soul neither *has* to feel nor think, if it is so disposed. Nor does it have to initiate action. One traveller may notice smoke and fire beginning to grow at the edge of a wood and do nothing. Another observing it and also thinking of its possible cause by careless campers will take action and inform the local fire fighting service.

The human soul then, is that in us which thinks, feels and wills. It is not of a physical nature. Nor can these three activities be physically perceived. Not even the greatest brain surgeon or cranial investigator assisted by the most refined scientific equipment, can see thinking taking place. For thinking activity does not take place in the brain. Certain *results* of thinking, or its absence, are perceptible there, as well as the effects of the activity of our sense organs, but that is another matter. We know that people think, have all manner of feelings and carry out all kinds of will impulses, but we have to go beyond mere physiological investigation to be aware of the existence of the soul.

An educator who has no awareness of the non-physical nature of the soul will be prone to tackle his work with the positivistic, reductionistic attitude developed in the modern theoretical, materialistic sciences. He* will also not be able to understand the nature of the individuals before him. We are all aware that we possess a unique individuality, whose existence we acknowledge whenever we use the word 'I'. But how this is related to our lives within our earthly bodies has to remain an unfathomable mystery if we cannot understand that the soul, though not material, is nevertheless absolutely real. The individuality, the 'I', the human spirit (all equivalent terms), exists within us as the captain of this soul.

In many of life's decisive moments this spirit of ours has to determine how much to rely on what its three lieutenants variously advise it. To rely solely on one of them may be to court disaster. Take the case of marriage. Just to be swayed by emotional attraction and compatibility of sexual urges – part feeling and part willing – will lead to the wish for a new, different partner before many months have passed. On the other hand, sole reliance on a clear critical assessment of the proposed partner's talents and activities (similar interests, health, educational background, artistic or sporting talent, wealth, temperament, political views, ability to cook or mend furniture and so on) could be equally disastrous. The heart's feelings – the real deep feelings of the soul – need to be listened to first, but clear thinking about what being married to such a partner is going to mean in the future is also essential. Yet something more is also required – a spark of will which one can trust. Only the captain can make the final decision. Only decisions made by the 'I' in clear consciousness, helped by the three soul activities, will give grounds for hope of a successful outcome.

Preface

In Britain's most critical moment during the Second World War Winston Churchill quoted from W.E. Henley's poem[1] in which the approach of death is contemplated. The poet had surveyed his successes and failures, his good and bad deeds, his thoughts, feelings and actions as a whole. The verse Churchill quoted well illustrates the role of the human individuality.

> *It matters not how strait the gate,*
> *How charged with punishments the scroll;*
> *I am the master of my fate,*
> *I am the captain of my soul.*

Among the physically invisible aspects or entities of the human being referred to above, there is another which can be named our *genius*. Unlike descriptions of things or beings in the physical world, where no one body can occupy the same space as another, these inner entities are fluid and can flow into and out of each other. What is called genius (which is certainly not the product of physical genes) has qualities of a soul nature but can be perceived as mentor and guide to the ego or soul captain. This genius has an intelligence much deeper and more widely embracing than what we call our intellect, but can also inform it, just as it can nurture other parts of our thinking activity and can penetrate our artistic feelings and willed actions. It may reveal itself as literary, scientific or artistic genius. It is there in everyone, but is frequently dormant; and when it does stimulate us and help develop our creativity we tend not to use the term 'genius' unless the creativity is of very high order.

With all the foregoing in mind let us turn to the subject of mathematics. *In every person, every child, there lives a mathematical genius.* Never should a teacher even think (let alone say): 'This particular child will never understand maths. It's beyond the talents which the gods (or his genes – if you want to be materialistic) have endowed him with.'

The genius is asleep to begin with, and rests within the beat of heart and lung – the true womb of arithmetic – and in the bones and muscles of the limbs – the true womb of geometry. Through encouragement, especially in the singing of songs and the making of music, one part of the genius can rise up to the level of the larynx and collar bone and begin to dream. The other part can move along the arms to the hands when a child is helped to draw in a colourful and healthy way; it too begins to dream, this time a geometrical kind of dreaming. When the two parts or aspects ascend to the head, later to unite, the full genius can awaken and mathematics can become a conscious activity possessed by human thinking.

What role mathematical activity plays and can play vis-a-vis the sciences of the physical world on the one hand and the sciences of the soul and spirit on the other will be dealt with in the following chapters.

It may seem an utter contradiction to maintain in one paragraph that the soul's activities are non-physical, non-material and then in a later paragraph to refer to parts of the human body which allow the equally non-physical genius to rise from sleep, passing through other bodily regions as it first dreams and then awakens. But just consider the word 'heart'. We use the word, on the one hand, to denote the physical organ which controls the pulsing blood in us. Has it not happened to many of us when meeting an attractive member of the opposite sex that our blood speeds up in response to our perceptions? We can be grateful to the heart that it prevents the blood beat speeding out of control. But hold on a moment. Is this really just a physical matter? We can learn to control, even master our instincts. In every situation, any activity in which we may find ourselves becoming engaged, not just love affairs, we can ask ourselves, 'Is our heart really in it?' This does not refer to the physical heart. Nor is it merely a useful metaphor. The genius of language understands that as well as a physical heart we have an invisible, non-physical heart, which has an intimate relationship with the anatomical one. So too, when we use words like 'hands' and 'head', it is not necessarily just the physical parts of our body we are indicating. It is via the invisible head, heart and hands that the human soul and human spirit can mediate with and control our physical body.

May it not be that at some future time in evolution – provided we have worked for it in the right way, with the help of the powers with whom our genius may put us in touch – we shall even be able to begin to control our livers and all other organs, too? At such a time the work of doctors and hospitals would become very different. To say then, that in becoming mathematically active our genius has risen from heart to throat to head is neither a physical nor just a metaphorical reference. How this movement can be taken account of in the practical teaching of mathematics will be shown in the chapters that follow.

Pursuing such considerations of the invisible (spiritual) but essential activities taking place in the human being, a whole science of the spirit can be evolved. This was what, in fact, Rudolf Steiner[2] did in the first quarter of the 20th Century. All that is developed in this book owes an immeasurable amount to the inspirations for further research which he made available at that time.[3] This science of the spirit is also known as anthroposophy, the essential basis for which is to be found in Steiner's fundamental book *The Philosophy of Freedom*.[4]

Preface

Before attempting to teach mathematics, whether this be arithmetic, algebra, geometry, trigonometry, calculus, computer programming or chaos theory, it is important to ask what sort of subject it really is. To this the first and second chapters will be devoted.

The aim of every teacher of mathematics is to bring about a confident capacity in his pupils to be able to move freely within the particular realm which is being focused upon, be it the life of number, the emergence of geometrical form and its metamorphoses, or the applications of mathematical ways of thinking to practical situations and technical tasks in the world. Over 40 years' teaching experience of the subject have amply confirmed for me that when children and young people have the good fortune to be taught in a single school from the ages of six or seven to eighteen by a small number of teachers whom they learn to know intimately (and vice versa), progress can become wholesome and stable. Such conditions obtain primarily in the Rudolf Steiner (Waldorf) schools, which were founded in 1919, and of which over 700 now exist spread through all continents of the world. But the realisation of the importance of not changing children's teachers at the end of every year or so is found in many other good schools, too. In Waldorf schools this realisation is complemented by teaching maths in block periods of roughly a month every term for the first two hours of the school day, in addition to having regular practice lessons of short duration in the weeks when the block period – called 'main lesson' – is operating in other subjects such as English, Science, Geography or History.

This book aims to present helpful, practical ideas and suggestions for mathematics teaching in school – or indeed for anyone who may wish to relearn, or failed to learn in his own schooling. The focus however, is on the way teaching can be developed in a Waldorf school. It is to teachers pioneering in these schools, who in many countries labour with inadequate salaries (Britain at present offers less funding support for such schools than any other government in the world – zero at the time of writing) that this book is dedicated.

Important note to class teachers – especially in Steiner Waldorf Schools

The treatment of all the mathematical topics applicable to the 7 – 14 age range in the chapters ahead is a comprehensive one. Very few of the topics which can justifiably be introduced to children over these eight years have been left out. This does not imply that *all* the topics which *are* included must be dealt with by a teacher to achieve an adequate mathematical education. Many of them certainly are essential, but it has to be left to the individual teacher to select which developments will achieve optimum progress for the particular group of children he is responsible for. Every school will have its own recommended mathematical curriculum for each age of childhood. To what extent this parallels the curriculum outlined here (see Chapter 10) or the national curriculum propounded by a government department is a matter for that school and its teachers.

Both the suggestions for curriculum and the examples for children to work at are made with a very wide ability range in mind. The way in which they are introduced here will show, however, that every child from the apparently most innumerate to likely future university graduates in mathematics and the sciences can benefit from a broad variety of numerical and geometrical experience. The criticism that much of the work in the chapters ahead is too difficult for an 'average child' is invalid. It misses the point. Experience shows, however, that such criticism will continue – often arising through fear on the teacher's part that his own ability is insufficient to grapple with all but the basic mathematical topics in primary schools.

Before we get to grips with the nitty-gritty of Maths teaching, however, let us first look at how mathematics has been perceived through the ages, particularly in regard to its spiritual significance. As I hope will become clear in the course of this book, this aspect is one which, albeit indirectly, can and should inform even the most basic levels of mathematics in schools.

---

* Rather than using both masculine and feminine forms on each occasion, I may alternate from chapter to chapter. The human individuality is essentially neither masculine nor feminine, and this alternation serves only to highlight that fact.

Introduction: *Mathematics and the Mystery Schools*

§1. Greek Teachings

The previous practice and knowledge of mathematical activities was a prime requirement for students (called novices in those days) seeking to enter Greek Mystery Schools. Plato declared, 'God geometricizes.' His predecessor Pythagoras required his students to work in mathematics for most of the time in their first year course, before subsequently being initiated into the world's deeper mysteries – Where have we come from before being born? What happens to us after death? What is the origin of our earthly home? What do the stars reveal? How can one be trained to hear the harmony of the spheres? When are the best times to open the inner ears to listen to the conversations of the Gods? Why are we at first unaware of our true tasks and destiny in life?

There are no extant records of the Pythagorean school written by its participants, but several convincing stories have come down to us through various biographers, foremost among whom is Iamblichus.[1] Eduard Schuré [2] has presented an imaginative account of what took place, based upon spiritual perception. More recently Ernst Bindel,[3] a mathematics teacher in the first Waldorf School in Stuttgart, Southern Germany, has written an enlightening book on the mathematical side of Pythagoras' work and teaching. After studying these and other books and developing inner sources of perception – again through the good offices of one's genius – the following description emerges.

A novice wishing to enter the school in Croton (whose ruins are to be found on the Calabrian coast of modern Italy) had first to give away all his possessions to others, or if he so wished, to the school. He was then required to attend an interview with the one we would nowadays call the principal of this college or university. Pythagoras' first question to him would be 'Can you

Teaching mathematics

Pythagoras

Introduction: Mathematics and the mystery schools

count?' On giving a positive answer the student would be bidden to show evidence of this. 'One, two, three, four –'. 'Stop!' requested Pythagoras. 'What you take to be four has the strength of ten, and the teaching given here will reveal its significance.'

A student of the stories of King Arthur and the Holy Grail may be reminded at this point of Sir Galahad who sang 'My strength is as the strength of ten, because my heart is pure.' This story goes on to relate that the valley in which he was riding echoed with the (divine) power of his song.

The novice was then given a tablet, told to go up a forested slope overlooking the school, spend the night in a cave there in which he would find bread and water, and come down the next morning to reveal to members of the school the results of his meditating upon the tablet. This tablet, well known to students of ancient Hebrew wisdom, bore the following triangular frame of hieroglyphs:

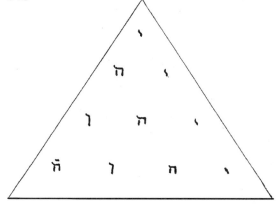

Only later would it be explained to the novice that the bottom line bore the name 'Jehovah' – or the unutterable name of God – written from right to left.

Next morning after spending a not wholly pleasant and comfortable night – lions and other beasts roamed the forests in those days – the novice would awaken to the distant sound of singing in the school below. The first school hour was given over to this activity. Its students, we might note, were rarely below the age of 30 and many were above 40.

On reaching the assembled ranks of the now quiet students, the novice would be asked to tell them the fruits of his meditation. He would certainly have observed that each side of the triangle contained 4 symbols and that the total number was 10. Most novices having disseminated these facts would be unlikely to say more. Though we might judge the procedure that followed to be somewhat cruel by modern standards of university admittance, the student body was encouraged to taunt the poor novice. 'You want to be accepted as a student here and that is all you can do? Surely you can do better than that!' The taunts would become ruder and more provocative. The whole thing was designed as a test of the novice's fitness to be accepted. If he eventually cried out corresponding insults in return, and then lost his temper completely, he would be gently taken to one side by Pythagoras and told he had failed the test – that of self respect. Should the novice on the other hand have bowed his head and admitted he was almost completely lacking in the wisdom needed for entry into the school, he was warmly embraced by the principal and led to the Temple of the Muses and given a brief view inside. There stood before him ten beautiful statues, the first one of which was called Hestia. She, the Muse of Silence, held a finger to her lips – for the first thing a student needed to develop was the ability to listen.

In the months which followed, the Pythagorean explanation of the tablet was made known to him. The four similar symbols (the Hebrew letter י or Jod) stood for the physical natures of each of the four Kingdoms (mineral, plant, animal and human). The three symbols ה , (Hebrew e or he) stood for the living natures of plant, animal and human, whilst the two symbols ו (Hebrew fau) represented the powers of animal and human to be conscious and have the ability to move their position on the earth. The tenth symbol ה , (the final form of ה) stood for the attribute which the human being alone among the kingdoms of nature possesses – that of self consciousness and responsibility. So the novice could now comprehend that what first appears to us as a fourfoldness – the kingdoms of nature – shows itself at a deeper level as a tenfoldness.

> One might at this point reflect upon modern vivisection and other medical experiments upon animals. The intention to gain 'therapy' for human beings at the expense of animals (causing them as 'little pain as possible' of course), is already morally highly dubious. Scientifically, however, it is even more doubtful whether the results of such experiments can give rise to remedies that will give lasting positive results in the alleviation of human suffering. The word 'positive' is used here because human suffering of itself is not necessarily an evil thing, even though we should do all we can practically and ethically to relieve it. Many a wise person has declared that 'suffering teaches'. What is gained from overcoming an illness can strengthen a person and help her progress. Measles in children is a well-known example. Parents who allow their children to be immunized against measles do not realize what opportunity for such strengthening they may be denying them. But returning to experiments upon animals: if the distinctions made in the Pythagorean

Introduction: Mathematics and the mystery schools

> triangle have substance – and a little thought will confirm that they are as valid today as they were 2500 years ago – then not only has animal consciousness to be looked at differently from human consciousness, but the same applies to animals' living substance. To those who consider a human being to be simply a very well developed animal and possibly the peak of animal creation (some dolphin lovers would no doubt dispute even this), such ideas will seem utter nonsense. They are recommended to read the writings of the Belgian biologist Jos Verhulst.[4]

Returning to the Pythagorean schooling course, the fact that there are four kingdoms of nature was felt to be an echo of the four great parts of the world, seen as a comprehensive whole. These were perceived as the interweaving of two pairs of contrasts. Imagining the whole world as a vast loom, the warp held the polarity of permanency and change. The weft mediated between the visible and the invisible.

The realm of the permanent and invisible belonged to the Gods, so the origins and deeds of the Gods formed the first great area of study in the Mystery school: Theogony.

Every morning we wake up to and at once become aware of something equally permanent in our life, but this is visible – the earth. Geogony, our earth and its origins, constituted the second area for contemplation.

Each night and series of nights when clouds do not obstruct our view, we see the starry worlds. The moon and planets in varying speeds slowly change their positions against the 'fixed star' background, yet the 'fixed stars' are also moving across the sky throughout the night. Everything is changing but visible. How all this came about in the dawn of time formed the third area of study: Cosmogony.

Finally the world is incomplete without the human soul, that is invisible but ever changing. The origin of the human soul formed the fourth vast area of learning in this Greek Mystery school. The whole is summed up in the following diagram

	permanent	
Our Earth		The Gods
GEOGONY		THEOGONY
visible ———————————————————————————— **invisible**		
The Starry Heavens		Our Human Soul
COSMOGONY		PSYCHOGONY
	changing	

xxi

Greek science, associated with the names of Socrates, Plato and Aristotle, revolved around another set of four formed from the interweaving of two pairs of antitheses. This is the well known set of four elements, but a careful comparison of this with the diagram above will show a qualitative isomorphism. In fact the idea of four elements takes its birth some hundred or so years earlier from Pythagorean perception of the four areas of world existence.

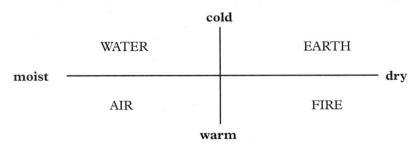

Earth in this set of four refers to what today we would call the solid state of matter, water to the liquid and air to the gaseous state. Fire or heat is that element which stands at a higher level than the other three in that it can change ice to water, water to steam, just as the ego can change the soul's focus of activity from willing to feeling to thinking – another sequence which can help in children's education, and which we will explore in later chapters. The modern physicist may also equate this state (fire) with atomic fission and fusion.

In a similar way Pythagoras taught how mathematics may be contemplated as four parts of an all-embracing whole. Once again a qualitative isomorphism with the world tetrad can be experienced.

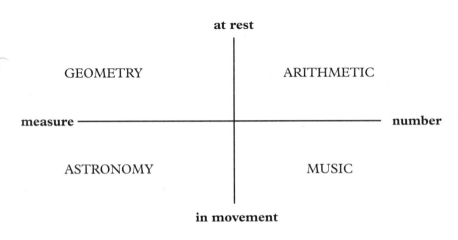

Introduction: Mathematics and the mystery schools

The founder of arithmetic is regarded by some as Abraham, directly inspired by Jahveh. Furthermore,

> *'The man that hath no music in himself...*
> *Is fit for treasons, stratagems, and spoils;'*

as Shakespeare wrote. (*The Merchant of Venice:* Act V). Both arithmetic and music are concerned with the invisible and spiritual activities of number. In what sense are number and measure antitheses or polarities? To be active with number requires no physical muscular effort; it is completely invisible and spiritual. Whenever we make measurements, whether with ruler, tape or eyepiece, parts of the body must come into play. To appreciate why music is number in movement, one only needs to remember how each musical interval corresponds to (indeed bears within itself) a fraction. Bow an open cello string, then place a finger exactly half way up the string and bow again. The new note is an octave higher than the first. In the same way, placing the finger $3/5$ of the way up, gives a note a major sixth interval above the open string's note. And so on – $2/3$ for a perfect 5th, $8/15$ for a seventh, etc.[5] Music consists in moving from one interval to another. Astronomy is so much more difficult than geometry or 'earth measurement' in that its measurements are always in flux.

It is often not realized that the first four of the seven liberal arts which formed the basis of university learning in the Middle Ages have originated from this Pythagorean tetrad. The four subjects described above constituted the Quadrivium, whilst Grammar, Dialectic and Rhetoric formed the Trivium.

In the Mystery school of Pythagoras all four appeared within each subject again in a manner not unlike that developed by Goethe in botany, when he showed how the whole plant can be revealed by looking into the transformations of the leaf. So, for instance, there are within arithmetic four progressions of numbers: arithmetical, geometrical, harmonic (originally astronomical) and musical progressions. Practice in calculations concerning these four – summation, algebraic expression and application to practical problems – belongs to the education of sixteen year-olds in a Waldorf school.

Geometry (for example in spiral forms), astronomy and music were given similar treatment in the ancient Mystery school. The interweaving qualities of four developed in the novices the mobile and meditative capacities required in subsequent training years for penetrating and experiencing those sublime realms of the spirit which mathematics as such cannot reach.

§2. Mathesis

'Mathesis' was a term used in earlier times to denote the learning of number properties, but which included the contemplation of their extra-numerical significance. How different are the numbers 7, 10 and 12! The first is prime and the last is abundant or excessive. The factors of 12, i.e. 1, 2, 3, 4 and 6 add up to more than 12. 12 is the lowest integer for which such abundance first occurs. This makes 12 mathematically special. But it also occurs in the number of months in a year. Dozens used to be of common usage when selling eggs or loaves of bread. Before decimalisation we had 12 pence in a shilling, and our inch as a twelfth of a foot is fast falling into nemesis. Our cousins in the U.S.A., God bless them, are putting up effective resistance, as far as linear measurement is concerned, to this abstract and intellectual French innovation, which has no basis in 'man as the measure of all things'. The matter of 'twelve-ness' goes further. Why did Christ have just twelve apostles? Why are there 12 signs of the zodiac? It is easy to dismiss this as mere consequence of the astronomical incidence of 12 full moons in the course of the year. The 12 here is not exact, however, so a sceptic could also take this as evidence of the immature thinking of earlier civilisations. Such judgment, however, may be regarded as a natural consequence of a cynicism that recognizes only material realities.

Like 12, the number 7 has mystical significance. What is 7 mathematically? Besides being prime it is the lowest number of equal parts into which a circle cannot be divided exactly using ruler and compasses. Again we have a sort of refusal to conform, this time to a spatial demand. The 7 planets visible to the human eye ('planet' meant wandering star in earlier times) are those refusing to conform to the 'fixed' nature of the stars everywhere else in the heavenly domicile. Where the number 7 shows itself, it is almost always in the rhythms of time. The 7 days of the week take planetary names, of course. English uses 3 of them but Italian has incorporated 6 of them. Longer periods of time, like the periods into which human life between birth and death can be divided, are arranged in sevens. Shakespeare[6] and Steiner had much to contribute to this theme. 7 is the number through which time incarnates itself.

We have ten fingers and ten toes. An evolutionary genetic accident? As a number it stands between 7's primality and 12's abundance. Mathematically, 10 is a deficient number, for the sum of its factors is 8, which is less than 10.[7] At one time not so long ago there was a society in Edinburgh campaigning for base 12 to be adopted rather than 10 in our counting process. An opposing society in Paris campaigned for a base 7 system. But Greek moderation has prevailed. 10 is the number which suits our earth activity, especially but not only in monetary affairs.

Introduction: Mathematics and the mystery schools

Probably the most significant example of mathesis is to be found in St. John's gospel.⁸ The third occasion on which the risen Christ appeared before his disciples was when some of them had failed to land a single fish from their nocturnal expedition. 'Cast the net over the other side!', they were bidden. Quickly the net was filled with 153 fish. Wasn't the writer of the gospel being a bit too fanciful or even pernickety? Couldn't he have said 'about 150 fish'? It was Thomas Aquinas in the thirteenth century who solved and explained the riddle.⁹ Just as Pythagoras had exclaimed that 10 is the strength of 4, or the creative revelation of 4, so Aquinas showed that if another equilateral triangle is taken whose base consists of 17 items, above which are rows containing 16, 15, 14. etc. and finally 3, 2 and 1 at the top, the total is 153. And what is special about 17, whose creativity is revealed in 153? Seventeen is just what it says – seven together with ten. Through Christ the creative wisdom-filled planetary world is united with the earthly world. In a mosaic in Ravenna this scene is depicted with the fish-filled net in the form of a triangle. Surely no accident in design. Its artist, too, knew – or at least his genius did – the secret of this triangular number 153. ¹⁰

xxv

§3. A holistic overview

A satisfying and inspiring experience of wholeness is achieved when tracing the development of mathematics in this way. Now embracing modern rather than just ancient concepts and ideas, a complete survey of all that is mathematical can arise. Just taking the domain of number itself as the whole, the following survey emerges:

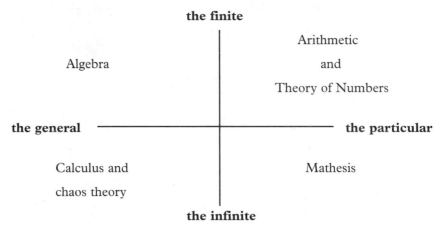

	the finite	
Algebra		Arithmetic and Theory of Numbers
the general	———————————	**the particular**
Calculus and chaos theory		Mathesis
	the infinite	

No greater work has yet been written on the first of these four areas of mathematics than by Hardy and Wright.[11] Just to take one example in this area, one can list part of the succession of prime numbers (those which have no factors other than unity – and, of course, themselves):

$$5 \quad 7 \quad 11 \quad 13 \quad 17 \quad 19 \quad 23$$

At first it may appear that there is a law by which each number is derived from its predecessor – alternately add 2 and 4. This 'law' however lets us down once we go further, for 6 has to be added to get 29, the next prime. That no law can be devised for an unbounded set of prime numbers is a hallmark of this domain. It is as if prime numbers bear such a trait of individuality that they reprove us for even contemplating some kind of racial characteristic among them.

In algebra we generalise. The best example of this is $x^2 - y^2 = (x + y)(x - y)$. Whatever pair of numbers is chosen, the quickest way of finding the difference between their squares is simply to multiply their sum by their difference. Thus $(11^{1}/_{2})^2 - (8^{1}/_{2})^2 = 20 \times 3 = 60$. The labour saved from the process of turning into improper fractions, multiplying the results

Introduction: Mathematics and the mystery schools

by themselves, etc. is enormous. Such a procedure as the one shown is of great value in practical problems such as calculating the cost of laying cylindrical oil pipe lines or determining the distance sailed to the north when a ship sails a particular distance on a straight course, such that it moves a certain distance westwards.

In calculus and chaos theory alike we are concerned with the infinite. In the former we can ask what happens if first we evaluate $1^{1/2} \times 1^{1/2}$ (answer $2^{1/4}$), then evaluate $1^{1/3} \times 1^{1/3} \times 1^{1/3}$ (answer 2 and $^{10}/_{27}$), $1^{1/4} \times 1^{1/4} \times 1^{1/4} \times 1^{1/4}$, $(1 \text{ and } ^{1}/_{10})^{10}$, and so on. For the answers in the sequence do not increase without limit. In fact they converge towards a particular number: 2.71828.

What kind of number this is and what it is to 10 decimal places, for example, only calculus can determine. It is in fact the number denoted by **e**, the initial letter of its discoverer Euler, the Basel mathematician.

Chaos theory is concerned with similar questions, but for which algebra ceases to provide a foundation after the first couple of steps. The formula $y = Kx(1 - x)$ is calculated using some value of K between 0 and 4 and some value of x between 0 and 1. Then using the same value of K and using for x the first answer y, a new value of y is calculated. The same procedure is then repeated a very large number of times. Once again, in a large number of cases (values of K), a limit is approached just as in calculus. But there are also a large number of cases where the behaviour of the answers (y value) becomes chaotic. The calculation procedure would be humanly impossible without the aid of the computer. Only within the last 19 years, in consequence, has chaos theory been able to be developed. Its applications in such diverse realms as biology, water flow, weather patterns and commerce are only now being refined, causing scientists to acclaim the chaos theory as the third great achievement of the century after relativity and quantum theory. It has also had another far-reaching consequence: for many decades, physicists, chemists, zoologists, etc. found each other's work increasingly remote. Even within a special branch of one of these subjects, a researcher who might wish to converse with an acquaintance in another part of that branch would be faced with unfamiliar scientific language. The revelations of chaos theory[12] are slowly beginning to allow healing of this atomistic separation of scientists to take place.

xxvii

§4. Mathematics and paths into the spiritual

The world of mathematics is a threshold world. On one side lies the world of nature and all the stimulating events and problems of the material world. On yonder side lies the invisible world of spirit, without which the domains of psychology, ethics (Christian and other), sociology and practical philosophy lack meaning. But this is not all. Just as the practical application of mathematical thinking in the one direction has led to the greatness of modern technology, so it can be applied in the other direction to help us progress along what has always been known as the path of knowledge and inner development, embracing cognizance of worlds higher than the physically visible and material one.

The first stage on the spiritual path is usually called 'study', consisting of developing clear perceptions of all that the senses present to one in ordinary life. This requires us above all to keep our feet upon the ground, avoiding any tendency to fly off into exotic realms of fantasy. (This latter tendency is what so many 'spiritual disciplines', often deriving from ancient Eastern traditions, fail to prevent;[13] it is also what modern drug culture promotes so effectively.) Such 'study' also includes the perusal of what adepts, initiates, philosophers, religious advisors and wise people, not only in the past but particularly in the present have to say about the path ahead. Openness and positive critical discrimination are what matter at this stage. Any tendency to believe what is heard or read, perhaps because of some charismatic trait in the speaker or writer, needs to be avoided. It is at this first stage that experience of arithmetic – knowing through practice the life of its number relationships and being aware of its objective truth – is such a help. Not the content of arithmetic but its quality is what gives support to us here.

The second stage, pictorially described by Eastern sages[14] as the development of a two-petalled lotus flower and described by Steiner as Imagination, is the acquisition of a new kind of seeing. This is not with the physical eyes, although the region at the root of the nose between the eyes is associated with the spiritual organ of perception so developed. People who have experienced near-death tell of suddenly finding themselves in the midst of a vast panorama in which is depicted the whole of their life, containing events stretching back to the age of three or even further. It can also happen through other similar circumstances – such as crossing over a gap containing a thousand foot drop when climbing in the Alps, when the feet slip but a hand grasps hold of a projecting root or rock at the last moment. In between the two instants in time such a life tableau can present itself. It is, however, unnecessary to actively seek such dangers in order to develop the Imagination. A steady, sound and safe method is given in various books.[15] It is algebra,

Introduction: Mathematics and the mystery schools

or perhaps better said, the quality of spiritual or thinking activity employed in practising it, which is of help at the second stage.

In algebra a single statement contains unlimited arithmetical truths. $x^2 - y^2 = (x - y)(x + y)$, for example, which has already been examined. So does the life tableau contain an immeasurable number of previous events. External perception vanishes, but memory becomes exalted. In algebra too, the special case gives way to the general, all-inclusive.

The third stage, having to do with the unfolding of a 16 petalled flower, or of the Mars organ (the first two stages are also denoted as Saturn and Jupiter organs in some sources)[16] is called Inspiration by Rudolf Steiner.[17] To achieve this the labour-intensive achievement of the Imaginative panorama has to be washed away, the ordinary memory must vanish and the new experience includes a kind of musical sounding, but not of the familiar kind. Experience of calculus helps cognition here, for it contains the essence of the Inspired step. Both the numerator and the denominator of an algebraic fraction have to be reduced towards zero (a washing away); only in the limit is the differential coefficient achieved. Something is seemingly born out of nothing – but of course the very functionality is retained in the mathematical process. This corresponds to the deep moral motif retained in the spiritual ascent to the third stage. Stories are told of musicians inspired in their compositions. Mozart was once about to step into a carriage in Vienna when, with foot raised, the whole of a new symphony flooded into his consciousness. His next task was to return home and laboriously write out the score. Such is an example of a genuine Inspiration, apparently born out of nothing.

Arithmetic, algebra and calculus are qualitatively isomorphic with the first three stages of the path to acquiring knowledge of higher worlds. Even at the fourth stage, that of Intuition in Steiner terminology, there is something of a mathematical nature (mathesis) which may help, but the essential message received from one's mathematical genius at this point is as follows. 'So far along the path I have been able to render some help to you. On your further path you have to leave me behind.'

Mathematics embraces many wonderful spiritual qualities, but it does not embrace 'being'. You cannot possibly describe a friend in mathematical terms. No formula can ever suffice to describe the shape of a tree, even though living bud profiles have become the subject of an exact geometrical science,[18] and fractals[19] can be used to depict complicated but non-living fern shapes and other plant and animal forms.

The fourth (Intuition) stage has also been given the names 'Sun organ' and '12 petalled lotus flower'. It occurs only when one is able to 'become one with' another being, whether a living or so-called 'dead' human individual [20] or a higher being such as an angel, elohim, deva or even an ill-disposed spiritual power. This is the stage when we may be able to help others or be helped by them in a far-reaching way. The dangers of illusion, present at all stages, become particularly intense here as they do in succeeding stages, which lie beyond forms of mathematical insight. Other kinds of danger present themselves too, the further one progresses. At the Intuition stage it is, for example, necessary to know how to healthily extricate oneself from 'oneness' with another being.

To behold mathematics, not as some kind of atomistically constructed edifice, or giant self-increasing green monster like those pictorial representations used in videos, but as a whole and wholesome spiritual entity – this is the prerequisite for a healthy evaluation of the subject. We have now briefly traced the 'Mystery School' aspect of mathematics. Before looking at how this may relate to mathematics teaching in general, let me sum up this chapter with two quotes by mathematicians about the scope and significance of mathematics:

1) Professor Arthur Cayley,[21] speaking about the range of modern mathematics, said:

> It is difficult to give an idea of the vast extent of modern mathematics. It is crowded with beautiful detail, a tract of beautiful country seen at first in the distance, but which will bear to be rambled through and studied in every detail of hill-side and valley, stream, rock, wood, and flower.

2) Professor Louis Locher-Ernst [22] concludes one of his projective geometry books with the words (which are also applicable to all mathematics):

> The primal phenomena may be simple and the consequences of these phenomena transparent, yet the configurations appearing to consciousness retain something mysterious, a certain inscrutability; and each time we think about them they appear as fresh as on the First Day.

Chapter 1:
Mathematics and Education

§1. Its invisible nature

How different this subject is from history, geography, the sciences, language and its development, practical crafts, arts like painting and sculpture, gymnastics and comparative religion! In all these subjects it is necessary to move some parts of the body – eye muscles, vocal organs, hands – in consulting books or people or in viewing external phenomena. But as inmates of concentration camps discovered, it is possible to develop considerable mathematical proficiency whilst being physically very restricted. Even in geometry we do not actually need to draw forms. That we do so could be interpreted as a kind of inner laziness on our part. However, the beauty of a large, beautifully constructed geometrical drawing is always worth contemplating, though it can never be perfectly accurate. The elements of mathematics are themselves invisible and perfect. 4 x 3 is always equal to 12 in our number system based on 10. That 4 x 3 equals 15, if we use the base 7 number system, constitutes no valid objection to this. Five general planes in space always have ten lines of intersection. Between any two irrational numbers like π and $\sqrt{10}$ there are always an infinite number of rational numbers like $3^{1/7}$ Straight lines are perfectly straight and circles are perfectly round (each of the points on a circle's periphery, in other words, is exactly the same distance from the centre).

Perfect things like straight lines and circles or the answers to questions like 'What number times itself makes 2?' simply do not exist in the physical, material world. So whence comes the word 'perfect'? If anyone doubts the existence of a spiritual world at work within the full range of human experience, let him answer that question. And let any brain expert who believes only in the reality of matter point out which cortextual strand of brain substance can be magnified to reveal the value of π; the first ten decimal places will do for a start!

So mathematics is concerned in the first place with invisible, immaterial but exact and perfect entities. Even more remarkable from a social point of view is the fact that to any clear mathematical problem there is one correct answer, not a series of debatable answers as in politics. That a quadratic equation has more than one solution does not argue against such a statement, for in this case there is just one exact pair of answers. The satisfying thrill experienced by the mathematical wrangler, who, when having failed to solve a problem one evening, awakens next morning to discover its answer, is due to the confirmation which his genius has given him that the spiritually perfect is eternal. No less satisfaction comes to a child when out of his own efforts the wonderful realisation dawns that 3 × 7 makes the same as 7 × 3.

The author can point to a most significant experience in his own life which led him to become a mathematician. It was in 1940 when the Nazi armies had reached the English Channel, and their victory in expelling the British from Dunkirk had, typically, been hailed by Churchill as a great British evacuation success. Then there loomed the danger of Britain being overrun by the Nazis and their evil philosophy. As a sixth former in a well-known northern grammar school I went to school next day. Our maths teacher addressed us, saying that if this dire danger was realised, sons would be forced to betray and tell lies about their parents. Untruth would prevail everywhere. 'But,' he said, 'there is a set of things the Nazis will never be able to pervert – and they are the truths of mathematics.' Pointing to the wall outside the classroom windows he concluded by saying, 'Let them put me against that and shoot me. These truths will not be altered a single jot.'

'That is all very well,' someone might remark, 'but maths is abstract, it has very little to do with real human problems.' On the contrary it has a great deal to do with them, especially given the way mathematics is taught in schools. In the last decade of the 19th Century and in the first decade of the 20th, Russian children were taught arithmetic in a synthetic way. They always had to take parts and portions of things, and put them together to form a single result. 'What happens when 3 is added to 4?' According to the philosopher Immanuel Kant[1] the result, 7, is not contained in what is given, and can only be found in the first instance by sense perception. In real life, however, taking an actual visible situation as he preferred to, rather than examining the inner mental process of thinking, all seven things are there from the start ('a priori' in Kantian terminology) and we, through our observation and intellect separate them into two groups. The real question in life is 7 = 4 + ?, i.e. if I have seven things altogether, and I hold four of them in my left hand and the rest are somewhere else, say in my right hand, how many things must I be holding in my right hand? The real process is one of analysis, not synthesis. So when teaching what will be referred to later as the

Chapter 1: Mathematics and education

second stage of arithmetic, to 6 and 7 year olds in a Class 1, the above problem of philosophical origin can be formulated as follows.

'Look, children! I have 4 candles in my hand and today let's suppose we are going to celebrate Margaret's birthday.' Margaret is a girl in the class and perhaps I am actually holding up 4 new cylindrical pieces of white chalk. No explanation of the substitution is needed, for at that age their imagination is more than equal to the situation. 'So, children, put your hands up if you think you can tell me how many more candles I need to take out of the cupboard to celebrate Margaret's birthday properly.'

A further examination of such procedures with Class 1 must wait until the relevant chapter. The point here is to notice that just because something is not yet visible (the birthday celebration) it does not mean that the number indwelling it (the sevenness of its candles) is unknown. Rudolf Steiner, in his first published philosophical book,[2] would – if he had been using this relationship of 3, 4, and 7 – have countered Kant as follows: 'Whilst Kant would maintain that in 4 + 3 the sum 7 is by no means contained and we must call on our sense of sight, it is actually impossible that I have no clue in the subject-concept which directs me to the predicate-concept. When I think 4 + 3 I really hold 7 mathematical units in mind, only not all at once but separated into two parts. If I think the group of mathematical units all at once, this is absolutely the same thing.'

Of course Kant was not implying that sense perception is always needed to achieve additive results; memory is the chief help in finding the answer to such numerical problems. Neither he nor anyone else would maintain that to add 287 to 648 you have first to make a sense-perceptible experiment.

To return to children in Russia at the turn of the century: the capacity for synthesis was fostered in them to such a degree that the natural primary capacity of analysis (going from a whole to its parts) was left undeveloped, the desire for it unsatisfied. What child would enjoy trying to put together the cogs, springs and fingers of a watch if she had not first had the joy (unshared by its owner!) of taking the whole watch to bits? When these Russian children reached adulthood, the urge to experience what they should have experienced earlier may well have expressed itself in their acceptance of Bolshevism[3] – a highly analytical approach to remedying the dreadful social ills in Russia at that time. Its successor, totalitarian Communism, with all its attendant evils, can thus, in part at least, be traced back to a mathematics teaching that failed to acknowledge the presence of invisible but no less real wholes. Just as Russian education in 1900 suffered from the consequences of imbibing philosophy propounded by people like Immanuel Kant, so also have more recent educational ideas, chiefly through people such as Skinner, who effectively followed in Kant's footsteps.

§2. School Mathematics Today

The teaching of mathematics in schools in general today has many shortcomings. A primary cause of the minimal interest children and young people often develop at particular ages, whether at 11, 14 or 17 is far too great a reliance on text books in schools. Television programmes which act as substitute teachers do not improve the situation either. Learning mathematics has an important social aspect for children. It is different for the adult who can work without physical or visible assistance if she so chooses, as suggested at the start of this chapter. The child needs to hear and watch the teacher elucidate each mathematical topic, be fired with the enthusiasm which a good teacher can stimulate in her for tackling the questions to be faced. Direct conversation between child and teacher and listening to the questions and comments of others in the classroom (these are almost impossible with electronic boxes, and only partially so with textbooks) are indispensable for healthy growth in mathematical proficiency. Yet many fine ways of teaching are to be observed in many different schools despite bureaucratic pressures from the education authorities and financial pressures from the TV companies and textbook publishers. At primary level especially, much that is imaginative and stimulating can still be found. When teachers plan their work with the children in such a way that most of the mathematical examples prepared for the class have been fashioned out of their imagination as teachers, then even the least able children respond positively.

A second barrier to learning and the joy of learning is the increasing imposition of examination and assessment procedures. How often one meets people who recall passing some examination and have completely forgotten six months later what they crammed into themselves for the sake of getting a piece of paper! This is less true of examinations and assessed projects in mathematics, but the restrictions of rubrics, marking criteria, etc. play their part, more detrimentally at the younger age levels. There is no harm in giving tests, indeed children need and want them. They want to know two things: how they are progressing themselves, and how their peers are doing. Competition with oneself is healthy. Instead of feeling one is competing against others, children can be helped to feel they are members of a whole class which is also competing with itself.

How a teacher can grade the difficulties of work set for a whole class of very mixed ability will be dealt with in Chapter 5. The feeling of a slow and weak child that she is working at the same mathematical topic as the brightest ones helps her immeasurably. At the end of a morning's work with younger children the teacher can call out the answers to all the sums or problems whilst the children mark their own efforts right or wrong. Then the children can call out in order how many each got right and the *cumulative* total for the whole class can be calculated. It is a delight to behold an occasion when a weak child has contributed several more marks than usual to the class total, and the whole class cheers.

Taking tests should not promote anxiety, fear or over-seriousness. They should have no consequence beyond a teacher's praise or encouragement to do better the next time. Internal or external league tables are rubbish and an insult to the very being of mathematics, as well as the human beings reduced by them to statistical data. This is not to say that external examinations have no place at all in a good school. They have a positive role to play, but not before the age of 16, by which time a teenager had developed true independent judgment.

What use has learning mathematics for life as a whole? The passing of examinations is certainly not its sole function. Nor is it merely for commercial excellence and money making – as illustrated in the well-known Socratic dialogue in which the student who ventured such an answer was offered a halfpenny. The right answer to the question is the same today as it was in Greek times: the prime value of learning mathematics is that it develops our thinking, our real, willed, independent thinking, a thinking capable of directing its powers to cognizing both the material world and the invisible world within.

The attempt has been made in this and the previous chapter to show the breadth and scope of mathematical activity. I have explained why the mathematical approach in the initial training in Pythagorean (and other Greek) Mystery schools was important. Similar approaches are valid today too, if the requisite modernisation is first made. It is not, of course, the task of a teacher of mathematics to give any kind of esoteric training to classes in a school, but an awareness of the subject's unique position in this respect, and especially its organic wholeness, can bring about inspired lessons at all ages of childhood and adolescence. It is the presence of imagination in the teacher that kindles pupils' interest so that they can be led to employ their thinking in finding intuitive solutions for all manner of mathematical problems.

In conclusion a table of qualitative isomorphisms is given below, which the reader may wish to contemplate. It should be noticed that each stage is indispensable as a springboard for developing the succeeding one and is also then contained within the latter. Clear exact thinking, for example is indispensable for genuine Imagination, Inspiration and Intuition (see previous chapter). In the 'types of number' row, each column is a subset of the one which follows.

Qualitative Isomorphism

Realm	1st stage	2nd stage	3rd stage	4th stage
Thinking	Ordinary Clear and Exact	Imaginative	Inspired	Intuitive
Mathematics of number	Arithmetic and Theory of Numbers	Algebra	Calculus and Chaos Theory	Mathesis
Types of Number	Integral (Whole numbers)	Rational (Fractions)	Irrational e.g. $\sqrt{2}$	Transcendental e.g. π
Directed Numbers e.g.	Positive $+5$	Negative -5	Complex $\sqrt{-1} = i$	Supercomplex i^i

Chapter 1: Mathematics and education

Such characteristics of enhancement can be found in other directions too

Families of lines in 3D	A line pair	Regulus	Congruence	Complex
Projective Geometry	Axioms of Incidence	Desargue's Theorem	Pappus' Theorem (the fundamental theorem)	Metric gauges (to give e.g. Euclidean, double elliptic or polar Euclidean types)

or a simple sample taken from the Pythagorean school

Progressions	Arithmetic	Geometric	Harmonic	Musical
e.g.	6 12 18 24	3 6 12 24	3 4 6 12	6 8 9 12

In each case there is something of an echo of a fourfold structure and evolution in the human being, and of the four kingdoms of nature. Mathematics has evolved out of the human being. No wonder its structure reflects this!

Chapter 2:
What Stimulates the Child?

§1. The child up to the age of 6 or 7

For the young child play is the greatest learning experience of all. The essence of play is imitation, through which he lives into the activity of all that surrounds him. Whatever he sees or hears adults doing he wants to copy. The origin of the child's imitation is to be sought in the baby's sense of taste, which seems to penetrate every other sense in his body. The movement of a baby's toes when milk passes his lips and tongue, suggests that even the body's extremities participate in tasting. Imitation is a second stage, a continuation of this tasting activity – it allows the child to 'taste' the whole world around him by making it part of himself. Soon it is not confined to 'drinking in' human actions but everything else in his environment as well – animal noises, the sighing of trees in the wind, lorries and aeroplanes, water rushing through taps into the bath. A third stage develops as the child's imagination begins to add something of himself to his imitative life – and here play becomes so important for him. He experiments. Perhaps he has watched his mother taking potatoes from a dish and distributing them to the family's plates. Later, when left untended for a while he may be found sitting on the hearth rug by an empty coal scuttle surrounded by black lumps, his hands, lips and cheeks having experienced their colour, too. If this example seems a bit dated (it happened with the author's son), substitute fish fingers for coal, or the contents of a handbag, a paintbox, etc. according to personal taste. A slightly older child will use the lumps of coal (or whatever is to hand) to build towers, and whilst being at first surprised at the way these tumble over, start to enjoy and repeat this process.

Playing alone, with parents, and with other children both young and old, is not only an *enjoyable* activity for the child. It is as serious a business for him as employment is for a parent. To view it as nothing more than a childish 'stage', as a kind of less important forerunner of sport and games, is a terrible error. Equally damaging to a child is the opposite error of providing him with simplified versions of adult technology, assuming that the earlier he becomes familiar with them, the more quickly he will 'get on' at school and be prepared for mature adult life. Gadgets of all kinds fill the modern home and children are quick to master them. In this there is no harm, for they see and can understand the final physical results of pressing buttons. A door is opened, a washing machine swirls around its contents, a light bulb is illumined and so on. But to provide children of 4 or 5 years of age (or even 2!) with simple computers is absurd in the extreme, for such children have no innate means of understanding the significance of the flickering shapes which assault the sense of sight. Of course, children may be fascinated by everything that moves. The TV is a very efficient baby sitter for this reason. But such electronic machines pervert and destroy life's up-building forces in the child, whereas real play nurtures them.[1] The best games to play with children are those made up on the spot from the child's and parent's imagination, using things and events around them – for there are creative possibilities lying hidden in everything that the world naturally displays to our senses. 'Toys' which are often manufactured to be used in one particular way only, can be a hindrance rather than a stimulus to creative imagination.

There are many life situations which cannot be directly imitated physically, but the child still needs to engage in copying them inwardly. Here lies a fourth stage of tasting activity. It comes about by listening to stories. Often parents tell a teacher that they can't tell stories to children, because they don't know any. Such a situation is easily remedied. Advice on the best kinds of stories to tell at different ages is easily obtained and a little reading preparation soon provides enough material. The direct communication possible through *telling* stories rather than reading them to children is so different, so much more enjoyable and beneficial. A parent (or indeed a teacher) has only got to try it once to see the effect. No matter how poor a story-teller one may feel oneself to be, the child will rate one's efforts very highly and much prefer to be told a story day after day, instead of listening to what is read from a book. The child in his imagination feels himself present among the events narrated. At one moment he is the king or queen, next he is a wolf or a gnome. He inwardly imitates and can freely choose to play these roles himself, in whatever way he wishes. This is not so easy with films, in which the imagination is fed over-specific images that are harder for it to 'digest'. In contrast, the creative story teller necessarily leaves a tremendous amount to the listeners' imagination. The birth of human freedom owes much to such activity. After listening to a story, which is best repeated on successive days to young children, they will enter into acting it with rich fantasy. Activity, both outer and inner – human, not mechanical or electronic! This is the most nourishing food for sustaining a young child's creative potential.

Chapter 2: What stimulates the child?

§2. Early Arithmetic (especially Class 1)

When should a child begin to learn arithmetic? In this form the question is not very sensible. He begins to count through watching and copying others do it, sometimes at the age of two or three, sometimes a year or two later. He couldn't do this if at the same time something within him (the genius in his heart and lungs) didn't stimulate him to meet what his senses offer him. Older brothers and sisters (often far healthier teachers than parents) may get him to copy what they are doing on their fingers. Provided lots of other activities interest the child, it would be foolish to attempt to stop the child becoming interested in counting and sharing things out numerically. It is only when arithmetic is imposed upon him that subtle dangers to health can arise.

> What is really happening to the child between birth and the age of 6 or 7? At birth he inherits his body from his parents, a physical and living model, in and with which he is at work until about the age of 7, when the foundations of his own physical development for the rest of his life are complete. The emergence of second teeth in a normal healthy child at about this time is a sign that these foundations have been laid. His own teeth replace the inherited ones. Of course, none of the 'body building' is a conscious activity. The inner being of the child, assisted by agencies much more sublime than human, works from the invisible and spiritual into the bodily organs and structure. A stage is then reached when the very forces used to achieve this are freed to undertake the next step. Between the ages of approximately 7 and 14, the living rhythms of life are fashioned, memory and habits evolve. Learning the three Rs forms a part of this new development. Should the latter have been forced (enthusiastic suggestion from parents and the manifestation of their own self-gratification is also forcing) upon children in earlier years, some of the forces prematurely transferred from body building to begin this new job will cause subtle deficiencies in the organs, the consequences of which may not be observed until the age of 40.

By the age of 7 most children are ready and eager to learn arithmetic. They are aware instinctively that now is the time to enter upon a new stage of learning. The faculty of imitation is still alive in them but it needs transforming and channeling in new directions in response to the birth in them of their own etheric body. For the exact meaning of this term in the science of the spirit, Steiner's fundamental books can be consulted.[2] Children now rely on the firm but loving authority of their teachers, among whom must naturally be included their own parents or guardians. As mothers and fathers often find out to their cost, a shared, consistent and agreed authority at home is rather important. Beside the corporate authority of the school and its teachers as a whole, to have one teacher, who teaches perhaps up to two thirds of all lessons given in the first two years or so, acting as central teaching authority, is ideal for the child. Parents may wonder whether such emphasis on one single authority figure is warranted: They may question whether a particular teacher appointed to this admittedly very responsible position is really a fit person to take charge of their own, naturally very special, child. This becomes even more alarming for parents considering a Waldorf school when they learn that one particular teacher may well be the central figure of authority for their child for up to 8 years! Well, a harassed teacher might be forgiven for retorting that maybe the child also ought to change his parents with greater regularity! Needless to say, the Waldorf way of educating only succeeds when frequent opportunities are made, both at school and at home for the parents and teacher(s) to converse with each other about the child's progress, difficulties and needs. This, together with frequent sharing of observations and suggestions among the whole body of teachers one or two evenings a week is a prime test of how good a school is.

Even though the teacher of the first class knows that many of his girls and boys can already count quite well and may even be able to do some sums, he will do well to act as if they know nothing. In any case a child likes the class to be taught what he already knows; it gives him confidence. So the teacher might start with a tale like the following. (Assume a September day with a chill in the air.) 'Look, I picked up this dry old stick on the way to school. (It's best to have really done so.) Tonight I shall want to light a fire with it at home. At the moment it's too long for that. I shall have to break this *one* stick into many pieces. But first, children, can you tell me other examples in the world where there is just *one* thing? See, I'll write **one** (I) on the blackboard.' Whilst this is carefully done the children consult their memory and imaginations. Then come the answers. 'One sun!' 'One earth!' Some children, whose parents have, perhaps unfortunately, allowed them to watch science fiction videos, may say, 'That's not true, there are lots of them!' You reply that only things you have been to or have really seen or touched yourself are allowed as answers. Then come other answers. 'We've only got one mother!', 'One class teacher!', 'One door!' (into the classroom) and so on. Sometimes you may get 'One God!'; often 'One big world!' sums it all up and it is time to break the stick into two (not equal) parts. 'Look, I am writing the number *two* (II) on the board. What do we have two of in the world?' Once someone says 'Two eyes!' you have a hard time making sure the children only answer one at a time. On one occasion a child answered 'Two lights!', which on

Chapter 2: What stimulates the child?

enquiry turned out to be the sun and the moon, one for the day and one for the night. In similar manner one piece of the stick can be broken again to give three pieces. Always the children will find answers. 'Our cat has just had three kittens!', 'Three big windows in the classroom!', and once a girl said 'Three round the plate!' – knife, fork and spoon, of course.

Each time, the new number can be written on the board. Roman numerals are best since their forms correspond to fingers and hands – by far the best aid to help children count and do sums. The number V is a whole hand with thumb outstretched. A teacher might hold up an apple by the stalk and cut thin horizontal slices for the children to look through towards the windows. The number five lives in every apple! So too does sixness in every daffodil. With ten the children immediately cry 'Ten fingers!' and 'Ten toes!' and the symbol X is a picture of crossed hands or feet. The original symbols IIII and VIIII are preferable to the more recent IV and IX as the latter already depict a thought process beyond what is actually perceptible.

Having introduced all ten symbols (the first part of a single lesson suffices) the cardinal nature of a number needs demonstrating. If one has eight oranges or classroom lamps, it doesn't matter in which order you count them; you always get the same answer. Children like to test this out, each member of the class choosing a new way. They won't run out, since the total number of different ways of counting them is 40320. At this point the lesson needs to change from being teacher-centered to child-centered. Let them make coloured pictures in their large main lesson books, illustrating all ten numbers. The four legs of a dog will come in one picture, a seven-coloured rainbow in another. No doubt at least one child (probably a boy) will draw nine aeroplanes in various formations, whilst another (probably a girl) may illustrate how nine tarts can be made from a rolled out piece of pastry. In each case the Roman number will be added to the picture and a lively teacher will quickly write down on spare pieces of paper the word LEGS, TARTS, etc. for particular children to copy into their books. One might ask any of the quicker children, who have tidily and beautifully completed this task, to see how many times they can draw three or four different coloured horses in order, one behind the other.

On another day the number sequence can be extended to XX. But now the ordinal nature of numbers needs to complement their cardinal nature. Have the children form a ring inside the classroom or out in the playground or field. Let them clap their hands as they step in time round the ring, calling out all the numbers in order from one to ten to twenty. Later, perhaps another day, let them walk backwards and recite the numbers going downwards. So many variations of such procedures are possible they do not need to be listed: children throwing balls or bean bags to each other and calling out the appropriate number as they catch them, counting whilst using skipping ropes, sitting down and standing up – there's no end to what can be done. Of course, one vital exercise is to count while the right hand grasps the correct finger of the left hand (I to V), then changing right and left (VI to X), then turning over first the left and later the right hand to count up to XX.

Complementing these activities one can introduce rhymes like 'One, two buckle my shoe' and songs like 'Green grow the rushes, O!'; and all these rhythmic activities can continue and extend beyond the arithmetic main lesson of about one month – when the main focus will change to writing and later reading – for the time needed for such exercises is no more than 5 or 10 minutes each day.

By letting all but 10 children sit down, getting 7 to make a ring, then allowing the remaining 3 to run in to join the ring, so that everyone holds hands again in a widened circle, X = VII + III is experienced. This can be the beginning of almost countless variations. And what about the symbol for 'equals'? Well, perhaps you could have a long log balanced near its middle on another log and have a nice game of see-saw. The children will see to it by arranging themselves appropriately, that no consideration need be given to that erudite concept in physics known as the law of moments. The 'equals' sign is just a simple way of a drawing a log.

The minus sign is a simple way of drawing an outstretched arm, which itself can be referred to as a means of giving something to someone else. We can call such sums not 'taking away' but 'giving away'. One major aspect of evil in the world today is surely that people are often too intent on taking rather than being willing to give.

The division sign could be derived from the picture of someone with a hand under a plate of sandwiches and the other one on top about to share out the food to a group of hungry people.

The multiplication sign can be looked at as a picture of a sower of corn, arms and legs outstretched – recall the wonderfully rhythmic way this used to be done before the age of farm machinery, and get the class to imitate it. The quality of multiplication is felt in imagining the twentyfold or hundredfold return when the ripe corn is reaped.

That the way arithmetic is introduced has far-reaching moral effects can be understood by contemplating the above examples.

The first stage of actual arithmetic occurs through demonstration in which everything is visible for the children. Going on from the experience of their own bodies being units in a group, a teacher can, the next day, bring in a bowl of oranges, get a child to count how many there are and then empty the bowl into three piles, say. Further counting by other children will culminate in the verification, for example, that XII = III + V + IIII. It can

Chapter 2: What stimulates the child?

then be shown how XII is also I + XI or I + II + III + III + II + I and so on. Now let the whole class be divided up into about 7 or 8 groups. Let them push tables together and give each group a basket of walnuts or beautiful stones – not raspberries or caterpillars, of course. Let the children play! They can make all sorts of rearrangements, play shop or whatever else stimulates their arithmetical fantasy. Later in the lesson they can make coloured pictures in their books of examples from wider contexts, for instance of a court jeweller distributing a casketful of jewels according to the relative ages of three or four princes or princesses – always completing the drawing by a statement below it of the whole number and its additive parts.

The second stage is what may be called the imaginative stage, in which at least one of the numbers is invisible. Stories made up on the spot by the teacher (with a little forethought the previous evening) begin this new stage, in which greater concentration is demanded of the children. 'Mother squirrel has been collecting nuts for her three baby squirrels. From one tree she gathers five nuts and from another seven nuts. How many nuts has she now? She shares them equally among her babies. How many will each receive? In the course of five or ten minutes a lot of questions can be formed in this spontaneous way, all demanding quick oral answers, although in the first few days of introducing such stories one will need to go slowly. The children will be asked to use their fingers in the right order to reveal the answers. The stories should be shorn of extraneous details. What kind of landscape or forest there was, what event woke up mother squirrel that morning, what kind of nest or tree hole it was, whether the babies were nice and warm – such imaginative elaboration, though perfectly valid at a 'story time', is not right for a number lesson, since it promotes dreaming in the children rather helping them become wide awake in the sphere of numbers.

> Whilst it is of great value to *introduce* any educational subject to children by means of pictorial presentation – and each topic within that subject, too – there is a danger in adopting a similar attitude to the *development* of the subject or topic irrespective of its nature. When teaching reading and writing, or history, or art, the pictorial element always needs to be present. Mathematics teaching, though, is quite different in this respect. Human feelings and thought pictures nurture the essence of literature and history, but mathematics is essentially a *will* subject. The will has to be brought into thinking. While the introduction to mathematical topics does require the pictorial element – only in contemplating the pictorial is a growing human being left free, for pictures do not compel – this needs to give way to a musical element in the development of such topics. To use

15

> Rudolf Steiner's terminology, whilst literature and history rely on Imagination, mathematics relies on Inspiration. Mathematical progress depends upon overcoming and freeing oneself from the pictorial and living in sense-free concepts. This is why all pictures used in introducing mathematical topics need to be practical and precise. Teachers who like to bring fairies and gnomes into Class 1 arithmetic need to be aware of the dangers indicated above. To describe a situation like the following is also false in respect to elemental spirits:
>
> 'Once upon a time there was a gnome who had gathered eight beautiful jewels in a basket. After running through a vein of gold in the rocks he found that his basket only contained five jewels. Can you help him to decide how many jewels he must have dropped in the rocks?'
>
> This is an untrue picture, for it is actually in the nature of a gnome to know things immediately. He doesn't have to think through a problem like us poor human beings. Perceiving and thinking are not two separate activities for him. The gnome³ is awake in timeless 'at-one-ness'.

It now becomes important to lead the imaginative stage from general class oral activity to silent, individual written work. When one child is asked a question, even though the rest of the class remains silent, it can happen that the child gives the right answer without having consciously worked it out himself. The presence of the rest of the class, many of whom know the answer, has helped the child. He has taken the answer from a sort of subliminal telepathic atmosphere. This he can't do where written work is concerned.

The problem about the birthday party candles described in Chapter 1 belongs here, where it can be turned into a written problem. From the blackboard the child copies the following, the situation already having been explained to him. (The drawing will be four thick white strokes, not these wretched rectangular outlines.)

VII =   +

Chapter 2: What stimulates the child?

He has to count the number of candles, enter IIII in the space below them, and then fill in the last space. A similar task in subtraction could be

– it having first been explained that the birthday child had arranged some glasses into which orange juice would be poured at his party; but that only six children could come, so some glasses had to be put back in the cupboard.

Multiplication and division sums can be composed in like manner and it is good, as in oral work, to take all four rules at once since this is what happens in actual life. To work at nothing but addition for a week, then nothing but multiplication for another week, etc. can give children a feeling that mathematics is something abstracted from or foreign to the real business of living. None the less there will be occasions when concentration on a single process becomes necessary to develop a particular faculty.

When the 4 rules are introduced to a class 1, the teacher can bring about a livelier and deeper response when he is aware of children's temperaments. The four temperaments[4] are yet another consequence of the Pythagorean tetrad described in the Introduction. As in each of the examples given there, one takes two pairs of opposite qualities. The first, not now permanent / changing, cold/ warm, at rest/ movement or finite/ infinite – but *introvert versus extrovert* (like the other polarities, qualitatively similar to each other); and the second, not visible/invisible, moist/dry etc. (also qualitatively similar), but *satisfied / dissatisfied*. This gives rise to a simple way of understanding the four temperaments:

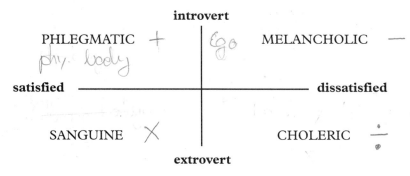

There are remarkable correspondences between these temperaments and (i) the four principles of the human being, (ii) the 4 rules in arithmetic.

Physical body	Ego	+	÷
Etheric body	Astral body	−	×

The reader is left to supply the two pairs of opposite qualities in each of these tetrads; a good imaginative task – just consider what adjacent zones have in common and ensure that the opposites have qualitative similarities to those in the other tetrads shown earlier.

With the above interrelationships in mind consider the example given of addition in the imagination stage of arithmetic. It is just this kind of question which especially interests phlegmatic children. They above all other children are the most disappointed if the ringing of the school bell marking the lesson's end prevents a teacher from completing the telling of a story. For they love wholeness. So, referring to Margaret's birthday in Chapter 1, make sure, when you have asked the children to raise their hands if they know the right number of candles, that you choose a phlegmatic to give the answer.

The answer to the question about glasses ready for orange juice in this chapter is best sought from a melancholic child. Melancholics have the keenest eye for detail and want to reduce the number of any kind of extraneous things. One has to watch that their handwriting does not become too small. In any situation at all embarrassing to them, they may wish that a hole in the floor would open up, down which they could slip and hide. They are a little too 'ego-aware'.

Sanguine children love variety – don't let them sit by the windows if you want to keep their attention. The example given in the chapter ahead where it is necessary to imagine turning over the pages of a book of stamps and do a multiplication sum, stimulates children of this temperament.

Finally, a choleric child loves to be in charge of a practical task, the more onerous the better, especially if he can tell others what to do to help. The example about rearranging chairs and the need to divide, also in the next chapter, is the kind of sum the choleric enjoys.

Naturally all children must do all 4 kinds of sums. The above choices for first answers simply gets the process going. When this is successful, a teacher will feel as if he has been conducting an orchestra. First the drums softly roll (phlegmatics), then the violins introduce the theme (melancholics). This is taken up by the woodwinds (sanguine) and finally the brass section (cholerics) bring the movement to a resounding climax.

Chapter 2: What stimulates the child?

It is necessary to emphasize at this point that the 'temperament principle' of correspondence shown here only applies to the 7-14 age range. Beyond puberty these relationships become quite different.

In the three parts – in the order they are written down – of each numerical example of the 'imagination' type of sum in the 4 rules, one can at once detect the presence of the three soul activities:

thinking   **feeling**   **willing**

Take the birthday candles example. First our attention is drawn to the 4 candles which are perceived. In our perceptions there is always an element of feeling involved; without this feeling we would never be able to remember what we have perceived. The 4 is the given part of the sentence

$$7 = 4 + 3$$

The 7 refers to the result, the goal or purpose of the event, and as such is the thought-borne element. The 3 concerns the actual deed, what has to be done to realise the goal; it is the will element.

Contemplation of the above will lead to the realisation that the procedure we go through in every intentional, conscious action in life, follows a precisely similar course. For example, we may be appointed to a new position in which we find ourselves among a new group of people. The first thing is to perceive and get to know these people and the way they work, as well as understanding the nature of our own job in the new environment. We 'feel out' the whole physical and human situation. Later on it may well occur to us that everything would be much more efficient and satisfying to everyone if things were organized in a slightly different way. Now we have a purpose. How to achieve the goal will require our will, including all the necessary tact we can develop.

| The goal conceived in **thinking** | = | the perceived given situation which we also **feel** | x | the change needed brought about by **will.** |

(Instead of **x** we could write **+**, **–**, **÷** or some other appropriate symbol). The third part is the part we don't see. Our life of will is never a gift from past experience. It has to do with the future, in which we need to have confidence. Further examples will be given in the next chapter.

The final stage concerns the third kind of sums, which are of the kind usually found in printed sets of questions in text books. Examples simply require the completion of statements like:

$$7 + 6 =$$

$$17 - 9 =$$

$$6 \times 3 =$$

$$12 - 2 =$$

This type of question is of practical importance for developing memory, quick accuracy and as a first step leading toward long multiplication and the like two years later. Compared to the previous stages, the third one, which could be called the **computation** stage, is already based upon thought, whereas the second (imaginative) stage has a feeling base and the first (demonstration) stage is based on doing, on the will.

By the second or third term in the first class the Roman numerals will have been replaced by the Arabic ones we commonly use, whose forms, beautiful though they are, have been subject to a lot of metamorphosis during their introduction into Europe. The capital letters of consonants originated from pictorial representation (ideographs) and are justifiably so derived in teaching children to write and then read, e.g. S from a picture of a swan and K from a picture of a king with foot forward and arm commandingly outstretched; but this doesn't work with the modern numerals used in our arithmetic. The Arabic originals were transformed for deployment in Europe through the initiative of Christian churchmen, so it is understandable that the symbols for planets, themselves endowed with crosses, transform as follows into our modern numerals.

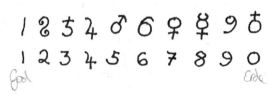

In the higher row, the sun (6) has a clockwise radiance above, whilst the smaller moon (9) has an anticlockwise radiance below. The zero, that brilliant discovery of the Arabs to which we owe so much, corresponds to our earth, around which we see everything else in the cosmos move. The one, 'all alone and ever more shall be so', belongs to God and the two to his prime mover. The correspondence of the remaining seven numbers to planets is illustrated in the work of Cornelius Agrippa[5] who called the magic squares of order 3, 4 etc. the Saturn, Jupiter etc. magic squares, in which the sum of the numbers in each row, column and diagonal, are always the same:

Chapter 2: What stimulates the child?

```
    8  1  6              1  15  14   4
    3  5  7             12   6   7   9
    4  9  2              8  10  11   5
                        13   3   2  16
```

It is 15 in the first case, 34 in the second, and $1/2n(n^2 + 1)$ in the nth case. The formation of such squares provides an excellent exercise for children at various ages – purely numerical for 9 or 10 year olds, algebraic for 13 year olds and as part of the theory of numbers for 18 year-old students.

Returning to the planet-numeral correspondence, this is not a suitable thing to present to young classes, of course. Our modern numerals surround children everywhere and they have no difficulty in making the transition from Roman numerals. A teacher might show how there is one stroke for 1, two strokes for 2, three for 3 – but the real story will have to wait until they are in an older class.

The extent to which arithmetic can be developed in a Class 1 must depend upon the nature of the particular group of children in it and what their teacher feels is best for them. Numbers extending to a hundred, the learning of the 2 times table and probably the 3x and 10x as well, and a full familiarity with the four rules and their simple applications to problems constitute the essentials. One of the great arts in teaching mathematics is to indicate further development in the subject coming in the year(s) ahead, with a light touch. So let the children recite what eleven tens and twelve tens make, even though the results go beyond a hundred.

The importance of daily rhythmic work with numbers cannot be too highly stressed, both orally by the class and by individual children, with and without limb movements. It is also good to have the class make the movements of clapping, jumping, walking, skipping and throwing with lips silent, the numbers simply being *thought*, and only voiced when, say, the teacher closes his eyes or scratches his left ear. All sorts of humorous little tricks can be of service. Maths has to be good fun.

Equally important is the choice of writing materials. At least A4 size blank paper books are needed. The crutches of printed ruled lines inhibit artistic expression and illustration and prevent development of the discipline required by the children to keep numbers and letters to the right size and alignment. Some less able children may for a time need a clearly ruled black line sheet placed under the writing page, but this crutch too should be dispensed with as soon as it can be. Coloured crayons or pencils are good writing tools, but wax crayons need conical ends; wax rectangular blocks are hopeless for numerals. Care needs to be exercised in how frequently a child swaps one colour for another. To write the answer or whole in one colour, the numbers occurring in the parts of the sum in other colours, the equals and addition signs in yet more colours, is going too far. It is, after all, arithmetic that the children are doing, rather than a 'number collage'.

Nor should one go to the other extreme. One evening whilst the author was taking a course in Russian at a technical college in the North Midlands, the lecturer apologised to our adult class for using coloured chalk: 'I know they are only used for backward children,' he said. Oh, dear!

In a two hour main lesson focused upon arithmetic the first half hour can include singing, movement, general (non-mathematical) recitation of verse, and then the oral and limb-active arithmetic. Following this will be the teacher-prompted review by the children of what they learned yesterday, then the teacher's introduction of new or consolidated work; and then there has to be up to an hour's steady written work in arithmetic. This may be relieved towards the end by the teacher telling a quick, short but interesting story unrelated to arithmetic, or a small part of another longer one; or perhaps the class will be taken outside to count the cows in a field or the buses going along a busy street at some moment, etc. The danger of a teacher's focus blurring so that child-centered written work becomes squeezed into a mere half hour, has to be avoided. The author still shudders at the memory of one class he visited in a school, where in a two-hour main lesson, a mere *ten minutes* written arithmetic was done by the children, half of it copied from the blackboard – a good example of how to cause boredom.

§3. Stimulation of mathematical activity up to the age of 8 or 9 (going on from Class 1 towards Class 3)

As the scope of arithmetic widens, the imaginative preparation of lessons has to intensify. The danger of writing a book such as this is that a reader may fall into the lazy habit of using the examples given here, instead of making up fresh ones for himself. The teacher's own creativity is a vital aspect of all teaching, and communicates itself to children in a mysterious, dynamic way. There are many ways of introducing units, tens, hundreds, etc. in a Class 2, of which the following is just one.

'Imagine a large apple orchard ready to be harvested. The workers carefully pick the apples and arrange them **ten at a time** in rows in a tray until the tray is filled up with **ten of these rows** of apples. Let's draw one of these trays.' (Let the children count as you quickly draw circular patches of red in the spaces, going as far as shown:)

Chapter 2: What stimulates the child?

```
OOOOO OOOOO
OOOOO OOOOO
OOOOO OOOOO
OOOOO
```

Someone carries a completely filled tray to a large box resting on a trolley, while another tray is filled. When the box is filled, with **ten trays** in it, it is wheeled to a trailer, which can take **ten boxes**. At the end of an hour there are two filled up trailers, four filled boxes for which there is no space on the trailers, six full trays which can't go into the boxes and one partially filled tray like the one in the drawing above. The whole collection drawn on a smaller scale would look like this if you were a bird flying over it:

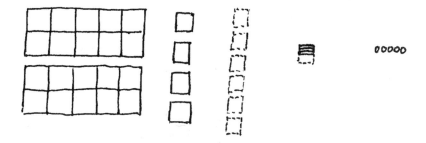

Now write the following list on the board and have a child write underneath each word the appropriate number.

trailers	boxes	trays	rows	apples
2	4	6	3	5

At this point the children can be asked to copy what has been drawn on the board, adding colour and detail to their taste, but also writing down an extra row of numbers to indicate a similar happening in an adjoining orchard. They then have the task of finding out the result of combining the two harvests. Whilst they are doing all this a set of similar sums can be written on the board to get on with, when they've done the first sum.

```
  24635          3604          12164      etc.
  71222          4235            804
      7
```

23

Teaching mathematics

The teacher can slip in towards the end of maybe twenty such sums, a couple like:

    5621   360
    <u>1763</u>   452
            and 823
                        <u>762</u>

to see what the quicker and cleverer children will make of them.

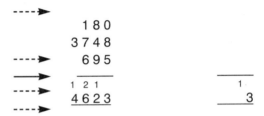

The new steps needed for doing the last two sums will be talked over with everyone next day, the significance of zeros as well, with a new set of sums incorporating 'carrying' written up ready for class. It is essential for the teacher to have decided well beforehand where to write the crutch, bearing in mind that she won't want to change boats in mid-stream when it comes to long multiplication in Class 3. Out of five possible places the one shown above has great advantages over the others in this respect.

Also in saying 'thirteen' in adding up the end column, the small number one can be written down first, then the larger number three after it, as is normal in the number thirteen, but just a bit lower.

The transition to the mathematical terms units, tens, hundreds etc. from apples, rows, boxes, etc. is easily effected after a day or two, and one can proceed to subtraction, short multiplication and division sums.

An interesting opportunity to apply the moral dimension of maths occurs with the first of these. Consider the sum 300058 − 2476. Instead of saying take away 6 from 8 like a tax collector, the large number can be pictured as giving away something of itself. After '8 give away 6 leaves 2', what next?

          300058
     −   <u>2476</u>
                 2

5 is not sufficiently well off to be able to give 7 away, so he or she asks his/her older brother or sister 0 to help. 'I'd like to,' 0 replies, 'but just a minute! I'll ask my older brother.' So this conversation continues until 3 says, 'Certainly,

Chapter 2: What stimulates the child?

I'll give you one of me, but that will be worth ten to you.' The series of donations which then takes place is indicated by neat crossing strokes, the noughts becoming nines, and the final givings away are quite easy.

$$\begin{array}{r} 2999{}_1 \\ 3\cancel{0}\cancel{0}\cancel{0}58 \\ -2476 \\ \hline 2 \end{array}$$

It's not so easy to devise a friendly conversation for the opposite way some people do subtraction sums, in which they tend to say 'As you can't take 7 from 5, then take 7 from 15 and next take 5 from 10 (instead of 4 from 9). The school staff should agree on which method they will use. New children coming in from other schools may of course have learnt other methods. Problems disappear, though, as one steadily dispenses with written crutches when doing sums on the board,

Multiplication and division of up to 5 digit numbers by a single numeral belong to Class 2 and (for brighter children) factor multiplication and division, e.g. by 28:

$$\begin{array}{r} 3193 \\ \times 7 \\ \hline {}_{1\ 6\ 2} \\ 22351 \\ \times 4 \\ \hline {}_{1\ 2} \\ 89404 \end{array} \qquad \begin{array}{r} 3193 \\ {}_{3\ 1} \\ 4\overline{)12772} \\ {}_{1\ 5\ 5\ 1} \\ 7\overline{)89404} \end{array}$$

Along with, indeed preceding, the doing of written sums must come lots of oral practice of 'tables' in many forms. During Class 2 all the rest of the tables up to 12 need to be learnt, each one in three ways (at least). Thus:

6 is 1 times 6,
12 is 2 times 6,
18 is 3 times 6 etc.

is archetypal – going from whole to parts. But this alone is of little use for helping children do written sums. One needs as well:

One 6 is 6,
Two 6's are 12,
Three 6's are 18 etc.

for use in written multiplication *and*

> 6 goes into 6...1,
> 6 goes into 12...2,
> 6 goes into 18...3, etc., to help written division.

Learning number bonds is also helpful:

> 9 and 9 make 18,   and 9 from 18 makes 9,
> 9 and 8 make 17,   9 from 17 makes 8,
> 9 and 7 make 16...   etc.

until
> 9 and 1 make 10.

> 8 and 8 make 16,   Instead of 'make' or 'makes'
> 8 and 7 make 15...   some teachers prefer 'is' or 'are'.

until
> 8 and 2 make 10.
> 7 and 7 make 14...

And so on until
> 5 and 5 make 10.

Class recitation of tables is a valuable rhythmic exercise, not only done standing, but with clapping, moving round a big circle, etc. This, however, is insufficient for children's individual, independent learning. The first beginnings of written mental work should begin in Class 2. On a spare sheet of paper given to each child, let the answers be written down for a set of ten questions called out slowly by the teacher, e.g.

> 1. How many 4s in 8?   6. Multiply 9 by 4
> 2. How many 4s in 12?   7.   "   9 by 5
> 3. How many 4s in 16?   8.   "   9 by 6
> 4. How many 4s in 24?   9. What is 9 times itself?
> 5. How many 4s in 36?   10. What times itself makes 16?

Then call out the ten answers, getting each child to mark his own work. After that ask for hands to be raised for 'all correct?', 'eight or nine right?', 'five, six or seven right', and with a smile, 'less than five?' A teacher's approving, shining eyes directed at those who have improved on earlier totals is all that is needed to complete such testing.

Chapter 2: What stimulates the child?

As the following years go by – and this can be done regularly, right up to Class 9 – let three successive sets of ten questions be asked, extending the examples to money, lengths, angles, percentages and so on. The speed of asking can be increased. By a Class 6 or 7 the children will have to write one answer down quickly whilst listening to the next question; ten questions in fifteen seconds. It is stimulating for the teacher too, to have to make up questions on the spot and write answers simultaneously on his own piece of paper.

The encouragement of discovery in the whole land and life of number needs to be active in the teacher throughout every class in the school. That no one can pour knowledge or skills into a child in the way beer can be poured from a jug into a mug is a wonderful fact. All the time one is telling the children as little as possible, simply trying instead to create the conditions whereby the children draw conscious awareness and inner mobility out of their thinking soul and spirit. From a simple suggestion in Class 2 – that to learn the 7 times table, help for the lower answers might come from tables they know already – they learn the commutative law (e.g. 4 x 7 = 7 x 4). By Class 3 one can ask the class to copy and take further the following list:

$$8 \times 8 = 64$$
$$1$$
$$9 \times 7 = 63$$
$$3$$
$$10 \times 6 = 60$$

when the numbers in the first and second columns increase and decrease by one each time. So:

$$5$$
$$11 \times 5 = 55$$
$$7$$
$$12 \times 4 = 48$$
$$9$$
$$13 \times 3 = 39$$
$$11$$
$$14 \times 2 = 28$$
$$13$$
$$15 \times 1 = 15$$
$$15$$
$$16 \times 0 = 0$$

Put the number differences 1, 3 etc. between each pair of results as shown. Afterwards do another list. Weaker children might begin with 4 x 4. Those with a high opinion of themselves might start with 20 x 20 and soon maybe wish they hadn't. So the children themselves discover the amazing fact that they always end up with a string of all the odd numbers in order. 'Why?', they ask. 'That is something you will find out when you are in Class 7 or 8. By then we will know about something called algebra,' you reply. Wonder has been stimulated and all knowledge – of every kind, not only mathematical – begins with wonder.

Both teachers and children can go on to discover other exciting number patterns. Numbers can also be arranged in pictures and their relationships discovered in geometrical forms. A 6 x 6 beginning in the previous example can be exhibited in the picture of a clock, multiplying its numerals horizontally. What happens if you do this diagonally? Or maybe with curved lines? How about putting a 3 times table round a figure eight? And suppose you are not always multiplying, but adding or...?

Running in parallel with number development must go the experience of forms. The very first lesson in Class I can be the experience of the difference between a straight and a curved line. The teacher, who will have begun by getting everyone to stand up facing him with really straight backs, slowly draws a vertical line on the blackboard – not too thin; it might even be a centimetre wide. Then having bidden everyone sit, keeping straight backs (to start with), let the children in turn come out and draw their own straight lines with their own choice of coloured chalk, length and width. An interesting picture of the class emerges – what variety! Yet everyone has within him the awareness of his own straightness. On a second blackboard the teacher can draw a curved line, almost a semicircle perhaps, and again the children follow suit. How different the picture becomes now! Ask the class what they feel about the two pictures. The hidden qualities of the children's own activity will be experienced anew when they are asked to make their own two pictures with many such lines in their books, on successive pages.

Form drawing is a subject in itself from Class 1 onwards. Whole books have been written about it.[6] Repeating patterns constitute one development from the beginning described above. Using the whole width of the paper, sequences like these, in large size, are practised with a coloured crayon.

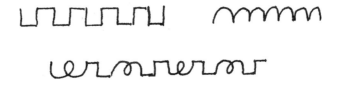

Chapter 2: What stimulates the child?

Drawings like the third one will not be given at the beginning, of course, but it illustrates one practical application of form drawing – that of teaching cursive writing the following year.

Another kind of form drawing which, in the author's view, needs introduction fairly early in Class 1 (some people prefer to delay this to Class 2, for reasons which seem to me not very clear) is often called symmetrical drawing. Children either carefully draw a vertical line down the middle of their paper, or use the line made by folding the page exactly in half, then opening it out again. Then they copy a form which the teacher makes on the left hand side of a similar line drawn on the board. Without further visual assistance from the teacher they have to complete their page with a form on the right which balances the one on the left as nearly as possible. These forms and balancing forms are drawn freehand. Such drawings are not easy for some children but they are just what they most need. For this activity is probably the most effective counter to dyslexia[7] that exists. An extension of the first kind of drawing (i) is shown in (ii) where the relationship to letter forms is obvious.

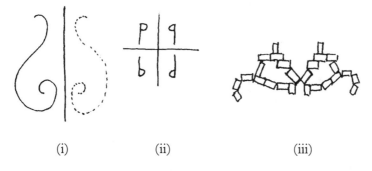

(i)   (ii)   (iii)

In (iii) is indicated the beginning of a symmetrical theme achieved by first issuing children with a large number of 1 by 2 cm. rectangles cut from sheets of coloured paper whose other side is adhesive – or the children could make such rectangles themselves. Many pairs of irregular forms of varying size, colour and shape could also be used. When left to make their own patterns, quite involved and often beautiful symmetrical results are achieved, often by those who are not at all good in number work. Such work belongs to Classes 3 and 4 and could accompany the Main Lesson topics of house building or physical measures in Class 3, and fractions in Class 4. Paints, fibres and clay naturally give further possibilities. Work with fixed building units should not be overdone, however. The discipline of exact drawing, controlling arm and finger to achieve curved forms, has the greatest value.

Large freehand form drawing has so many possibilities and extensions for both teacher- and child-inspired discoveries of the beauty of both linear and area forms: in- and out-going spirals (good, respectively, for children with sanguine and melancholic tendencies in Class 1), nestings of squares and diamonds (Class 1 or 2), structures symmetrical about a vertical plane, using either a whole large piece of clay or many small brick-like pieces of clay (Class 3) are some of them.

In a subtle way, child development in the early part of the class teacher years – the full understanding of which requires the teacher to train himself in the perception of the etheric body's evolution – is related to the 3 dimensions of space.[8] Experience of the linear, i.e. actively moving along straight and curved lines – both physically in classroom or playground and then in imagination, and on the page or sheet of paper – suits the character of Class 1 children. The two-dimensional experience of the whole page through coloured areas is more satisfying for Class 2, whilst down-to-earth three-dimensional work is what Class 3 wants. Both the Main Lessons in farming and building (including protection from the elements generally, such as with clothing) in Class 3, serve this need.

§4. Working with Class 3

Class 3 arithmetic, besides developing skill in long multiplication and long division, includes all the various kinds of measures about which children need to know. The whole phenomenon of time is of special interest to the nine year-old, for whom the stories of the Old Testament answer many questions about how the world began, and how human generations evolved from Adam and Eve's descent from Paradise to Earth. The Old Testament gives a strong impression of the need for older, experienced, wiser people telling younger, inexperienced people what to do, and guiding them. A simplified Old Testament is an excellent reader for the class and the main lesson with this focus contains a prime opportunity for telling children the simple human physical facts about how babies are conceived, as well as the meanings of all ten commandments.

From Spring, beginning in any one year, 25,920 is the number of times the circling zodiacal stars have to pass behind the sun before they stand in the same relation to it at another beginning of spring. 25,920 years was felt by the ancient people of India as the time it takes the great God Brahma to breathe in and out once. 'How many breaths do *we* have in a single day?' you ask the children. An experiment in quietly counting the number of breaths they take averages about 18 in a minute. Multiplying by the number of minutes in an hour, and the result by the number of hours in a day they can calculate 18 x 60 x 24 = 25,920, the same number as before! Then you can ask them how many times in life they go to sleep for the night (a breathing out of their souls from their bodies) and wake up again (breathing the soul in) next morning. They will have been taught already that there are 365 or 366 days in a year, so this is shortened to 360 to make the sum easier. The bible speaks about 'three score years and ten' as the normal span of human life and this can be increased a bit to 72 to balance the decrease to 360. So the answer is 360 x 72, i.e. 25,920 again! All three instances are approximations but the remarkable numerical agreement stimulates wonder, a feeling that what happens in our own lives and in the heavens are in tune with each other. Breathing is felt to be of a universal nature.

When the class has learnt the numerical relationships of years, months, weeks, days, hours, minutes and seconds (this is a good moment to ensure that everyone in the class can tell the time on a clock properly), sums such as the following can be set.

How many calendar months in 7 years?

How many years in 132 successive calendar months?

How many weeks in 56 days?

How many hours in 5 days?

How many minutes in 360 seconds?

Measures give excellent further practice of multiplication tables. Liquid measure using 8 pints to the gallon and 8 gallons to the bushel may seem archaic, but so are the cubits they may read about in the Old Testament. Moreover, a good springboard is provided for base 8 arithmetic in an older class by finding, say, the total amount of milk produced in three cow stalls given the amount of bushels, gallons and pints coming from each one. Before any sums to do with capacity are set, here is an excellent opportunity to let the class play with thimbles, medicine bottles, cups, jugs, teapots, flower vases, buckets etc., filling them with water, seeing how many vesselfuls of one kind will fill another vessel and so on, introduced so effectively in state schools thirty or more years ago. The wise teacher will naturally wait for a dry day and have the children perform these experiments in the open air, one toying with the thought of a future career behind a public bar perhaps, another in a café or as a chemist.

Another educative experiment is to have the whole class line up with their heels against the wall of the school building and have them place heel to toe successively as they walk across the playground to determine its length in feet. The wide discrepancy in answers shows the need for a standard foot. In the first place some handsome prince's foot may be suggested as basis for measurement. It is unlikely that even a junior women's libber in the class would press for the foot of the princess in the circumstances! Here is the right moment to issue to the class rulers with a foot of inches on one side and 30cm on the other. All the old English measures are fine for Class 3, for the inch, foot and yard originate in the human body, the furlong from the length of a furrow and so on. In addition further excellent practice of the tables arises (3x, 8x, 12x, even 22x). The metric system of lengths based upon a false calculation of the earth's circumference in Napoleon's time, can be taken up a term later.

So can litres and the metric measurement of weight. Hundredweights, stones, pounds, and ounces no longer serve much purpose today, apart from knowing how heavy we are.

The order of introduction of the measures follows a descent from the more cosmic to the more earthly. Least cosmic of all is money. It was Christ's third temptation, turning stones (or gold, money) into bread which caused the Cosmic Being his biggest problem.[9] Adding up costs in shopping lists, knowing what change is required from a £20 note and how it is placed into one's hand form part of the essential mathematics in Class 3.

In a Class 3, long multiplications present few lasting difficulties provided clear, tidy arrangement of the sums is demanded and not more than three digits in the multiplier are used. It is again helpful to look ahead to future years' work, however, and first multiply by the leftmost digit. Thus we first multiply here* by 200. Notice the value of using crutches in the way mentioned earlier. If the children's writing is allowed to become too small, the less visible distinction between the numbers of the sum and the crutches will lead to errors in addition. It is in later years when having, for example, to multiply 7.49 by 2.56 correct to two decimal places, that the method of first multiplying by 2 will pay dividends. For the answer of 19.17 is unaffected by the column on the far right.

$$\begin{array}{r} 749 \\ \times 256 \\ \hline {\scriptstyle 1} \\ 149800 \\ {\scriptstyle 2\ 4} \\ 37450 \\ {\scriptstyle 2\ 5} \\ 4494 \\ {\scriptstyle 1\ 2\ 1\ 1} \\ \hline 191744 \end{array}$$

*

Chapter 2: What stimulates the child?

Long division however, can become the last straw for the less able child, if it is not taught properly. It is here that a child can inwardly throw in the towel. 'Maths just isn't my subject!' This is exacerbated when crossings out begin to breed like greenfly on a cherished rose bush. There is in fact no need whatever to guess the numerals in the quotient and then alter them if they prove wrong, or to use a piece of rough paper to do trials. Let us divide 89631 by 23. In Class 2 the children will have used their familiarity with the 4 times table to divide 3572, say, by 4, as follows:

```
      8 9 3                    or half mentally
 4 ) 3 5 7 2
     3 2                               8 9 3
     ___                               3 1
       3 6                     4 ) 3 5 7 2
       ___
         1 2
         1 2
```

The first, not the second, method is best used for long division, but wholly so, that is to say we now need the 23 times table. So write this down first, adding 23 to each row to get the next number, checking that the 10th number is 23 with a 0 following it. The lines included after each three numbers help to view the separate numbers which will later be chosen from the whole column. After doing a few long division sums the first column 1, 2, 3. can be omitted. Now the proposed division is straightforward; it's just a matter of seeing where the various dividends lie between the rungs of the ladder.

```
  1.      23         3897
  2.      46         23)89631
  3.      69         69
  4.      92         206
  5.     115         184
  6.     138         223
  7.     161         207
  8.     184         161
  9.     207         161
 10.     230
```

Isn't this a rather long business, having to construct a 23 times table first?' Certainly it is, but everything is clear; guessing is unnecessary and tidiness and beauty in lay-out is preserved. Moreover no one in adult life ever does long division. We use hand calculators. It is not, therefore, a question of saving time when teaching long division. The chief value in teaching it is once again the development of clear, exact thinking. If this is considered a bit superfluous in modern technologically-oriented life, then you may as well give out calculators in Class 1. So much the worse for the future of civilisation!

There is, however, little point in dividing by a number with three or more digits, although a teacher could have examples of division by 127 or 349 up his sleeve to produce for talented pupils who have soon accurately finished the set of questions the class has been asked to do.

This leads to the whole problem of varying ability within a class of children. In a Rudolf Steiner (Waldorf) School there can sometimes be a very wide ability range. In many school systems not only are the children in a particular one-year age range streamed into different classes according to their general intellectual abilities (a practice avoided in Waldorf Schools), but they are further arranged in sets for mathematics lessons too, according to their proficiency.

Underlying the choice of mathematical topics in each class of a Waldorf School is the judgment of what topics help the whole development of the child in each chronological age. Children who are 9 years old naturally question authority. A child may even surreptitiously elbow a bowl of flowers off a cupboard just to see how the teacher will react to the damage. If the child is not asked to clean up the mess, fill another vase with water and arrange the fallen flowers in it, then next day replace the broken vase, preferably buying a new one out of his own pocket money, he will have been denied the answer to his inner (perhaps sub-conscious) question. This in turn may lead to his failure to begin developing that essential inwardly directed authority we call self discipline. In spiritual scientific technical language the age of nine is when an ego presentiment projects into the etheric body and heralds the second of its three formative steps between the ages of roughly 7 and 14. Such invisible maturation is independent of either physical maturation or 'developmental age' – the term often used in educational psychology as an assessment biased in favour of solely intellectual performance.

> All children of 9 require education in the need for guidance and authority, which is revealed to them in house-building, farming, Old Testament stories, etc. Learning about measures and long division is part of this. It is unhealthy and unsociable for the brightest at maths in a class to be engaged in a different topic or branch of the subject

> from the weaker children. Such arrangements can sap the confidence of the weak ones or at least cause them to feel inferior. It does not help the clever ones, either, to be treated as sheep, as opposed to goats. But whereas everyone in the class can be engaged in the same mathematical topic, the weaker ones will need to concentrate on its simpler aspects whilst the clever ones tackle harder problems as well.

Examples of sets of questions for written work are given in the next chapter. They are devised with the thought of about an hour's written work for the whole class being needed daily. In the first 5 or 10 minutes the teacher's energy is occupied in helping the weakest third of the class who will do well to succeed with the first third of the questions set. Then he can help the middle third of the class who by now have progressed beyond the easy earlier questions. After that, the brightest third of the class, having done all the (to them) really easy questions, may require some advice about the later, difficult questions. From Class 3 onwards the teacher can save himself a lot of time by having all the answers available at the foot of the set of written questions, but not in the same order as the questions. For easy reference they can be arranged as an increasing set of numbers. Then a child who finds that his answer appears in the answer list can tackle the next question without bothering the teacher. It is worth stressing that a smaller number of correct solutions is preferable to a large number of correct ones interspersed with many incorrect ones.

It is important to make a habit of collecting up the children's books and marking them, or confirming that their own marking of answers was done correctly. In Waldorf Schools teachers encourage their pupils to regard their written work, complemented by coloured illustrations, as works of art in the making. This leads to the treasuring of completed books and gives the creators of their contents a valuable reference and record of the progress they have made, both then and for future years. No such book can be perfect, although striving towards near perfection provides a good stimulus. Arithmetical errors are bound to occur here and there. A sum done wrong can receive a small cross by its answer and if time permits the correct sum with appropriate tick included later. A fetish that no errors or mistakes of any kind should disfigure a completed book (whether in spelling and grammar, numerical accuracy or in historical or scientific fact) is unhelpful and is caused by a self-centered desire (by teacher or school rather than by pupils) to erect breath-taking exhibitions of colourful and faultless work. It is, of course, an excellent thing to show admirable artistic and academic achievements, but to have special books containing nothing but correct arithmetical solutions to problems, copied from practice books where mistakes don't matter, would be an awful source of time wasting. We learn so much by making mistakes and later correcting them; this too, is worth showing. Whatever the mathematical context or topic in a particular class, whose membership is solely determined by the chronological (as distinct from developmental) age of the children, there is plenty for the cleverest and weakest to get their teeth into. Never need it happen that a weak child or his parents should feel that more is being demanded of him than he can cope with. Equally unnecessary is it for a talented individual (or again his parents) to complain that he hasn't enough work to do of a challenging kind. Some of the best schools in the earlier part of the century in this county were our village schools. Only a few now exist. The teachers had a big age as well as ability range to deal with. In many cases they developed fine, imaginative presentations. Younger children could listen in to lessons given to older ones and vice versa, and the content was the same for both the more gifted and less able children. We just don't need the strait-jacket techniques of streaming any more than we need rigid national curricula. But fortunately, with good sense to sift out from the latter what we can use, and with imagination to transform it, we can invest the substance of our teaching with wholesomeness even within such constraints.

There is no limit to ways of stimulating children in mathematical activity. It is only when we lose sight of the essentially human, fail to read child nature and its inner development at each age, that we don't choose the best subject matter or fail to find healthy imagination in ourselves to encourage their learning. Dull theoretical or unsuitable technological influences then creep in. There is a simple way of finding out whether we are succeeding or not. The children will tell us by their eyes, the way they breathe and smile. When at the end of the main lesson block, whether it is maths or some other subject, they extravagantly and maybe shortsightedly declare, 'This is the best main lesson we've ever had' you know you have not failed to stimulate them.

Chapter 3:
Suitable examples for children's written arithmetic in Classes 1 to 3 (6 to 9 years old)

§1. Class I

Several examples have already been given in Chapter 2. Since children are not yet able to read words at the beginning of this class, questions need to be pictorial in form. Careful copying from a blackboard is in itself a real exercise. Before they do this it is good to look through with them all the questions on the board, which you have set for the class that morning. Make sure they know what you want them to do in the whole set before they copy the first question; also make sure the board drawings are large ones.

Demonstration type

Each child can have a little basket or box of small nuts or stones from which to extract and arrange piles demonstrating the sums. Then by copying these arrangements she can complete her drawings and write the appropriate Roman numerals below them. The nuts and stones can naturally represent anything – oranges, jewels, people, animals, money… The use of freely chosen colours will enhance the drawings. The teacher's descriptions and explanatory words are indicated in brackets.

1. (apples, picked and placed on these plates – choose how many you like for the other two plates, but don't leave any unpicked. Put numbers instead of dots underneath.)

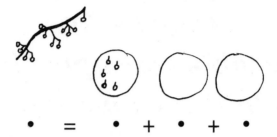

• = • + • + •

2. (bales of hay for cattle in four fields)

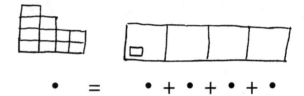

• = • + • + • + •

3. (eggs put into three baskets)

• = • + • + •

4. (each box has to have the same number of caterpillars)

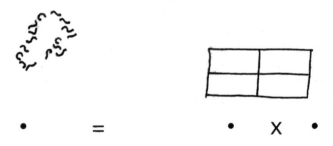

• = • × •

5. (each part of the sky has to have the same number of stars)

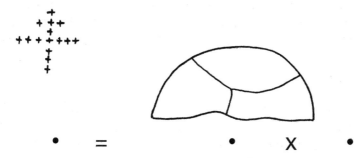

• = • X •

6. (put these rings into as many triangular boxes as you like, but each box must have the same number of rings)

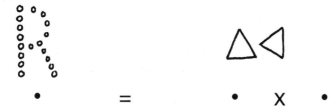

• = • X •

7. (use the red spots to make dominoes where each domino is a double)

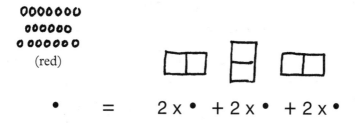

• = 2 x • + 2 x • + 2 x •

8. (arrange all these flowers in vases so that each vase has one more flower than the one before)

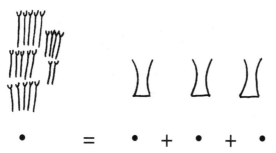

• = • + • + •

All these examples, it must be stressed, are not intended to be photocopied for children, nor even just copied from this book on to the blackboard. They are here to stimulate the teacher's own imagination. She will find her own contexts and produce much more interesting examples out of herself.

Imagination type

Here we dispense with nuts and stones. The children have to use their own fingers and their imagination. The only drawing to be made each time is the one copied (and perhaps made with greater beauty). This represents the *given* element (what is seen). The goal or result is shown in Roman numerals. The child has to count what is seen and then decide what has to be done, expressing each result also in Roman numerals. The two examples in Chapter 2 could be complemented by two more in the form of a completed birthday story. Here is another story.

1.(A carpenter took these planks out of his store to make a shed, but found that he needed 19 altogether. How many more did he fetch from the store?)

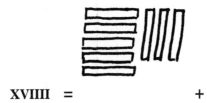

XVIIII =   **+**

2. (He brought these bolts with him but only used 8 of them. How many did he return to his store?)

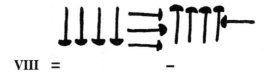

VIII =   **−**

3. (He had these tacks to fix pieces of felt to the roof, but each piece needed 6 tacks. How many pieces of felt could he fix?)

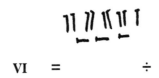

VI =   **÷**

Chapter 3: Examples for classes 1-3

4. (The floor needed 20 beams. He could carry this many at once. How many journeys did he have to make from the store?)

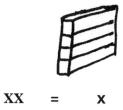

XX　=　X

Smaller numbers could be used in such examples to begin with, increasing their size in later examples for the cleverer children.

Computation type

A few questions using Arabic numerals in the imagination type of sum might be done at first. Then pictures as well as Roman numerals can be dispensed with altogether.

1. (How many pages of stamps do you need to stick one stamp on each of 24 letters to be posted?)

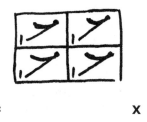

24　=　　　　X

2. (I only need 8 of these pound coins. How many can I give to my friend?)

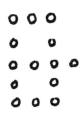

8　=　—

3.   11 = 3 +
4.   5 = 10 ÷

Then come the sets of questions on the 4 rules in a purely computing manner. Remind children that question 17 can also be read as 'How many threes in six?'

5.	2+7=	9.	6−3=	13.	4x2=	17.	6÷3=
6.	4+3=	10.	9−4=	14.	3x3=	18.	12÷2=
7.	7+6=	11.	14−6=	15.	3x5=	19.	17÷1=
8.	14+4=	12.	20−15=	16.	6x3=	20.	16÷4=

Later on a teacher could write a sum on the board (still in Class 1) but cover up one number with her hand and ask the children to say what it must be before removing her hand. Then with another sum she could use the backs of her wrists to cover up a number. With a third sum she could just draw her wrists, and with a fourth write X. Children could then do sums where they have to replace X by a number. When teaching algebra in Class 7 it is good to be able to say, 'Actually you learned to do algebra in Class 1'.

So: $6 + 2 = x$ $x =$ (What is x?)
         $3 \times x = 12$ $x =$
         $20 \div x = 5$ $x =$
         $x - 9 = 4$ $x =$

There are, of course, many ways of introducing written sums in Class 1. A teacher might say to her class, 'Eight swallows were sitting on a telephone wire, then 3 flew away.' She writes 8 − 3 = on the board and asks everyone to copy and complete the arithmetical sentence to show how many swallows were left on the wire.

To bring in additional variety it is good to consult various text books in public libraries, to look at examples suggested in National Curriculum publications and – most helpful of all – look through the written work done by children in previous Class Ones including those in other schools. There follow some examples of wider range – needing oral input from the teacher.

1. Copy and write down the neighbours (above and below) of 35, 19, 50.
2. Can you do those in Roman numerals, too?
3. Make a list of the numbers between 10 and 20 which don't come in the 2 times table.

Chapter 3: Examples for classes 1-3

4. 'Guess how many marbles there are in this glass. Write down your guess.' 'Now, count them', (you say to one child, who empties the glass, marble by marble.) 'Now write down by how many you over- or underestimated the total.'
5. Draw a triangle and mark the middle of each side. Join up these middle points. How many triangles are there in the whole drawing?
6. Draw a square and its diagonals. How many triangles *altogether* can you count now?
7. Write down all the Roman numerals you can make using just 7 sticks. How many did you find? Which is the highest number?
8. How many more numbers can you find if you can use at most 6 and at least 1 of the sticks?
9. Draw a clock with Roman numerals on it. Now write outside each number another one to make it a 24-hour clock.
10. Draw a clock with modern numbers on it. Join up all the numbers that come as answers in the 2 times table with red lines and all those in the 3 times table with blue lines. Have any lines become purple?
11. Suppose you were to share out 28 crystals among a group of girls so that the oldest received 1 crystal, the next oldest 2 crystals, the next oldest 3 crystals and so on. How many girls would have to be in the group?
12. See if you can draw this picture carefully, using different colours for squares and diamonds. Then draw one more square inside and one more diamond outside.

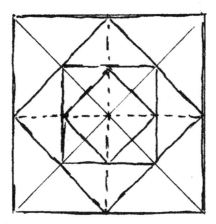

To do these questions, children will need to use their fingers, or in some cases small baskets of nuts or stones.

> Some teachers whose Class One contains a preponderance of slow learners, and also some teachers of an older school of thought in Waldorf schools may consider that some of the questions in this section are too advanced or too abstract or intellectual for Class One. Whilst one can sympathise with such a view – for certainly the danger is always present of going beyond what the nature of a seven year-old requires from us – the following remarks are in place here:
>
> i) 'Intellectual' in Rudolf Steiner's use of the word simply means analysis or going from the whole to the parts;
>
> ii) it is only when one stops with these parts, ignoring their origin (a failure in modern particle physics), and fails to use the synthesising power of reason to re-attain the whole in a more comprehensive way, that one may be justified in using the word 'intellectual' in a derogatory way;
>
> (iii) 'abstract' means to take something out of its context, for example quoting from a lecture, usually without fully understanding its significance in the whole lecture.

§2. Class 2

Besides the frequent, diverse oral practice of all the multiplication tables and number bonds in addition and subtraction, examples of the following kind need to be done regularly in written work. The list below might be regarded as an hour's revision test towards the year's end.

1. 35
   +24
2. 718
   −213
3. 32
   × 3
4. 2) 128
5. 424+3 + 31
6. 58+26 + 13
7. 375 − 158
8. 153 × 4
9. 5)5125
10. 616+4127+358+91
11. 15006 − 1297
12. 142857 × 7
13. 12)379248
14. 2166 × 27
    (multiply 2166 by 9 and then the answer by 3)
15. 33792 ÷ 44
    (similar method)

Chapter 3: Examples for classes 1-3

16. Subtract 29 from 917. Then divide the answer by 7, showing the remainder.

17. Work out the 13 times table.

List of answers:

6	64	104	217	1025
13	65	117	458	5192
26	78	126	505	13709
39	91	130	612	31604
52	96	143	768	58482
59	97	156	888	999999

Since so much depends upon the teacher composing and working out simple examples of the 4 rules each evening before the lesson, further examples of this kind for Class 2 need not be given here. But notice the value of writing on the board along with the questions, but not in the same order, a set of answers. Children will notice if their answer to a question comes somewhere in the list. If so they don't need to ask you if their sum is correct and much time and energy is saved for helping children who are having problems.

A beginning can be made in Class 2 with written problems, first copied from the board, then read aloud by the whole class, then by one or two individuals weak at reading, then discussed between teacher and class. Indications written on the board by teacher or child might follow, then everyone can get down to the task individually in their own book.

Two examples:

1. If a hundred and sixty-five tadpoles were shared equally among five tanks, how many tadpoles would live in each tank?

2. The swan carried the princess for thrice four weeks across the great sea. Seventy-two times did she see the sun rise in her journey, but the other mornings were dark with clouds. How many dark mornings were there?

Practice in changing numerals and large numbers into words and vice versa belongs to Class 2.

§3. Class 3

It is important that before children reach the age of 10 they learn to handle whole numbers with at least 3 or 4 digits in each of the processes of the four rules (or four operations). This means that they should have achieved some proficiency in long multiplication and long division. The class teacher should try to ensure that at least two thirds of the children have managed this by the end of Class 3. For looking ahead, the main work in Class 4 mathematics will concern fractions and decimals. Weakness in handling whole numbers could well be a serious hindrance in learning about these new number experiences. The examples below (answers in brackets) indicate a progression from easier to harder sums.

1. 312 x 21   (6552)   – no 'carrying'.
2. 1102 x 43   (47386)   – "   "   , but use of zero.
3. 24 x 42   (9828)   – a little 'carrying'.
4. 574 x 67   (38458)
5. 97 x 85   (8245)
6. 234 x 567   (132678)
7. 9999 x 111   (1109889)   *   (53
8. 1471 x 143   (210353)   106
                                                    159
9. Work out the 53 times table.*   212
                                                    265
10. 1272 ÷ 53   (24)   318
11. 2769 ÷ 71   (39)   371
12. 2002 ÷ 22   (91)   424
13. 69741 ÷ 123   (567)   477
14. 50001 ÷ 23   (2173, remainder 22)   530)
15. 100000 ÷ 101 (990, remainder 10)

When children spot shortcuts, e.g. in question 12 divide by 2, then 11, or in question 15 don't write out the 101 times table – certainly allow this. There is little value in dividing or multiplying by a 4 digit number, but you might have a couple up your sleeve for clever ones who soon rattle through the questions set for the class. It is also instructive to get children to do the reverse calculation, so from question 5 do: 8245 ÷ 85 and from question 13 do: 567 x 123. Learning about measurement gives rise to a big range of problems and this provides the opportunity to give a lot of practice in problems written in sentences, as distinct from pure number problems. On the simplest level you can ask the children to fill in the spaces:

Chapter 3: Examples for classes 1-3

1.   5 weeks   =   days
2.   3 years   =   calendar months
3.   63 days   =   weeks
4.   120 seconds =   minutes
5.   3 days   =   hours, and so on,

also doing similar things with liquid measure, length and weight. When it comes to questions involving whole sentences or paragraphs, then it is best to photocopy a set of such question in your best handwriting and let the children later paste these into their own main lesson books alongside their arithmetic. Here is a range of such questions.

1. Mary went for a four day hike. She walked 10 miles the first day and it took her 5 hours. Next day she walked 11 miles and 2 furlongs, taking her 5 hours and 20 minutes. On each of the last two days she walked 12 miles and 3 furlongs taking 6 hours and 20 minutes each time. How *far* did she walk altogether?

2. How much *time* did Mary spend walking altogether?

3. Each of eight big families ordered 1 gallon and 3 pints of milk from the milkman. How many gallons altogether did he have to supply?

4. I went into a confectioner's shop and bought:
     3 loaves costing 83p each,
     4 packets of biscuits costing £1.20 each and
     2 cakes costing £1.95 each.
   What change should I get from a twenty pound note?

5. The floor of a building is 15 yards long, 12 yards wide, and it has to be covered with square concrete slabs, each side of every slab being a yard in length. How many slabs must be used?

6. If one of the slabs were marked out in inch squares, how many of these inch squares would there be altogether on this slab?

7. Three heavy men weighing 15 stone 12 pounds, 16 stone 9 pounds and 17 stone 6 pounds stepped carefully into a light boat which would sink if more than 50 stone were placed in it. Did the boat sink?

8. Robert bought 25 coloured pencils each costing 35p. His change from a £10 pound note consisted of a small coin and six slightly bigger ones of a different shape. What were all these coins?

9. How many centimetres are there in 5 kilometres?

10. A roll of cloth 70 yards long has to be cut into pieces 8 feet long. How many pieces will there be and what length of cloth will not be used?

11. If the roll were 70 metres long instead, and pieces 2 metres 60 centimetres long were required, what would the 2 answers be then?

12. A cubical tin in which every edge is 10 cm long will hold a litre of water weighing a kilogram. If a quarter of the litre is poured away, what will the remaining water weigh in grams? What depth of water in millimetres will there be now?

Naturally, simpler examples of the above need to be set first, for the reasons given in Chapter 2. So if the morning's written work is about length – and we will suppose that metric lengths will be introduced later in the month's main lesson block – you might have:

1. How many inches are there in 2 feet?

later,

7. The fields of a farm all ended along the bank of a straight canal and each field was a furlong in length. Altogether the canal ran along two and a half miles of the farm. How many fields were there?

later,

13. A goods train had a diesel engine 4 yards long and 33 trucks each 19 feet long. Every coupling space was a yard. The whole train was longer than an eighth part of a mile. How much longer? Give the answer in yards.

As usual, include the three answers in a list below the questions, i.e. 20, 24, 26. It doesn't matter at all that the weaker children will not have time to get anywhere near question 13. They will feel, however, that if they had a much longer time, they would probably have been able to do that question too, with a little help. Next morning, though, they will watch the teacher doing question 13 on the board, helped by suggestions from the class, as revision of the work of the day before. Some of the cleverer ones may be inspired by the beauty and clarity of the teacher's lay-out on the board in comparison, maybe, with their own. Once again the social divisiveness caused by making different ability groups work at different assignments, in turn brought about by examination league tables and other apings of professional football, has to be avoided.

§4. Practice periods

It is important, certainly from Class 3 onwards, that each week, in addition to main lessons of up to 2 hours daily, there shall be 2 or 3 forty minute 'extra main' or practice periods taken by the class teacher. During a maths block of main lessons they will be devoted to practice of the English language. During other blocks these shorter periods need to be used for arithmetic (and drawing exercises). Here it is not a case of introducing new topics but of practising what has been taught in earlier maths blocks. For learning maths is like learning foreign languages, which also need regular practice.

So later in Class 3, such a forty minute slot would include a five minute introduction by the teacher, 30 minutes quiet individual work by the children and a 5 minute ending for them to tick or cross their answers whilst the teacher calls out the correct ones. The assignment may be:

1. Add up 329, 41 and 106.
2. How many gallons are there in 56 pints?
3. A collection box for a charity contained the following coins: 21 pounds, 35 x 50ps, 52 x 20ps and 17 x 5ps. What was the total money collected?
4. How much less than a million is 7 times 142857?
5. Subtract 16m 74cm from 19m 39cm.
6. In how many of the 12 multiplication tables does the answer 36 come?

7. Copy and add more lines so that every 2 spaces are balanced by the line between them.

8. Fill in the blanks in this addition sum.
```
      2 5 7
   +  • 1 8
      3 8 • •
```

Teaching mathematics

9. The first day of a certain leap year was a Sunday. Every day in that year except Sundays I put 5p in my savings box. How much had I saved by New Year's Eve in that year?

10. Divide 67081 by 259. What do you notice?

11. Each winter day a farmer cleaned out 2 hundredweight of dung from his cow stalls. How many tons of dung did he clean out in November? *(Do we really have to do this one, Ron?)*

12. **RON** with each letter 'turned round' looks like this: Do the same separately for each of 8619. Your four figure number will now be bigger. How much bigger?

Answers (except for question 7 and 8):
1, 2-65, 3, 5, 7, 15-65, 49-75, 259, 297, 476.

The children could do these questions in any order they liked. Afterwards you could invite them to do others for homework, but let this be quite optional at this age.

Chapter 4:
The Heart of Childhood

§ 1. Child development

When we review the school life of children up to the age of nine, the following picture emerges:

Spiritual Scientific Phases	Soul Emphasis	Class & Age	Child 'says'	Waldorf Curriculum Indications
Physical body complete in basic structure as its building process reaches beyond the age of 6.	–	Kindergarten	Love me along with other children.	Creative play and imitation.
Physical body adjusts to physical surroundings. Building force is released to develop habits, memory, rhythms (ether body).	W I L	I 7	Bring rhythm and good habits into my play and my store of fantasy.	Writing. Fairy stories. Numbers and the 4 rules.
Settled posture (ether controls physical). Astral presentiment in etheric body.	L	II 8	I feel at ease in my actions. Teach me about courage, cleverness and worthy goals.	Legend & fable. Multiplication tables.
Ego presentiment in etheric body. It practises control of life forces.		III 9	Who are you as a being of Will? Are you really acting for my benefit? Whence comes your authority? What do you know about practical life?	Old Testament stories. Farming, dung, building, measurement.

The first column indicates the activities of each of the four earthly parts of the human being. For an elucidation of them, various works of Rudolf Steiner need to be consulted.[1] Instead of 'ether body' the alternative term 'body of formative forces' is perhaps more appropriate here, for the physical body alone would be no more capable of growth and finer complexities than the stone statue of a human embryo. It is this invisible, cosmos-centred rather than earth-centred ether body, which surrounds yet also penetrates, that makes all life, growth and enhancement possible. The so-called astral body of emotions, centred in the realm of 'moving'[2] rather than 'fixed' stars, whose proper development does not begin much before the age of 14, starts to delicately influence the two 'lower' principles somewhat earlier. The same is true of the actual human individuality or ego, except that the latter's true emergence occurs at the age of 20 or 21. Presentiments of it, however, tend to take place at three year intervals, rather like the limit veils in modern mathematical chaos theory. So it is that the 3 year-old child can say 'I' rather than just 'me want...' or 'Johnny wants...'. The 6 year-old wants to assert himself in a school, not just in a kindergarten. The 9 year-old experiences the opposition of 'I' and world – hence the need for a teacher's kind but firm authority at that age. The child doesn't say aloud the sentences in Column 4, but we need to be awake to his unspoken and only half conscious requests.

Of the three human soul activities, the will is the dominant lieutenant in the first three school years. Feeling and thinking are there too, of course, but it is the movements of arms and legs, lips, eye focus, lungs and blood beat – all with increasing control – which is of greatest importance. The soul's captain, the ego, not yet fully in control physically of his ship, has to rely a lot on this particular lieutenant.

> Nowadays the word 'ego' is often given a derogatory connotation in many well-meaning circles. E.g. 'There is too much ego in people, we have to overcome it'. It is true that egotism is a strong negative element in society. But it would be a great pity if the word 'ego' had to suffer a similar fate to that lovely English word 'gay', becoming confined to only one narrow kind of definition.

From the latter part of Class 3 to the end of Class 5, the 'feeling lieutenant' becomes of central importance to the captain. This age (9 to 12) really is the heart of childhood. Everything is of interest to children during this period, from long past civilisations, their practical and social achievements, their myths and poetry to the living world of plants, animals and human beings in the world today. The 12th year of life has been described as a Rubicon. In Class 3 children love the Old Testament stories and how the one God rewards and punishes the Children of Israel (with a land flowing with milk and honey and with awful pestilences). But by the beginning of Class 4 they are aware that there is not just one single authority in their world. Teachers and parents sometimes have different and maybe conflicting views on children's behaviour. Mum and Dad may have varied standpoints too. So in European schools Norse mythology is so satisfying to Class 4, for *many* gods now appear, and there is even conflict between them. As well as looking up to the mighty Odin and Thor, how they love the naughty exploits of Loki! In Peru there are similar themes in pre-Inca myths; these take the place there of Norse mythology.

§2. Arithmetic

Is there some similar change in the realm of arithmetic? Does a new quality or theme enter into mathematical education, which if understood by the teacher will engender a corresponding welcome in the children?

Indeed there is. Fractions! Two distinct new qualities can be felt when you become acquainted with this new kind of number. First you realise that the word has evolved from the Latin verb 'to break'. (Loki loved to break up what his fellow gods created.) The name of the Yorkshire town Pontefract was derived from the broken bridge there. When you break up 4 into 5 equal parts, each part is $4/5$, a so-called vulgar fraction. If 12 is given the same treatment, however, you get a so-called improper fraction $12/5$ or $2^2/5$, a mixed number.

Perhaps it was Victorian standards of morality that account for these curious adjectives. The elemental world loves it when rocks are broken up in quarries and it is well known that coal miners (at least before modern power tools and automatic conveyor belts took over) often had perceptions of gnomes underground.[3] It is possible that the wonderful singing of Welsh male voice choirs is related to these phenomena as well.

If this quality of fractions alone were described to children, it might stimulate destructive impulses in them. The second quality, however, has to do with an opposite impulse. The fraction $4/5$ is just the same as $8/10$ or $12/15$. Whilst whole numbers have just one name, fractions have lots of names, rather like members of the royal family. Their fluidity gives them watery rather than earthy endowments, etheric rather than physical features.

Contemplation of all the other names of $4/5$ at once leads to intuition of the infinite wholeness of 4x and 5x tables.

This gives the key to how one can begin teaching fractions.

§3. Freehand Geometry

A significant change in children's drawings should come about in these 'heart of childhood' years too. The use of colour flourishes in new dimensions. Illustration of mythical events are a wonder to behold, often far surpassing what adults can achieve. In addition to this a geometrical quality can be fostered in a new type of purely freehand drawing. First teach the children how to draw an (almost) perfect circle after telling them this famous story about Leonardo da Vinci: One day he left the walled city to go for a walk in the woods. He only returned when it had grown quite dark in the evening. 'Halt! Who goes there?' demanded the sentry at the gate. 'Leonardo da Vinci!' 'Oh yeah? Hi! I'm the new Pope! Come on, you'll have to prove who you say you are!' Leonardo beckoned him and his lamp to a patch of dusty pathway, knelt down and with a finger drew a perfect circle in the dust. 'Ah,' cried the sentry, 'Only Leonardo could do that. Pass, friend!'

On the blackboard you demonstrate. 'I want you to first imagine a perfect circle on this board. You can't see it yet, of course. It is invisible. Now I'll go round it with my hand several times. You do the same on your white sheet of paper. No, that won't do, Jane. Your head must be right over the middle of the paper. O.K. Now let the point of your soft pencil go round your invisible circle slowly – but don't let it touch the paper.' On the board you then show how you let your chalk touch the surface here and there as you continue your circumambulations. Then let the chalk gently make a continuous contact and go round and round many, many times. It will look somewhat like a 1 or 2 year old's lovely scribble which he afterwards proudly tells you is a picture of his mother. Actually the latter is the 1 or 2 year-old's will activity, or a depiction of his own heart beating. You demand more exactness from the 10 year-old, but it will still necessarily be inexact. Then you take a harder chalk and carefully draw a clear circle in the midst of your softer circlings. When the children have done the same thing with a hard pencil, you can get them to rub out the soft black lead circlings, leaving a pretty good hard circle. Magic! Naturally they need to do all this a few times more.

Similar practice of drawing almost perfect straight lines is needed, but without repeated soft attempts. Moreover, it no longer matters where the head is in relation to the drawing surface. You can get the children to draw a vertical line through their circle to make a drawing just like one of the symmetrical drawings they made in Class 1 and continued to make in Classes 2 and 3. Do the same horizontally to achieve the drawing shown below.

Guess the middle points of the 4 arcs, then the middle points of the 8 resulting arcs. Now leave them free to elaborate. They might draw 8 diameters altogether and maybe colour alternate sectors blue and gold. They

Chapter 4: The heart of childhood

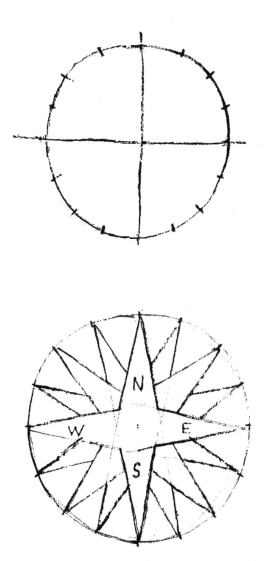

might draw 4 almost exact squares whose corners lie on the circumference and have light overlapping colours on the finished drawing. Another possibility, more difficult, is shown below, culminating in a ship's compass, with its NE, NNE, ENE, etc. added.

The innermost space embracing all 4 cardinal directions might then be coloured red, outside them 4 blue pieces, outside them 8 yellow little pieces; but colour choice is up to the children. When another circle, this time divided into 12 sectors, is drawn, still perfectly freehand, you have a fine basis for talking about fractions.

§4. The 4 Kinds of Integers (Whole Numbers)

It will be obvious that unless the children are thoroughly at home in their multiplication tables, fractions will present problems to them. By now the answer to 'What are eight sevens?' should be instinctively immediate. 'Fifty-six' should require no thought. In view of this a delightful section of number work beloved of the ancient Greeks can be introduced in Class Four prior to fraction work.

Every whole number can be analysed to see which smaller number divides it exactly. Going from a whole to its parts is always a healthy intellectual exercise. Later, the power of reason will step in to build up what has been revealed by these results into a confident skill in handling fractions. Take the number 12. Its factors are 1, 2, 3, 4 and 6, whose additive sum is 16, which is *more* than the number 12 with which we began. One does not count the investigated number itself as a factor – that would give the former too egotistical a quality. Numbers like 12, also 18 and 20, whose factor sums exceed the number being analysed, are called *excessive* or *jovial* numbers. 12 is the lowest such number – herein lies the wholly mathematical secret of twelveness.

Some numbers on the other hand are called *deficient,* e.g. the factors of 10 are 1,2, and 5 (sum 8, which is less than 10). The whole Greek civilisation was based on the need to achieve balance. 'Not too little, not too much, but just right!' So naturally people were interested in discovering *perfect* numbers. 6 is such a number, for the factors 1, 2, and 3 add to give 6 again. Perfect numbers, like perfect human beings, are very rare. Above 6 comes 28, then 496, then 8128, then a number in the millions and so on into huger sizes.

There are also *prime* numbers like 13 which have only 1 as a factor. All numbers are one of the four types described, the only exception being 1, but 'one is one and all alone and ever more shall be so.' The first prime number is 2, not 1, for a prime number is defined as a number which can only be divided exactly by 1 *and* itself – 'and' has no meaning in the case of unity. This section of number life provides excellent discovery work for the children. Don't tell them what sort of number 28 is, let *them* find out. If wished, a class teacher could leave this section to Class 5, just using the geometrical illustrations of fractions in Class 4.

Certainly more appropriate for the fifth class is a full prime number analysis of any composite number, e.g.

$$9100 = 2 \times 2 \times 5 \times 5 \times 7 \times 13$$

which is best done in a continuous short division form:

```
2)9100
2)4550
5)2275
5) 455
7)  91
    13
```
One tries 2 first and again for the next step and the next, where it doesn't work, then 3 which also fails, and so on up the list of primes 2, 3, 5, 7, 11, 13... until the last number itself is prime.

Beware of making a Pythagorean tetrad out of the 4 kinds of numbers.

perfect	deficient
abundant	prime

The qualities of 'deficient' and 'melancholic' have something in common; so too have 'prime' and 'choleric', 'abundant' and sanguine', but can we really suggest that 'phlegmatic' is the perfect temperament? Some teachers who have an unruly, boisterous and difficult class might, however, affirm such a judgment. Also it *is* true that phlegmatic children generally produce the best – the most exact and artistic – geometrical drawings.

§ 5. Curricular aims for mathematics in Classes 4 and 5 (ages 9 to 11)

By the end of Class 4 almost everyone in the class should be able to handle mixed numbers in each of the four arithmetical operations upon just two of them, e.g. able to do the sum $4^7/_{12} \div 3^1/_8$ (answer $1^7/_{15}$). However, there will always be two or three children for whom this will be an esoteric foreign language until Class 6 – more on that later.

The addition and subtraction of decimals and simpler examples of decimal multiplication and division also belong to Class 4, say as far as 19.43 ÷ 2.9, but leave for Class 5: 0.023104 ÷ 0.00076. (Answers 6.7 and 30.4). The beginnings of translation between the two 'non-integral languages' also belongs to Class 4, for instance expressing $3/4$ as a decimal and 0.6 as a fraction. Recurring decimals could be left to Class 5, e.g. expressing $2/3$ in decimals or $0.3170\dot{7}$ as a fraction (Answers $0.\dot{6}$ and $13/41$).

Class 5 gives both teacher and class a second bite at the cherry (perhaps using a new approach, whereby the troublesome stalk and stone have been removed or at least rendered less damaging to unwary teeth). By the end of Class 5, at least half a class of widely varying ability should be able to tackle with success a question such as $(2^{5/6} + {}^{3/8}) \times (81^{3/7} - 78^{4/7})$.

To reach the answer which is simply $9^{1/6}$, several subtleties need to be known. Many little errors in method may have developed in the children and require some painless (if possible) drilling and filling by the teacher's patient treatment. The odd tooth may even need extraction. Oh dear! This dental analogy is getting out of hand. It would of course be nicer if we were eating bananas. But the efforts the children (and teachers) have to make in mastering fractions are well worth while. They have to learn how to take the bit between their teeth – for it really isn't as bad as eating pomegranates!

Some years ago a bevy (if that's the right collective noun) of Her Majesty's Inspectors declared that working out fractions – especially those like the last dreadful example, was a shocking waste of children's time. Decimals were the in-thing, for example in computers, so teachers were advised to discontinue teaching fractions. A few years later it was realised that those children who had had no experience in fractions found it very hard to understand and work with algebra. So, of course, the said H.M.I.s quickly reversed their advice to teachers. It is good to notice that in contrast to earlier decades most school inspectors today have actually been teachers before their 'elevation' to inspector status.

It is important in these two classes to extend the application of arithmetic to practical situations in life. Averages – of weights, monetary gifts or a shop's daily takings during a week, a cow's milk production, distances walked to school by members of the class (car journeys don't count!) etc – form good contexts for addition and division. Pie charts can be introduced in relation to fractions. The 'rule of three' or unitary method is another good practical application of all the arithmetic learned so far and can be used especially in Class 5 as the first glimmering of the logic which will come in Class 6 geometry. This is based upon that most famous personality Caius, whose mortality made him immortal.

All men are mortal.
Caius is a man.
Therefore Caius is mortal.

So for the question: If 12 pencils cost £3.48, what will 7 pencils cost?
we write   12pencils   £3.48
               1 pencil   £0.29
               7pencils   £2.03

Questions involving a process known as inverse proportion, such as: If 4 people can between them complete a job of work in 6 hours, how long will it take 10 people to complete the same job? – should be avoided. For whilst the calculation

4 people	6 hours
1 person	24 hours
10 people	2 hours 24 minutes

is correct, the true answer is probably in excess of 8 hours unless you employ a pretty good foreman!

The transition from Class 4 to Class 5 can also parallel the change from freehand geometrical drawing to exact ruler and compasses constructions in geometrical drawing. Even the latter can never be perfectly exact, but awareness of this is not meaningful to the real nature of the child before the age of 12. Whilst freehand drawing needs developing further at every age of childhood and adolescence (whether with a geometrical slant or not), the skilful use of instruments enhances the child's confidence. Whilst she continues to appreciate what was achieved freehand in Class 4, the repetition of the same drawings in Class 5 that she did a year earlier but now by using compasses and straight edge gives her added satisfaction. Still more joy will come to the Class Fivers when they see how to have lots of circles in the same large drawing and begin to recognise several geometrical truths. This corresponds to the period in human civilisation when thinking activity took such a crucial step forward, i.e. Ancient Greece. The curricular aim here is not that of proving geometrical propositions, but rather of becoming aware of the truth and beauty of symmetrical forms in relation to circular milieus; for instance 4 equilateral triangles, 3 squares and 2 perfect hexagons all arising from 12 equally spaced points round a circle.

§6. Developmental Summary

Theoretical educationalists have laid stress in the last half century on the importance of 'developmental age' as against 'chronological age'. Unfortunately, the stress has been placed less on the first seven than on the last 6 letters of the word. Mind and body are only two parts of the human being. Even the word 'mind' refers to more than what is mental in the sense which many educationalists conceive. This 'more' is the individual human spirit. Furthermore, except for a few psychological qualities, the human soul is left out in pushing the 'developmental age' postulate. The word 'developmental' is being used in this chapter and section of it in a comprehensive sense. It is much more closely related to 'chronological age' in consequence. Continuing the table given up to Class 3 at the beginning of the chapter, with the same column headings, we obtain:

Spiritual Scientific Phases	Soul Emphasis	Class & Age	Child 'says'	Waldorf Curriculum Indications
Feeling of world astral influence on etheric body.	F E E L I N G	IV_{10}	How do you control temptations? What a lot of interesting things the world contains!	Norse mythology. Human beings and animals. Drawing, fractions, grammar, letter writing.
Feeling of world etheric influence on etheric body.		V_{11}	What does the world remember of the distant past? My heart beats for everything which lives.	Greek Gods and heroes. The plant world and the earth. Geography of one's own country. Geometry reaching into drawing.

The first column shows the spiritual scientific phases where the developing ether body in the heart of childhood receives the gifts of world astrality and world ether. The concept of 'ether' is quite different from the concept of 'ether' used in nineteenth century physics. Feeling remains the dominant soul lieutenant through these two years and only during Class 6 will it hand on its role of steering and look-out supervisor to thinking, under the direction of the ship's captain.

Some of the things which the child is silently saying and asking are shown in the 4th column and a brief selection of Waldorf curriculum indications are shown in the last column.

In teaching mathematics in whatever class, it is vital to be aware of what other subjects are being taught in that class and what phases of those subjects in particular. It is most helpful to the children when in Class 4, say, a lesson on fractions can include a reference to the wide variety of animal life. How different lions and eagles are! How different twelfths and elevenths are! In Class 5 many kinds of flowers are studied in a Botany main lesson – and look! The very same forms begin to appear in geometrical drawing. English grammar and the right way to set out the solution of problems in arithmetic (like the 'rule of three' examples) have a subtle affinity. No curriculum subject is healthy if it is surrounded by brick walls. The maths lesson can embrace every other subject – in moderation, of course. So too can maths be encouraged to make its appearance now and again in all other subjects – history, foreign languages, nature study, music and so on.

Chapter 4: The heart of childhood

It is particularly in the 'heart of childhood' classes that a real social feeling can develop, a feeling for each other among the children, for their teachers and for the whole school and wider community of which they are part. Opportunities for their teachers to come and share a meal with their parents and themselves at home are welcomed with joy by them. It is therefore also pertinent to seek social qualities within the pure context of mathematics itself. We shall meet these in the following chapter when examining the communicative nature of different whole numbers and the conversational isomorphisms of different geometrical shapes.

Chapter 5:
Suitable Examples in Classes 4 and 5
(9 to 11 year olds)

By this age children should be used to an hour's quiet individual work in arithmetic each day in the course of a two hour main lesson. An element of revision of what has been learnt in earlier classes is always helpful when included in written work.

§1. Class 4 Fractions

Questions set in the course of **approach to fraction work** could include

1. What is seven multiplied by itself?

2. 14 x 21.

3. How many times will the first answer go into the second answer?

4. What fraction of the second answer is the first one? – is it half, a third, a sixth or a tenth?

5. Draw a big circle. Divide up the circumference into 2 equal parts to start with; then into 6 equal parts, then into 12 equal parts, finally into 24 equal parts. Each point on the circle should be joined to the centre.

6. Colour one sector orange and the next two sectors light blue, then the next sector orange and the next two light blue again and so on until you have finished.

7. What fraction of the whole circle is orange and what fraction is light blue?

8. Investigate every number from 20 to 30 inclusive and say which numbers are deficient, perfect, abundant or prime.

9. What fraction of the numbers in the last question are abundant?

10. Make a list of prime numbers in which the lowest is 13 and the biggest is 43.

11. Terence spent a quarter of a £5 note in buying 2 oranges (19p each), 3 apples (12p each) and 3 bananas. What did each banana cost?

12. Do the same as question 8 using the range 496 to 499 inclusive. What do you notice?

Answers: 49, 294, 41, 37, 31, 29, 23, 19, 17, 17, 6, 2/3, 3/4, 1/3, 3/11, 1/6

Some clever children may regard the earlier questions as being too easy for them, rush through them and so make a mistake or be criticised by the teacher for untidy or inartistic finish. They will find much to get their teeth into in the later questions, however. You could also, if all 12 have been satisfactorily completed, ask them to fully investigate the number 360 to see why the Egyptians of old decreed that apart from sleep and meals everyone should work continuously for that number of days, every year; the rest of the year was a holiday of several days.[1] The working is shown below

```
        [ 360    x ]    1
          180    x      2        717
          120    x      3       + 93
           90    x      4        810
           72    x      5
           60    x      6
           45    x      8                    So 360 is very
           40    x      9                    abundant indeed.
           36    x     10
           30    x     12
           24    x     15
           20    x     18

totals    717          93
```

Chapter 5: Examples in classes 4 and 5

Next day a teacher could do that on the board – making individual children tell her just what numbers to write next, of course. It is wonderful how many numbers go into 360. The children can now appreciate why this number, so close to the number of days in a year, was chosen for angle measurement, 360 degrees in a complete turn. At this point you might introduce protractors to the class. N.B. fully circular protractors are far better than semi-circular ones – just try out both types practically! There now follows a list of fractions sums, in which the aim is to indicate a steady step by step growth of difficulty. It is not true to say that addition sums are the easiest ones. Also multiplication and division sums are much more 'full of life'. Even before them, however, come 'of' sums, since these are nearest to the child's experience. Naturally this is not intended as a set of sums for one particular day's work, although it might be useful in composing a revision or test set at the end of a main lesson block. The teacher will make up a set for each day according to difficulties experienced the day before and also the need to progress to the next step. One useful thing to be aware of is this: the more you give children sums to do which are easy and which they can do well, the more you educate the will. The more they have to struggle with hard problem after hard problem, the more you educate their thinking. The first can result in rosier and rosier cheeks, but also a tendency to misbehaviour and horse play. The second can produce quiet but pale-faced children. Once again the Greek call for moderation in all things (even in moderation) helps the teacher in planning the lessons.

1. $4/12 =$
2. $6/10 =$
3. $27/9 =$
4. $17/7 =$
5. $35/15 =$
6. $8 \, 5/6 =$ (as improper fraction)
7. $1/3$ of 12
8. $7/10$ of 20
9. $1/9$ of $18/19$
10. $2/11$ of $77/80$
11. $6/25$ of $35/39$
12. $1/4$ of $2 \, 2/5$
13. $5/6$ of $3 \, 9/10$
14. $30 \times 1/5$
15. $14 \times 1/3$
16. $2 \, 1/2 \times 1/2$
17. $3 \, 2/3 \times 1 \, 2/5$

18. $3^5/_7 \times 1^3/_4$
19. $10^1/_8 \times 4^4/_9$
20. $5 \div 1/_2$
21. $4 \div 2/_3$
22. $2^1/_2 \div 1/_4$
23. $9/_{14} \div 3/_7$
24. $1/_3 \div 1^{11}/_{12}$
25. $12^5/_6 \div 4^8/_9$
26. $1/_8 + 3/_8 + 1/_8$
27. $4/_5 + 3/_5$
28. $8^2/_7 \times 9^3/_7$
29. $5/_8 + 7/_{12}$
30. $23^3/_4 + 24^1/_6$
31. $5^{11}/_{20} + 14^8/_{15}$
32. $9/_{16} - 3/_{16}$
33. $3/_4 - 5/_{14}$
34. $80^9/_{10} - 1^1/_6$

Answers:

$2/_{19}$, $4/_{23}$, $7/_{40}$, $14/_{65}$, $1/_3$, $3/_8$, $11/_{28}$, $3/_5$, $3/_5$, $5/_8$, $15/_{24}$, $1^1/_4$, $1^2/_5$, $1^1/_2$, $2^1/_5$, $2^3/_7$, $2^5/_8$, 3, $3^1/_4$, 4, $4^2/_3$, $5^2/_{15}$, 6, 6, $6^1/_2$, $53/_6$, 10, 10, 14, $17^5/_7$, $20^1/_{12}$, 45, $47^{11}/_{12}$, $79^{11}/_{15}$

Notice that subtraction sums in which the fractional part of the second term exceeds that of the first term do not occur in the above. They can be left to Class 5.

In teaching how to do all these fraction sums the importance of finding appropriate pictures cannot be too strongly emphasised. One always needs to address the children's feelings to start with. Later they will (and should) dispense with the pictures and allow their thinking to work in pure numerical concepts. But the secret lies in making pictures which are *simple*. One day a teacher might bring a lovely ripe melon into the classroom. Good cooks might bake a fine round cake the day before, but in that case they should ensure that cake crumbs will not subsequently litter the children's desks.

With a long sharp knife cut the melon horizontally into 2 equal parts. The pips and soft stuff in the centre can be spooned out and put in the classroom compost bucket. Now draw on the board what has been done.

Chapter 5: Examples in classes 4 and 5

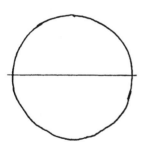

We began with one melon and now get two half melons. That is why we write a half as

$$\frac{1}{2}$$

but instead of drawing the knife each time, we just draw a line:

$$\frac{1}{2}$$

Go on to cut the melon vertically and also have 4 sloping cuts to obtain 12 slices. Also complete the blackboard drawing. At this point a story could be told.

'Once on a hot day a cafe proprietor had such a melon on the counter. Eight thirsty people came in and each had a slice. How much melon did each eat? Yes, 1/12. How much did they eat between them? Yes, 8/12. Later on a similar melon was produced for four very thirsty customers who each required a piece twice as big as before. How much melon did each one eat? Yes, 1/6. How much did they eat between them? Yes, 4/6. Later still, two giants who had been playing basketball came in and wanted slices twice as big as the last lot of customers had eaten. How much did each giant consume? Yes, 1/3. How much did they consume between them? Yes, 2/3.'

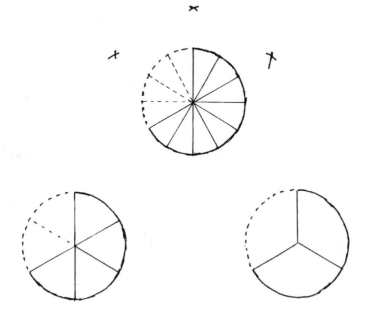

Different colours would enhance the beauty of these illustrations, to be copied into the children's main lesson books. 'Something interesting has happened. Can you tell me what it is? Yes, each time the café proprietor sold just the same amount of melon. So 8/12 = 4/6 = 2/3; and, if you look at what was left, 4/12 = 2/6 = 1/3. Yes, that's right, we put the number of slices on top – and call it the numerator, but underneath we put the number of times the whole melon had to be sliced to the centre – and we call that the denominator. Now, can you notice something else when you look at the two sets of fractions? Yes, that's right, the tops (or numerators) are all in the 2 times table, whilst the bottoms (denominators) are all in the 3 times table. 1 isn't in the 2 times table? It is, you know. It depends which way you say the table. Yes, 2 into 2 goes 1. Don't forget your *gozintas*.'

As a fitting conclusion to this part of the lesson you might slice up all 3 (or 4) melons into twelfths and have the class consume them.

Now you can give the class a whole set of sums in which fractions have to be reduced to their lowest terms. They just have to look at the top number and bottom number and remember in which times table both occur.

A day or two later the 'of' sums can be begun. Using a picture of 20 boats, say, show first what 1/5 of the flotilla is, then 2/5, etc. A couple of days later still, illustrate multiplication. Now, you really need to have done the simple area sums in Class 3.

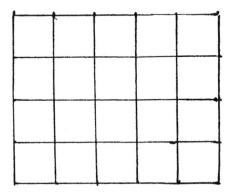

'Here is the plan of a small shed, paved with yard squares. How many paving stones are there? Now someone wants to turn the shed into a greenhouse, so a narrow 18-inch path is made, using pieces of paving stone. All the other slabs are removed and good soil is spread instead.

What area will be used for growing plants? The ticks show square yards, both whole and synthesized. The pieces left over can be rearranged as illustrated and clearly make 3/4 of a square yard. So the picture tells us that

4¹/2 × 3¹/2 = 15³/4

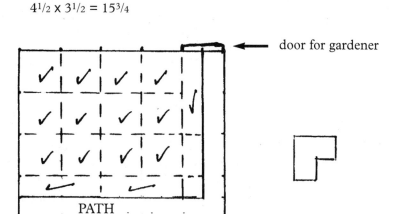

Perhaps one or two other illustrations of multiplying fractions will be shown. But now you can say, 'Look, I'll show you a secret. Instead of always having to make these pictures, there is a short cut. Do what you did before with "of" sums. Now multiply tops and multiply bottoms. Change the resulting improper fraction into a mixed number.'

$$\begin{aligned} & 4^{1}/_{2} \times 3^{1}/_{2} \\ = & 9/2 \times 7/2 \\ = & 63/4 \\ = & 15^{3}/_{4} \quad\quad \textit{It's the same answer!} \end{aligned}$$

Do not attempt to prove this by formal logic. Children have no interest in such logic. The picture together with the number sum *contain* the logic, which can be allowed to rise into full consciousness at a later age, say 14 or 15. For what is more important to children than logic? It is their written calculation receiving a tick from their teacher. So it's just a matter now of children learning the rules of the game. Now and again return to the picture process, e.g. calculate 2⁷/10 ÷ 3/5

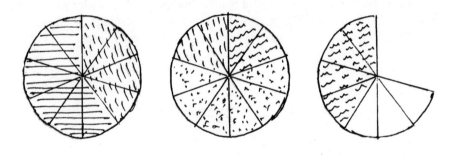

Imagine we have 2⁷/₁₀ Dutch cheeses. Cutting the whole cheeses into 10 parts each, we have altogether 27 pieces. ³/₅ of one cheese means 6 of these pieces. So how many times can we colour in 6 pieces? (a different colour each time, of course). 4 times, with 3 pieces left. But 3 pieces make half a coloured set. So the answer is 4¹/₂

Now without a picture:

$$2\frac{7}{10} \div \frac{3}{5}$$

$$= \frac{27}{10} \div \frac{3}{5}$$

$$= \frac{\overset{9}{\cancel{27}}}{\underset{2}{\cancel{10}}} \div \frac{\overset{}{\cancel{3}}^{1}}{\underset{1}{\cancel{5}}}$$

$$= \frac{9}{2}$$

$$= 4\frac{1}{2}$$

Same answer!

They will have learnt cross cancelling in earlier sums (notice the value of cancelling by differently directed strokes). As for turning a fraction upside down to multiply instead of divide, this can be understood by the simple example 3 ÷ ¹/₂, which can be translated into English as 'How many halves

Chapter 5: Examples in classes 4 and 5

are there in 3?' Demonstrate by cutting 3 apples in half if you really need to. The answer is 3 x 2 = 6. Dividing by $1/2$ is the same as multiplying by 2, which is the same as $2/1$.

Whether or not you have recourse to the simpler example, the magic is still there when you turn $3/5$ into $5/3$. For the real art of mathematics consists in taking short cuts. Children can appreciate the thrill of this just as much as a senior wrangler. Once I helped a rather inattentive boy to remember this step by turning him upside down in front of the class; far more effective than trying to be logical!

Little needs to be said about going on to addition and subtraction. If we take as an example $75^{5/6} + 23^{3/8}$, the whole number addition gives 98. Sixths and eighths can no more be immediately put together than can apples and bananas be combined as 'bapples'. A picture of how to transfer a heavy load between two lorries or trucks can help. To achieve equal truck floor levels, let down the tyres of one truck and blow up the tyres of the other truck.

But now be even more fantastic and blow up both denominators.
So $5/6 + 3/8$
= $20/24 + 9/24$
= $29/24$
= $1^{5/24}$

Then the whole answer is: $98 + 1^{5/24}$
= $99^{5/24}$

Never turn the mixed numbers in addition sums into improper fractions, of course.

§2. Class 4 Decimals

That these are just a special kind of fractions can be shown by asking the children to work out

$$3\tfrac{74}{100} + 25\tfrac{3}{10} + \tfrac{23}{1000}$$

By now they should be able to write down the common denominator just once in the next line.

$$= 28\,\tfrac{740 + 300 + 23}{1000}$$

$$= 28\,\tfrac{1063}{1000}$$

$$= 29\,\tfrac{63}{1000}$$

```
 740
 300
  23
1063
```

Then once again show how, by changing the form of expression, mathematics is the art of taking short cuts.

```
   3.74
  25.3
   0.023
  29.063
```

Emphasize the importance of having all the decimal points in a straight line, like the shining well-polished buttons down a soldier's tunic. Addition and subtraction sums should now present few problems. Multiplication is best first carried out by keeping decimal points below one another again. So for 7.42 x 5.3 begin by multiplying by 5; then, since the 3 is worth a tenth of what it would be if it had been where the 5 is, the result of multiplying by 3 has to be written one place further to the right.

```
     7.42
   x 5.3
    37.10
     2.226
    39.326
```

Chapter 5: Examples in classes 4 and 5

After much practice with these sums the class can (perhaps some months later) be shown that they can just do a multiplication in whole numbers: 742 x 53; then put the point in the answer by counting up the decimal places in each part of the question, adding and so counting back from the right in the answer (2+1=3).

Naturally it is best to work with short multiplication first and later with short division before going on to long division, but the principles are not different. Consider the previous example done backwards, i.e.

```
              7.42              1)    53
     5.3 ) 39 . 326              7)   371
            37 1                 4)   212
             2 22                2)   106
             2 12
               106
               106
```

Why has the point in the answer been shifted to the right? Logical arguments about compensated shiftings can confuse. It is much better to introduce the whole matter of rough estimates before tackling long division. Thus 39 ÷ 5 is about 7. So it is obvious where to place the decimal point in the answer. The *whole* list of multiples of 53, as in Class 3 long division, is no longer needed – except for the weaker children in the class – so trial multiplications are put at the side of the sum.

There follows a set of questions suitable for the conclusion of a week or two's work on decimals.

1. 3.5 + 6.2
2. 27.8 – 2.7
3. 712.38 + 9124.5
4. 2.67 – 0.428
5. 2.321 x 3.2
6. 16.7 x 0.129
7. 7.4272 ÷ 3.2
8. 742.72 ÷ 32
9. 74.272 ÷ 0.32
10. Add up 0.018, 63 and 8.788
11. Roughly how many times does 2.85 go into 39.444?
12. What is the exact answer to no. 11?

Teaching mathematics

13. A white line painted in the middle of the road, telling you not to drive across it, is 13.6 cm wide and goes on for 0.87 km. What is the total area of white paint in square metres to the nearest square m? Make an estimate first.
14. A dry stone wall consists of 13 layers of stones, each 11 cm high, and is topped by a layer of concrete. If the wall has to be 1.5 metres high, how thick must the concrete be?
15. A woman whose vital statistics are 42-24-42 (in inches) wraps a belt round her waist with 7 equally spaced holes in it, each 0.75' in diameter. What distance is there between the edge of one hole and the next? (to 2 d.p.)

Answers: 2.1543, 2.242, 2.321, 2.68, 7, 7.4272, 9.7, 13, 13.84, 23.21, 25.1, 71.806, 118, 232.1, 9836.88.

§3. Class 4 Drawing

Freehand drawing can include both artistic and geometrical examples. An example of the former – when there is no single 'correct' answer – is to copy the first form below and then complete the other two forms according to artistic feeling.

Other examples are given in Steiner's Ilkley course.[2] Geometrical free-hand drawings can be based mainly on the circle construction shown in Chapter 4. By dividing a circle into 5 equal parts (organized guesswork) the following can be obtained:

74

Chapter 5: Examples in classes 4 and 5

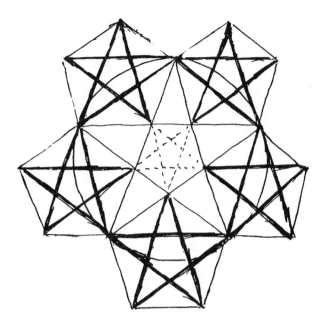

Colouring will bring out the 5 pentagrams standing round the larger inner one. Several circles can also be drawn. It helps after drawing the centre circle to put in all the heavy dots – which occur in straight lines.

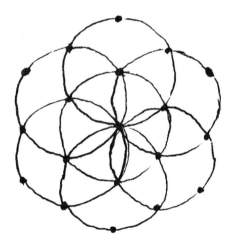

This drawing, when constructed with compasses in Class 5, will become a primary phenomenon of geometry – the seven circle net, which will be found to contain a large number of secrets of exact geometrical constructions. Naturally the children will want to use colours to produce flower petal arrangements.

§4. Class 5 Arithmetic

The work in fractions and decimals needs further development. Now can come the mixing of the 4 rules in fractions, but first ensure that a subtraction sum like $73^{1/3} - 68^{5/6}$ can be done easily.

$$\text{This} = 5 \frac{2-5}{6}$$
$$= 4 \frac{8-5}{6}$$
$$= 4 \frac{3}{6}$$
$$= 4 \frac{1}{2}$$

The 2 is unable to give away 5, so he asks the big 5 to help him. 'Yes,' says the big 5, 'I'll give you one of me and so I shall become 1 less, but one of me will be worth 6 to you…'

A complicated sum like $(3^{3/5} - 1^{1/3}) \div (8^{7/10} + 5^{3/4})$ has to be handled in the same way as someone preparing a good meal. Make sure you don't pour the custard on to the mashed potatoes or gravy on to the stewed pears. So keep the two courses of the meal on distinct parts of the cooking range, even though repetition in picturing the whole job has to be accepted. The sum is done as follows:

$$= \left(2 \frac{9-5}{15}\right) \div \left(13 \frac{14+15}{20}\right)$$
$$= \left(2 \frac{4}{15}\right) \div \left(13 \frac{29}{20}\right)$$
$$= \left(2 \frac{4}{15}\right) \div \left(14 \frac{9}{20}\right)$$
$$= \frac{34}{15} \div \frac{289}{20}$$
$$= \frac{\overset{2}{34}}{\underset{3}{15}} \times \frac{\overset{4}{20}}{\underset{17}{289}}$$
$$= \frac{8}{51}$$

Chapter 5: Examples in classes 4 and 5

Objections that a Californian pear-potato ensemble has been covered with a yellowish brown mess are left to the individual teacher to resolve, but I doubt whether children in Sacramento would be too worried.[3]

Remember that although such a calculation is unlikely to arise in some practical problem in technology, its value in stimulating the talent needed later in algebra is considerable. More complicated decimal sums can be set starting with simple questions like

$$0.0012 \quad \times \quad 0.0005 \quad = \quad 0.0000006(0)$$

and

$$350 \quad \div \quad 0.0005 \quad = \quad 700000$$

Pie charts and averages as well as the 'rule of three' belong to Class 5 age education. As the history of Ancient Egypt also arouses a lot of interest for 11 to 12 year olds, attention could be drawn to the work of Ahmes,[4] who delighted in relationships like $2/3 = 1/2 + 1/6$, $2/5 = 1/3 + 1/15$. Can the class find other examples where the first numerator is always 2 and the others always 1?

A further exercise for Class 5 can be in translating from one language to another, just as they are learning to do now with greater exactness in their foreign language lessons. Whilst translating $3/4$ into decimal language is easy enough (divide bottom into top and add noughts to the top when necessary, giving 0.75), $2/3$ becomes the endless 0.66666... abbreviated to $0.\dot{6}$.

A little harder is translating decimals into fractions.

$$0.3125 \quad = \quad \frac{3125}{10000}$$

which on cancelling by 5 becomes in turn

$$= \frac{625}{2000} = \frac{125}{400} = \frac{25}{80} = \frac{5}{16}$$

However $0.405405405405... = 0.\dot{4}0\dot{5}$

$$= \frac{405}{999} = \frac{45}{111} = \frac{15}{37}$$

This can be checked by converting back to decimals, but the real reason for putting 9s underneath the fraction line will only emerge in Class 10, where they will learn how to deal with geometric progressions.

Teaching mathematics

Here is a final set of mixed questions to conclude Class 5 arithmetic:

1. 5 skeins of coloured wool cost £20. What would be the cost of a set of skeins giving all the colours of the rainbow?

2. The heights of a group of Class 5 children are 4'6", 5'2", 4'11", 5', 4'3" 5'3", 5'4" and 4'8". What is their average height?

3. Change into decimals 3/5 and 8/9.

4. Change into fractions 0.72 and 0.72727272...

5. By changing to decimals find out which of these fractions is the biggest and which is the smallest: 8/11, 7/10, 5/7, 3/4, 2/3.

6. At a concert in Cairo the audience consisted of Egyptians, Syrians, Iraqis and Palestinians as indicated in this rough pie chart. How many people were there altogether?

   Calculate the exact number of degrees there should be in each angle at the centre and draw the pie chart accurately.

7. 66 souls came with Jacob to Egypt at Joseph's invitation. They included Benjamin and his children (11), Simon and his (7), Juda and Perez and theirs (7) and Levi, Reuben and Isashar and theirs (14). When Jacob together with Joseph and his children were also included to make the whole 'house of Jacob', the total became 70. [5] Make a pie chart for the 'house of Jacob' to show B, S, JP, LRI and ATO (all the others) in 5 sections.

8. (i) How many children did Joseph have?

   (ii) What fraction of the souls who came with Jacob did Benjamin and his children make up?

   (iii) Jacob had 11 children apart from Joseph, but only 7 are named above. What answer will you get if you add up all the whole numbers from 1 to 11 inclusive? What do you notice?

Chapter 5: Examples in classes 4 and 5

9. Here are two numbers, each with 9 decimal places:
    0.123456789 and 1.111111110.
    What is the result of
    (i) adding them together,
    (ii) subtracting the smaller one from the bigger one?

10. I doubled a number, then added 3 and got 15. What was the number?

11. Find how the second number below arises from the first number.
    $$\begin{array}{ccc} 2 & . & 11 \\ 3 & . & 16 \\ 4 & . & 21 \end{array}$$
    Then complete
    $$\begin{array}{ccc} 30 & . & ? \\ ? & . & 101 \end{array}$$

12. Find the difference between $40^{1/4} \div 30^{2/3}$ and $40^{1/4} - 30^{2/3}$

On this occasion no answers are given. The whole set could be photocopied and given to the class late in the last main lesson in Class 5 where a recapitulation of all the year's work (not only in mathematics) might take place. Before the children start to write, some time could be spent discussing what the first 6 questions mean and how to tackle them. At the lesson's end, the main lesson books would be collected by the teacher, marked overnight and returned the next day when all the questions could be done on the board, with the children writing down what they had not managed to do the previous day.

§5. Discovery situations

Many of the examples and problems given in this chapter can give rise to children making their own experiments with numbers and so making their own discoveries. It is healthy to achieve a balance between that more self-directed experimentation and working carefully through the teacher's carefully prepared sets of questions. The latter helps build the inner discipline of the children whereas the former lets them taste its fruits when freely searching for new revelations. This will become even more the case in the concluding section 6 on Class 5 geometry.

Recalling Chapter 1, Pythagoras showed how the creative power of 4 is revealed in 10. 1+2+3+4=10. An example in the previous section of the present chapter showed that 1+2+3+4+5+6+7+8+9+10+11=66. That result could also be exhibited in a triangle, but, of course, with a longer base and greater height.

So △4 = 10,   △11 = 66,   and △17 = 153,

remembering the story of the fishes at the end of St. John's gospel. This also makes for a discovery situation. Let the children see if they can decide on how to quickly work out

△5   △6   etc

And what about big answers like △100 ?

Also can they find a way of working backwards? Going to the final chapter of the Bible, what about

666 = △?

If you give them the Ahmes discovery problem, some children may discover that $2/19 = 1/10 + 1/190$, but it would be a crime in Class 5 for the teacher to tell them that

$$\frac{2}{2b-1} = \frac{1}{b} + \frac{1}{b(2b-1)}$$

They won't be ready to appreciate algebraic identities until Class 8. It is very doubtful whether Ahmes knew himself. He was clearly entranced by the fact that just as one can divide a whole (2) into two parts (1+1), there is something of a similar nature one can do with fractions.

§6. Class 5 Geometry

One of the great secrets in teaching any mathematical subject is to look a year or two ahead of where the class is at a particular moment and, with a light touch, anticipate their future work. 'What we are going to do now, children, is something you will learn about in Class 7 called the theorem of Pythagoras.' This remark together with the strange map they will have observed on a spare loose blackboard in the classroom when they entered it that morning, whets their curiosity in a healthy way.

Chapter 5: Examples in classes 4 and 5

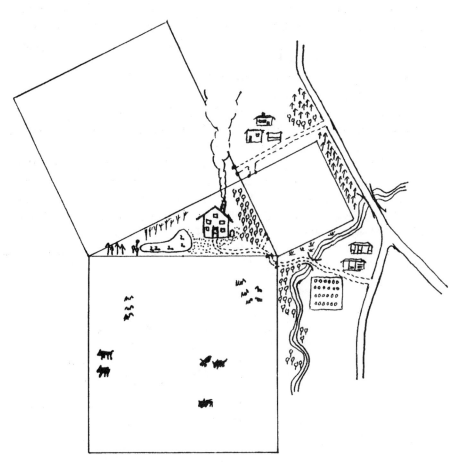

In Class 4 geography they will have drawn bird's-eye views of their local area, so now you explain that this is a similar view of a farm. The farmer has planted corn in 2 of his fields and his animals are grazing in the third field. Looking ahead to his plans for next year he knows it is wise to rotate his crops. Suppose he plants his corn in the big field next year and has his animals grazing on the grass he would plant in the other two. Will he be likely to get more corn next year or less?

Let the class argue about this. One child will observe that he will have a much bigger field for the corn, another that it will only be one instead of two fields. To find out the answer place the movable board on a couple of desks in the middle of the classroom and have the class rearrange itself. Now produce a packet of grain, sprinkle two heaps on the smaller squares, let 2 children use their hair combs to spread them out level and evenly. 'Are they equally deep in corn?' 'No?' Then sprinkle a little more grain on one of them and comb it again. Let the class look at these two cornfields with concentration. Now ask a third child to use his comb to rake all the grain from the two fields into the big one and then rake it into a smooth level square. 'So, what do you reckon? Not enough grain or more than enough?'

Smiling eyes accompany the words 'It's the same!'

Of course this is not a logical proof. It is a *feeling* appreciation of what will be proved and applied two years hence. Such an episode might take place in the last 20 minutes of a main lesson on decimals.

Next day a similar 20-minute slot could be occupied by the children constructing a square in their books and a congruent square on a piece of coloured sticky paper. Now comes a simple jig-saw puzzle-like riddle. Cut out the coloured square and cut it up so that when rearranged it makes two squares. These can be stuck on the page after the teacher's completed blackboard drawing has confirmed that their pieces have been cut and moved about correctly.

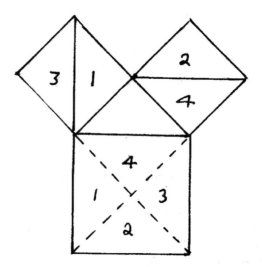

On the following two days increasingly interesting and harder 'jig-saw puzzles' can be given. Cut out the following 5-piece and 6-piece squares. The latter is the most general rightangled triangle. This still isn't a logical proof but a fully satisfying demonstration for children of 12. Rearranging the pieces is left as an exercise for the reader, who may find himself less able or slower at the task than many 12 year-olds.

Chapter 5: Examples in classes 4 and 5

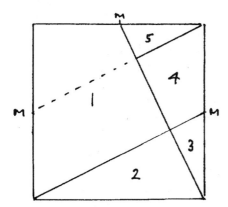 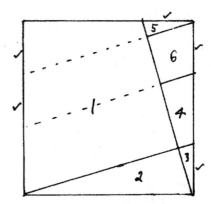

M indicates a middle point.   Ticks indicate equal lengths.

The main task in geometry for Class 5 is learning to use a pair of compasses, and a wise teacher will purchase these instruments for the class rather than let each child buy his own – which would result in much time-wasting screwdriver work for the teacher. Many compasses manufactured nowadays are quite hopeless.

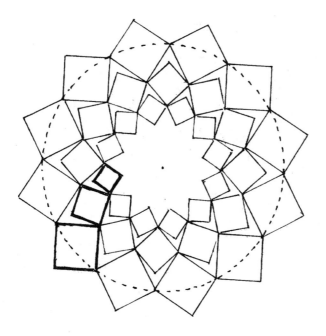

83

The 'seven-circle net' drawn freehand in Class 4 can now be constructed accurately, after which let the class experiment in any way they wish to produce patterns of delightful variety (except on their neighbour's rear quarters). Two examples follow, and other simpler examples can be found in *Education Towards Freedom*.[6] Children will naturally colour these flower-like forms but can be encouraged to leave some spaces uncoloured. Economy can enhance instead of swamping the form. In past years some Waldorf teachers left this work with compasses until Class 6, but this later class needs theorems and deductive work, whereas the obvious link with the Botany main lesson in Class 5, and the practical skill not unlike that achieved in sewing at that age, show how apposite Class 5 is for these accurate drawings of circles. The first drawing follows solely from the construction of 12 points on the circle shown. It can be extended both inwards and outwards with the same linear construction. Notice how all sets of squares, like the 3 bolder ones in the illustration, give rise to the whorls like those seen in flower heads.

The second drawing begins by dividing the dotted circle into 7 equal parts by the engineer's method – organised guesswork, and improving the guesses. Such forms cannot appear in the living world since the number of sectors is not divisible by 2, 3 or 5. Also 7 is not a space-dividing number for ideally accurate 'ruler and compass' constructions.

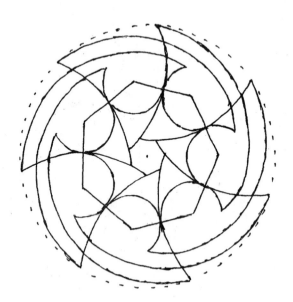

Finally much joy can be found in constructing parabolic envelopes, where all the lines are best drawn in a single colour. Just take any equal spacings of points on two outside lines.

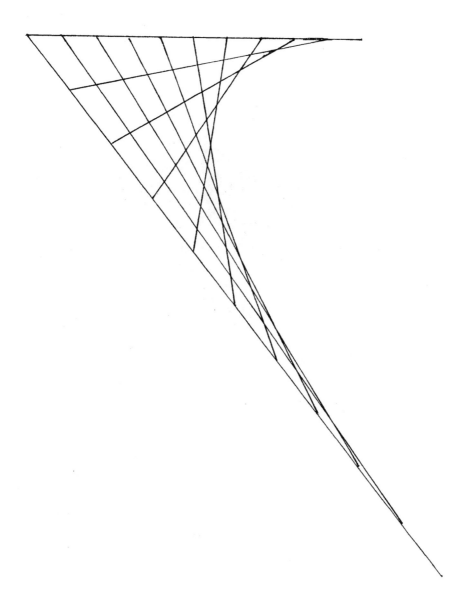

Pythagoras

Chapter 6:
Class 6 Mathematics
(ages 11-12)

§1. The Approach to Puberty

The three soul forces thinking, feeling and willing, directed by their ego captain, reveal themselves with changing emphases as the child grows up. In the kindergarten, willing is uppermost; from the age of 7 to 14 it is feeling, and beyond 14 the young person's thinking becomes the prime lieutenant. The other two are always active as well, of course. During the Class Teacher years (7 to 14), the three give additional underswells. An analogy here is the influence of the moon on tides. Besides the main monthly rhythm there is also a twice daily rhythm. The whole seven or eight years can be divided into three parts: first willing takes the leading role (roughly Classes 1 to 3) in the etheric body's development. Then in the heart of childhood feeling takes over. It is thinking which stands at the helm roughly from Classes 6 to 8, though the ego-individuality guiding it will not take the wheel completely until the age of 21. Continuing the scheme given in earlier chapters we may write:

Spiritual Scientific Phases	Soul Emphasis	Class & Age	Child 'says'	Waldorf Curriculum Indications
Feeling of world physical influence on etheric body.	Feeling	VI 12	Goodbye spiritual world! I want to know and control this one! Teach me science and how to use my life forces to shape the world.	Gym. Money. Geometrical law. Roman Law. Physics. Woodwork. Minerals.
Deeper ego presentiment. Awareness of etheric body's control over physical forms	T H I N K I N G	VII 13	Widen my horizons! I am filled with new wishes and longings. Does one need balance? How may I achieve this?	Chemistry. The Renaissance. Discovery of new lands. Equations. Archimedes' principle.
Awareness of life's possibilities. Astral body approaches ether body.		VII 14	What is happening in the world today? I am becoming different, but I want to be able to cope. How can I learn things for myself & live with my fellow men and women?	Epic and dramatic poetry. French & Industrial revolutions. Illness and health. Laws of locus and envelope. Sewing machines. Mechanics.
Practice and play of participation in life. Ego sends astral body down to ether body. Birth of young person's own astral body	Uncertainty about which should have emphasis	IX 15	I am lonely, but keep out of my inner shrine. Help me to develop new imagination and idealism. What is love?	History of Art. Organic Chemistry. Anatomy. Mathematics of possibility. Telephone and motor.

In Class 6 mathematics the rule of law needs presenting; crystal clear concepts but still approached with rich human feeling and applied to practical situations in life. Erotic tendencies which naturally appear as the teen years approach can only be controlled by the practice of clear thinking and the growth of idealism. It often happens that a class teacher notices a significant change when he or she meets the group of children taught since Class 1 after the long summer holidays. Class 6 seems to have become much taller and have a stabler stance than hitherto. Their individualities begin to hint at their closer involvement in decision making, and it will no longer do to treat the class as it was in Class 5. A new relationship is needed. To feel as if one were the tour guide of a party which also needs to make some explorations on its own, rather than act as a class mother or father, may convey the kind of change required. Authority is still essential – but indicate how glad you will be when you no longer have to use it. Humour is vital. Once when I was teaching Roman History to my Class 6, I had them all in the playground and remembering my days in the R.A.F. lined them up: 'Eyes right! Quick march! About turn!' and so on, in stentorian voice. They very much enjoyed it. But this would not have succeeded at an earlier and definitely not at a later age.

This is the age when half an hour's homework every night is justified and healthy.[1] Any untidy or sloppy work handed in next day needs to be immediately rejected, and an after-school fatigue imposed during which the required neatness can be achieved.

§2. Money problems and the approach to algebra

Rudolf Steiner made a telling observation in declaring that teaching children the intricacies of monetary dealings – profit, interest, etc – before the age of puberty, allows them to tackle the subject without developing feelings of acquisitiveness.

A preliminary step is to introduce a third number language. $0.15 = {}^{15}/_{100} = 15\%$. The last symbol simply consists in taking the 1 of the 100 denominator, lengthening it and making it slope slightly, then attaching the two noughts like berries to the stalk. Translations from each of the languages to the others makes a good exercise.

Ask the class to tell you what are the 3 real uses of money in the world. Saving up money is not really a use on its own; you need to have some idea of what you will eventually do with it, too. Soon they will appreciate that you can:

(i) buy and sell,
(ii) borrow and lend,
(iii) give and receive.

Later on they can be helped to understand how these 3 activities, if they are to be healthy, need to embrace 3 paramount human virtues:

(i) initiative,
(ii) freedom,
(iii) love.

All these activities are essential in the economic life of the world, yes, the last one, too. Whoever heard of a father at the end of breakfast time saying to his son, 'Did you enjoy the meal? Fine, that will cost you £2.50'. Without free giving the world would come to a standstill. Yet it is not only within families, nor even in well publicised charitable donations that this gift money operates. In attending a concert for example you come away at the end with nothing of economic value. It is something wholly aesthetic and spiritual that you have been given. The ticket you purchased to attend the concert was a recognition that the money handed over was partly to offset the cost of lighting, hire of hall, etc and partly as free gift to the musicians to enable them to live, have food and shelter and bring up their families. Taking collections of money at artistic events serves similar purposes.

Later in the curriculum young people in Classes 11 and 12 can go deeply into the threefold life of society: the spiritual-cultural life; the life of human rights; and economic life. An echo of all three occurs in each of them. In the last one can be observed gift money, loan money and purchase money.[2]

Where purchase money is concerned – the matter of straightforward buying and selling – the whole motive is to make a profit. So one might work through on the blackboard with the class the following 3 examples, in which the percentage profit has to be calculated:

1. Anna bought a record player for £80, thoroughly cleaned it and then sold it for £96.

2. Brian bought a second-hand car for £480, repainted it, advertised it and sold it for £552.

3. Catherine bought a new hat for £36. She found a lovely bird's feather in the woods, stuck it in the hat and then sold it to a 'friend' for £45.

Catherine proved to be the best business person (25% profit as against 20% and 15%), even though Brian obtained the highest difference between cost and selling prices.

What has freedom to do with loan money?

In olden times a peasant wishing to have a house in which to bring up his family would go to the lord of the manor, baron or hereditary landowner and ask for a loan of money to build or buy it. 'Fine,' would reply the latter, 'here is the money; but if I have a dispute with some other baron, then you'll have to serve in my army until you can pay me back what I have lent you.'

Today if you go to your bank manager and obtain a loan, he demands interest at so much percent per month until the loan is repaid. Should he also suggest that his lawns need mowing, you would no doubt make a suitably polite reply!

Interest promotes freedom, for by means of it we are no longer personally tied to servitude. Of course each of the three uses of money can be corrupted. Monopolies, Shylock syndromes and national lotteries are examples. Money, though, is not the root of all evil. It can be used for great good upon our earth as well as become subject to horrible degradation.

Compound interest can be left for Class 9, so it is best to have time periods of less than a year, to which simple interest can be applied, for most examples. Two examples to work through with Class 6 could be:

1. How much interest will I have to pay for borrowing £30 for three months at 12% per annum?

2. If I deposit £400 in a bank at an interest rate of $7\frac{1}{2}\%$ p.a., how long must I wait before I can withdraw £420?

In the course of doing these sums, fractions again have to be practised – and sometimes it is found that children who seemed to have little ability in fractions in Classes 4 and 5 suddenly become adept at them. The practical applications of money has helped their geniuses rise up to their heads. Thus

1. Interest = £30 x $\frac{12}{100}$ x $\frac{3}{12}$
   = £$\frac{9}{10}$
   = 90p

2. £420 – £400 = £20
   Time in months = $12 \times \frac{20}{400 \times 7\frac{1}{2}\%}$

   $= \frac{12 \times 20 \times 2 \times 100}{400 \times 15}$

   = 8

An example of how to make up a problem about gift money will be given in the next section.

After a main lesson block on money earlier in the year, a later block can be given to the beginnings of algebra. Returning to loan money, the sentence 'Interest is calculated by multiplying together the principal (or capital), the rate of interest and the time taken and then dividing by 100, becomes subject to a mathematical shortcut.

$$I = \frac{PRT}{100}$$

Even the multiplication signs are dispensed with.

All sorts of algebraic formulae can now be introduced and you can ask the class to guess what the letters stand for in the cases

$$A = LB, \quad S = D/T, \quad P = S - C, \quad C = L + S,$$

since all these examples of the 4 rules are within their own experience, but notice the special value of beginning with the simple interest formula. Why this instead of the simpler A = LB? The reason is that *you cannot make a picture* of the first, whereas you can draw a rectangle to show area in the second case. Algebra takes us beyond the sense perceptible, even though it is often useful in solving problems with a pictorial context. Even S = speed can be related to the distance shown on a map which can be traversed in a time of one hour and the P for profit or L for loss can be pictured in terms of two piles of coins.

Since, historically, mathematical development has very frequently anticipated natural scientific development – often by several centuries – it is quite allowable to use formulae as yet unproven in physics and chemistry lessons. It will not be until Class 7 or 8 at the earliest that the refraction of light formula $\dfrac{1}{u} + \dfrac{1}{v} = \dfrac{2}{r}$ will be established. No matter. The children are interested in using burning glasses to light fires, so work through the problem:

'A burning glass having a radius of 3 feet, is placed 9 feet in front of a hot flame. How far on the other side of the glass must a piece of paper be placed to set it alight? Use the formula $P = \dfrac{rf}{2f - r}$.'

Alliteration helps. So $P = \dfrac{3 \times 9}{18 - 3} = \dfrac{27}{15} = \dfrac{9}{5} = 1\dfrac{4}{5}$ feet,

or 1 foot 9.6 inches.

Chapter 6: Class 6 mathematics

§3. Examples for Class 6 (numerical and algebraic)

It is for the teacher to work out intermediary examples so that the difficulties slowly increase between some of those given below. Here the intention is to indicate the whole range of calculations which certainly the more able children should be able to do before the end of the school year.

1. Express in percentages $3/100$, $12/25$, $17/20$, and $5/7$ to 2 d.p.

2. Express in fractions 50%, 35%, 164% and 8.75 %.

3. I bought a faulty alarm clock for £45. After repairing it I sold it for £72. What was my percentage profit?
   (N.B. *Some* intelligent work or improvement should be expended on a bought article before it is sold again at a profit.)

4. A shopkeeper paid 30 dollars for a crate of 100 apples Later he found that 55 apples were bad. He sold the good ones at 40 cents each. Calculate his percentage loss on the whole deal.

5. A student going to a workcamp to earn some money had to borrow £120 from the bank for travelling and clothing expenses. The bank charged 10% per annum, but the student was able to pay back the loan only a month later. How much was he charged in interest?

6. A craftsman borrowed 6000 dollars from a bank at a rate of 10% p.a. in order to buy machinery and materials. Eight months later he received 7000 dollars from sales. After clearing his debts, what was his bank balance?

7. £9.90 interest was charged on a £160 loan after 9 months. What was the percentage rate?

8. In a class of 28 children, one girl became very ill and the rest of the class decided to send her a present costing £4. Seventeen of the class each gave 10p, eight of the class each 20p and the remainder of the class promised to make up the total needed by equal contributions. What did each of them give?

9. What was the average speed in m.p.h. when my mother drove 120 miles up the Ml in 1½ hours? Should she have been fined? (N.B. $S = D/T$)

10. $A = LB + E$. The entrance to a house is approached by a 3 sq yd piece of paving. This is joined to a rectangular patio 10 yards long and 5½ yards broad. Calculate the total area of paving.

11. $W = ECT$. Calculate the weight of metal deposited in gm if a current of 1.3 amps is switched on for a time of 500 seconds, the electro-chemical equivalent being 0.0014.

12. Two weights, the first heavy and the second light, are hung over a smooth pulley and released. Calculate the downward acceleration of the heavy weight.
$$a = \left(\frac{W_1 - W_2}{W_1 + W_2}\right) g$$
and gravity on a freely falling body produces 32ft per sec per sec; and the 2 weights are 9Kg and 7Kg.

13. Draw a block graph showing how the members of the class come to school (by car, bicycle, on foot, by bus or by train). Suggest changes which a national petrol and oil strike would bring about.

14. Turn the information in the last question into a pictogram. (It is a good age for children to become aware of some simple statistical devices, just as pie charts are good a year earlier.)

15. $(11c + 3h + 20s + p)$ and $(6p + h + 50s)$ show the cows, horses, sheep and pigs which a farmer has in two fields. If all the animals were placed in one field how would you show that?

16. Several bags of two kinds contain a mixture of screws, bolts and nuts as follows: $3(24s + 8n) + 4(9b + 3n)$. If all the bags were emptied out and then the same quantity of each piece of metal was placed in each of 6 new bags, how would that be represented?

17. N stands for a number. Find what N is and complete the subtraction sum:

```
   NN.4N
 - 60.N9
   ─────
     . 9
```

Answers to the first 12 questions are contained in: 580, 85, 80, 71.43, 60, 58, 48, 40, 35, 8¼, 4, 3, 1¹⁶/₂₅, 1, 0.91, ½, ⁷/₂₀, ⁷/₄₀

§4. Practical Constructions and exact Deductive Geometry

In Class 1, freehand drawing already contained two distinct aspects. One of them, concerned with the rich colourful illustration of stories, develops into pure art as the child grows up. Free of any geometrical influence it will continue to mature throughout the whole school up to Class 12 – and beyond. The second aspect embraces geometrical experience and has its origin in the child's awareness of his limb movements. The feet learn to move round a circle or along a straight line. The hands learn how to make a chalk or crayon execute these forms on a blackboard or large sheet of paper. Rhythmical repeating patterns and symmetrical forms are produced.

Class 4 saw a new stage in the second aspect of freehand drawing, when the forms became wholly geometrical, yet this too was balanced by other drawings containing a free artistic element – asymmetrical symmetries and the like. Class 5 experienced the power of using instruments. Compasses and ruler brought about an external exactness to meet what had been felt as a purely inner experience. Yet the inner experience will always continue to be the creative source, even when informed by external laws.

12 year-olds require geometrical drawing to be of practical use. How do you construct angles of exactly 60°, 30°, 90° etc? How are angles and lengths bisected exactly? The seven circle net contains the key, but instead of drawing whole circles only parts of them, arcs, need be drawn. Thus:

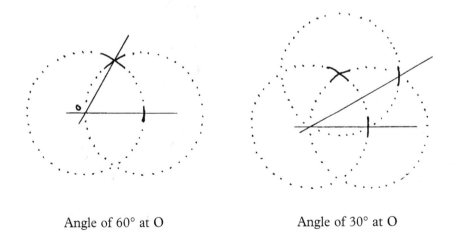

Angle of 60° at O   Angle of 30° at O

Angles of 90° and 45° at O

Bisection of AB

Dividing a line AB into 5 equal parts

(also constructing lines through A and B which are parallel – here they are at 60° to AB, but this is possible at any angle)

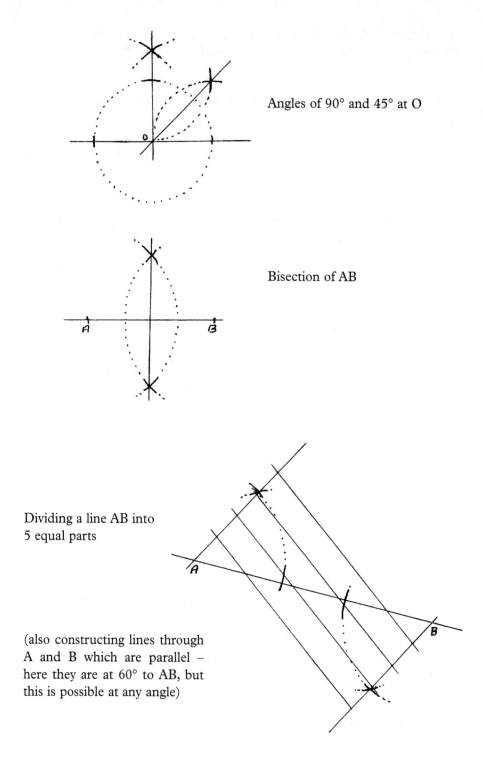

These and other well-known constructions from Euclid's Elements enable Class 6 to construct all manner of geometrical figures, for example a triangle ABC, where

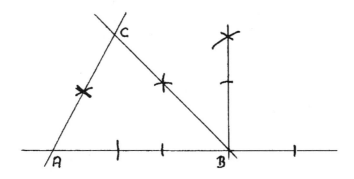

(i) Â = 60°, B̂ = 45°, AB = 5 cm;

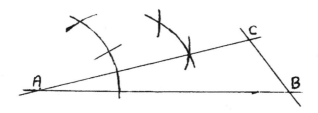

(ii) Â = 15°, AB = 7 cm, AC = 6 cm.

After several days work at such constructions some obvious geometrical facts of an axiomatic nature can be recorded.

1. A set of adjacent angles bounded by a straight line add up to 180°

2. Corresponding angles to parallel lines are equal.

The biggest help to children in learning such axioms lies in giving them numerical examples, e.g.

1. What is a?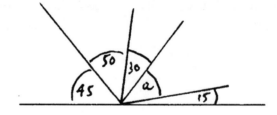

$$180 - (45 + 50 + 30 + 15)$$
$$= 180 - 140$$
$$= 40°$$

2. What is b?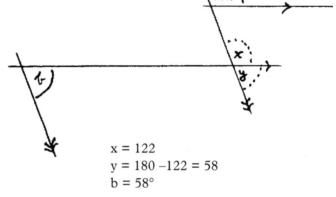

$$x = 122$$
$$y = 180 - 122 = 58$$
$$b = 58°$$

Whilst it is also obvious that 'vertically opposite' angles are equal and that alternate angles to parallel lines are equal, it is good to show that both these facts are also logical consequences of the two axioms above. The soul's thinking lieutenant gains much satisfaction in observing such consistency. Thus

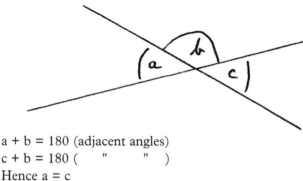

$$a + b = 180 \text{ (adjacent angles)}$$
$$c + b = 180 \text{ (} \quad " \quad \quad " \quad \text{)}$$
Hence $a = c$

Chapter 6: Class 6 mathematics

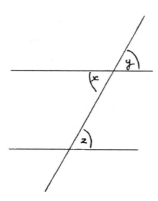

x = y (opposite angles)
y = z (corresponding angles)
Hence x = z

Instead of 'hence', you can use the old ∴ or the new ⇒ .

Only now are we in a position to lead Class 6 through its *most important geometrical experience*. Ask them to construct a triangle whose sides are 8 cm, 10 cm and 12 cm, say, on a piece of paper.

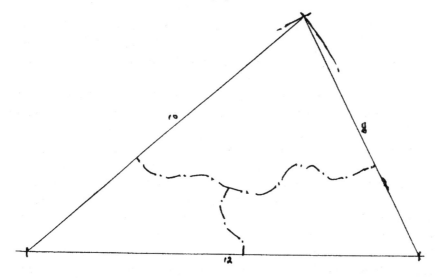

Then using their protractors ask them to write down the size of each of the three angles as accurately as possible. As a teacher you deliberately choose a triangle whose angles are not whole numbers – in fact they are not even exact mixed numbers. Then ask them to add up their three answers and write down the result.

Ask each member of the class to call out his final answer and make a list on the board. Variation between 178 and 182 will occur, perhaps with the odd 185 and a very precise 179¾ from a keen-eyed member.

'It ought to be 180, didn't it?' 'Oh? Why?'

Now get them all to use a pair of scissors and cut the paper into three pieces of triangle in any way they like, but keeping the angles to different pieces, then rearrange them.

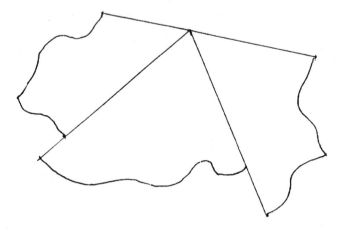

'It must be 180!' 'Put your eye at one end of the top line and look at it!' 'Well, it still *ought* to be!' 'Maybe so, but suppose we did all of this again with a differently shaped triangle – would that be sufficient evidence? Or would it be best to cut out a hundred triangles?'

Someone – and you hope without any prompting – will observe that the lines may not be perfectly straight. Get the class to put their eyes against window frames, door edges, desk lids, etc. 'My desk is awful!'

This can be a most precious moment. Not only is it clear that the physical world is imperfect, but you can ask the class, 'Where, then, does the word 'perfect' come from?' It's only something we can think and never see. But go on to emphasize that the real craftsman, carpenter or engineer has the idea of perfection in his mind when he makes something. He always strives his utmost to get as near to it as possible. Machines can also not achieve perfection – indeed they would not be able to work if there were not a tiny gap of a few thousandths of an inch between an axle and a bearing, for example. And what about a painter? Was Raphael completely satisfied when he laid down his brush on completing the Sistine Madonna? Dare one take this as indisputable proof that besides the physical world there must be a spiritual world? The wise teacher will not say this, but some children will be able to express it in their own words.

Only now can we prove that the three angles of any triangle, irrespective of size, shape, colour or what have you, add up to 180° or two right angles. (It is worth reading Steiner's proof and commentary in his *Theory of Knowledge Implicit in Goethe's World Conception.*)³. First construct a line through one corner of the triangle parallel to the opposite side. Then imagine breaking the whole figure into two parts without altering the shape and size. Pull it apart like a Christmas cracker.

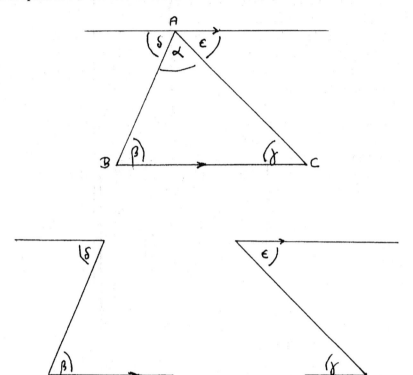

The proof, later copied into their books with colour added, looking first at the bottom left, then at the bottom right and finally at point A, is

$\beta = \delta$ (alternate angles to parallel lines)
$\gamma = \epsilon$ ("   "   )
So $\beta + \gamma = \delta + \epsilon$
Add α to each pair
$\alpha + \beta + \gamma = \alpha + \delta + \epsilon$
Since δ, α and ϵ add up to 180° (adjacent angles),
$\alpha + \beta + \gamma = 180°$.

> It is worthwhile for the teacher to meditate on this thinking activity, although this won't concern his children. They will, however meet its implications in a Class 11 or 12 main lesson block on Philosophy. The first steps – breaking up and examining the pieces – is the work of that part of our thinking activity we call *intellect*. It is *analytical*. The next step is *synthetical*, the part of our thinking activity we call *reason*; with it we build things up and so achieve *knowledge*. Without the application of our intellect followed by that of reason, which achieves the sought-for wholeness, the triangle would remain a mere percept, either of a sense-perceptible kind or as a perfected mental image. Only now do we know one of the essential attributes of the triangle. In Class 8 this will be carried further.
>
> One might also notice the role of the line drawn parallel to the triangle's opposite side. In Class 7 one can observe something similar, but in a different subject – a catalyst in chemistry. Drawing such analogies at the appropriate moment is the stuff of which education is made.

Returning to Class 6, the class should be given lots of numerical questions about angles to answer, from the simple 'What is α below?' and 'What kind of triangle must it be?' to the much more complex 'What is θ below?'

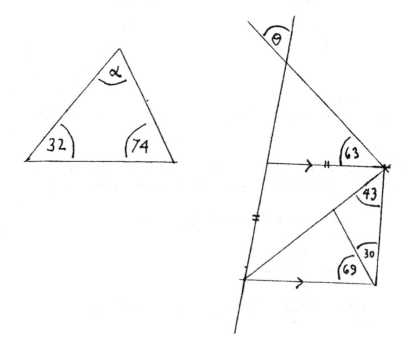

Instead of rushing into the midst of this maze, seeking the value of some unmarked angle, let the class recall the Greek myth, in which Theseus slaughtered the minator. Ariadne had given him a golden thread. He fixed one end outside the labyrinth and unwound it as he entered so as to be able to retrace his footsteps after the deed had been done. θ is, of course, the initial letter of Theseus in Greek.

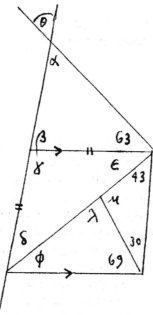

He steps inside, knowing α = θ. He can calculate α if β were known, since the 3rd angle of that triangle is 63. β is γ from 180 and γ would be known if only δ and ε were known. But the last two are equal because of the isosceles triangle there. Now ε = φ because of the parallel lines. Now because of the 69 we only need to find what λ is in order to calculate φ. However, λ + μ = 180 and 43 + 30 + μ = 180. Ha!!! μ must be 107. At that moment the beast has been slain. So Theseus just winds up the thread and returns to broad daylight.

One of the prime tasks of ancient Greek civilisation was the development of intelligence and clear thinking. Not only is this evident in the dialogues of Socrates but it can be seen in pictorial form in many Greek myths. The tales of Odysseus contain very many examples of this. It is the return journey which we accompany by writing

μ (which is the initial letter of minator) = 180 − 43 − 30 (angles of triangle) = 107
λ = 180 − 107 (adjacent angles) = 73
φ = 180 − 73 − 69 (angles of triangle) = 38

$\varepsilon = 38$ (alternate angles)
$\delta = \varepsilon$ (isosceles triangle) $= 38$
$\gamma = 180 - 38 - 38$ (angles of triangle) $= 104$
$\beta = 180 - 104$ (adjacent angles) $= 76$
$\alpha = 180 - 76 - 63$ (angles of triangle) $= 41$
$\theta = \alpha$ (opposite angles) $= 41°$

Short cuts are possible in two places, if the exterior angle theorem is known, i.e. $\rho = \sigma + \tau$.

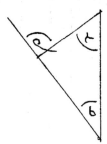

The class can join up the letters $\theta, \alpha \ldots \mu$ by a golden curving line. The form of the reasoning above is important and it is a great pity that many, indeed most schools in many countries have dropped this requirement from their curriculae. It should be noted in passing that the curriculum of Steiner (Waldorf) schools involves learning a little of the ancient Greek language in Classes 5 and 6, so the Greek letters should be quite familiar.

Another piece of deductive geometry belonging to Class 6 concerns congruent triangles. Every triangle has 7 metrical elements: the lengths of its 3 sides, the sizes of its 3 angles and the area of space it contains, but just 3 of these are sufficient to determine the rest.[4]

The 4 principal cases to be learnt are

| 1) 3 sides | 2) 2 sides and their included angle | 3) 2 angles and a corresponding side | 4) A right angle, the hypotenuse and another side |

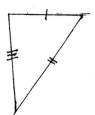 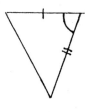 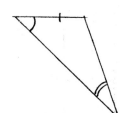 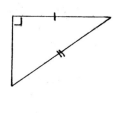

Chapter 6: Class 6 mathematics

The teacher's problem here is to find *interesting* examples where these criteria can be applied. Books often contain tasks for children which are dull because the property requiring proof is too obvious.

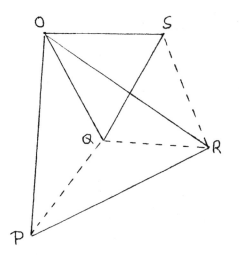

OPR and OQS are equilateral triangles. Which pair out of the 3 dotted lengths PQ, QR and RS are equal?

(Hint: consider the triangles OPQ and ORS.)

Nowadays preference has been given to movement geometry in schools generally. Transformations such as rotation, translation, enlargement and shear, however, belong properly to Class 7 when History and Geography main lesson blocks deal with the discovery of new worlds and how the African continent's shape can be transformed into that of South America or Australia. Already in Class 6, though, it is important to draw triangles in movement, e.g. the king's and queen's crowns and triangles in the same segment of a circle.

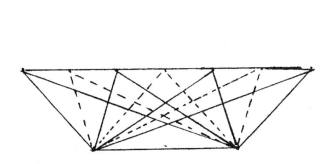 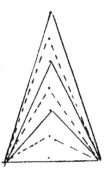

Colour always enhances such movement drawings. In Class 7 and Class 8 the teenagers will be able to look again at their Class 6 main lesson books and then deduce important geometrical properties from them.

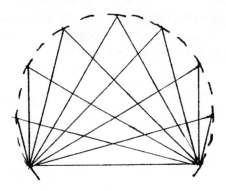

Notice, in this way of educating, that thinking always follows doing and feeling. Large scale drawings tend to give a richer experience than do the small scale ones and this section concludes with the envelope of a cardioide. We can see this boundary curve every day. Where and when? [5]

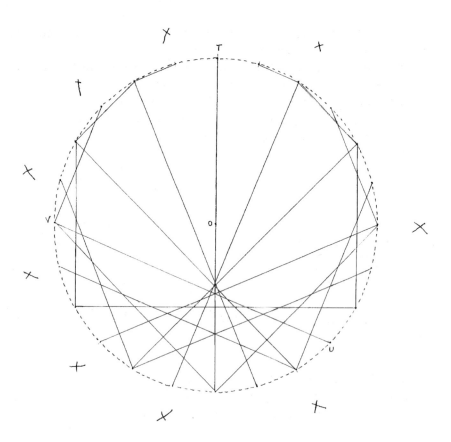

Chapter 6: Class 6 mathematics

§5. Geometrical examples in Class 6

The answers are given in brackets at the end of each question, but teachers are recommended to continue the practice of listing them at the end of the set of questions in a different order.

1. Calculate angles α, β and γ.

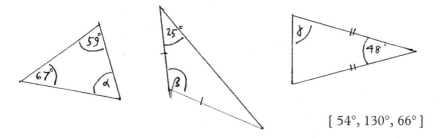

[54°, 130°, 66°]

N.B. The angles are not necessarily accurately constructed.

2. Calculate θ and φ.

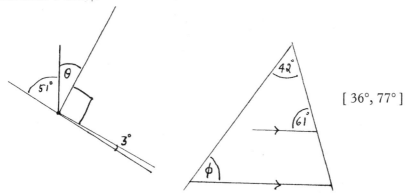

[36°, 77°]

3. AECD is a parallelogram and AB = AC. Calculate AD̂C.

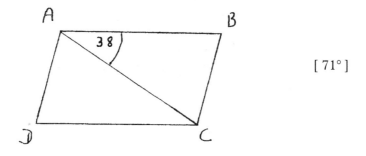

[71°]

107

4. O is the centre of circle ABC. Calculate the 3 angles of triangle ABC. Do you notice anything interesting?

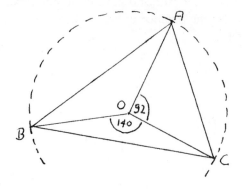

[70°, 46°, 64°]

[The central angles are twice the triangle angles.]

5. L and M are the middle points of AB and AC. N lies on the continuation of LM, and NC is parallel to AB.
  (i) Copy this accurately and prove that triangles ALM and CNM are congruent.
  (ii) Prove that NC = LB.
  (iii) Prove that triangles LBC and CNL are congruent.
  (iv) What can you deduce about the lines LM and BC?

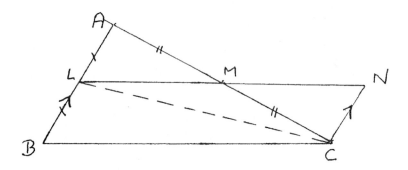

[(i)   In the triangles ALM, CNM
        AM = MC
        LÂM = NĈM (alternate angles)
        AL̂M = CN̂M ("   ")
        ⇒ they are congruent (2 angles and a corresponding side)

    (ii)   ⇒ NC = AL
            ⇒ NC = LB

Chapter 6: Class 6 mathematics

(iii) In the triangles LBC, CNL
LB = CN
LC is common to both triangles.
BL̂C = NĈL (alternate angles)
⇒ they are congruent (2 sides and the included angle)

(iv) ⇒ LN = BC and BĈL = NL̂C
But by (i) LM = MN
⇒ LM = ½ BC. Also LM must be parallel to BC.]

It may be better to have the whole class do question 6 before trying to do question 5. Certainly it would be better for the weaker children; (or you could tell them they could leave out question 5 – which you will do on the board tomorrow when recalling today's work). In this way wonder will be stimulated, for they will feel delight in the practical results.

6. Draw the following 3 figures, using any measurements you like, then construct (or measure out) the middle points of every line drawn.

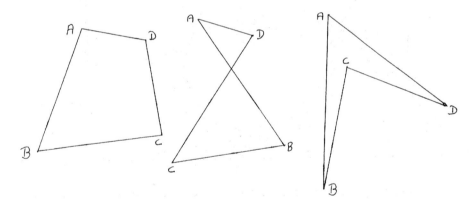

Now join up successive middle points each time,
i.e.　　middle of AB to middle of BC,
　　　　　"　　BC　　　　"　　CD,
　　　　　"　　CD　　　　"　　DA,
　　　　　"　　DA　　　　"　　AB.

What do you notice? Will it always work for any other 4-sided shape (called a quadrilateral)? Can you prove it?

[Each time a parallelogram is formed. To prove it, use the last result of question 5 in conjunction with diagonals AC and ED .]

Triangles may be classified in two ways. They are either equilateral, isosceles or scalene. If one angle is obtuse it is 'obtuse-angled' or simply an 'obtuse' triangle. If one angle is 90° it is a 'right-angled' or simply a a 'right' triangle. Otherwise it is 'acute'.

7. Decide what kind of triangle ABC must be if
   (i)   A = 19° and B = 57°   (scalene and obtuse)
   (ii) C = 12° and A = 84°   (isosceles and acute)
   (iii) B = 110° and C = 35°   (isosceles and obtuse)
   (iv) A = 37° and C = 53°   (scalene and right)
   (v)   B = 60° and A = 60°   (equilateral and, of course, acute)

8. Construct a triangle ABC, where AB = 12cm, EC = 15cm and CA = 18cm.

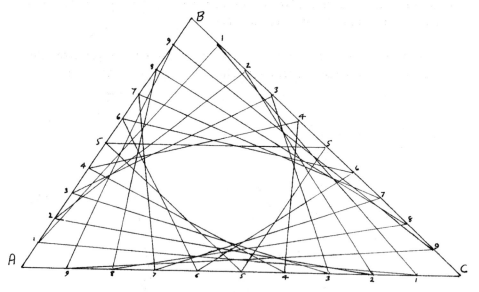

Don't show them this. Let them discover it. The form consists of 3 parabolic arcs or nets.

Using the ruler's millimetre scale, divide up each side into 10 equal parts. Making sure you keep going clockwise round the triangle, label the points between A and B from 1 to 9. Do the same between B and C, then between C and A. Make 9 new triangles by joining up all the 1's, then all the 2's and so on.

9. Construct a triangle PQR without using a protractor in which P = 45°, Q = 75° and PQ = 10 cm. Then measure the length of QR.

[8.16 cm]

10. Given that LM = 12 cm and LN = 9 cm and M = 40°, construct two quite differently shaped triangles LMN. Measure the two possible lengths of MN. [7.3 cm and 16.6 cm]

11. Draw a line 11 cm long and divide it, using rulers and compasses, into 7 equal parts.

12. Draw a line across the middle of the paper and mark a point P about one inch away from it. Construct a good selection of circles all passing through P and all having their centres on the line. What do you notice? (they all go through another point)

13. Draw this circle and its vertical diameter on a whole blank page, making sure that the line is in the centre of the page and that the circle's centre is 13 cm from the top. (This would suit A4 size paper)

Radius of circle = 3 cm.

Mark your own letter in the places shown.
Now divide up your circle into 12 or 24 equal parts. Stab each of your points on the circle, as well as your lettered point. Now rub everything out!

'What?!'

'Ah, but you still have the pricked holes, don't you?' 6

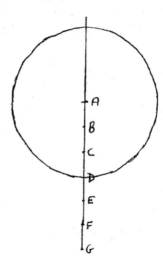

[Go round the class and give each child one of the seven letters A to G. You might give very weak children the letter A.   AB = BC = etc. = 1 cm.]

Using each one of the little holes on the rubbed-out circle as the centre, construct 12 or 24 circles, such that each circle passes exactly through the hole of the chosen letterpoint (D will only give 11 or 23 circles). Finally use one colour only to fill in the small 'circular triangles' on the border of the shape which has appeared.

[Illustrated below – using only 12 circles – are the shapes for cases A, C, D and F. They are respectively a circle, a limaçon (French for snail), a cardioide (heart shape) and another limaçon. Only the border-creating parts of the circles are shown.]

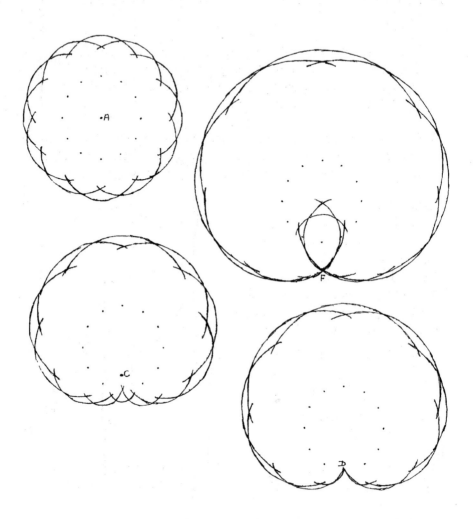

(The teacher could also request that the colours used range from red (A) via green (D) to violet (G) – i.e. a rainbow set – or some other sequence. Let sets of 7 drawings be mounted on the classroom walls. This gives a fine example of *metamorphosis;* and further intermediate shapes can be imagined.)

8. Construct a rectangle 8 cm across and 10 cm down, then inside it construct further horizontal and vertical lines to make a net with a 1 cm mesh. Starting in the middle of the top place a blob, over the crossing point. Then go 1 to the right again but 2 down, then 1 to the right and 3 down and finally 1 to the right and 4 down. Do the same on the left starting from the middle of the top again. Make a blob each time you stop. Imagine that the blobs are a set of balls thrown up by a juggler. Carefully draw the curved path which the balls will be moving along.[7] If the juggler had 2 more balls, one in each hand, where would his hands have to be? Now go outside with a friend and see if between you something similar can be done. Start with just 2 balls and increase the number steadily.

9. Carefully construct 36 points equally spaced round a large circle, using 10 degree divisions on a protractor. Join every point to every other. How many straight lines have you drawn altogether? Can you prove that? How many circle envelopes are clearly there in the drawing? Why?

Chapter 7:
Arithmetic and Algebra in Classes 7 and 8 (children of 12 to 14)

§1. Becoming a teenager

The young teenager is aware of a region, a realm in herself that had not seemed to be present previously. This is a private space to which other people, whether parents, teachers or peers, are denied access except under special circumstances – determined by the teenager alone. Membership of a peer group, whilst very important, is not the only thing that matters, despite the pressures involved in the pop music and drug 'culture'. Growing sexual awareness, first in girls and later in boys, is not the cause of this private inner space awareness. The two changes run parallel and their common origin lies in a new stage of human ripeness for life on earth. Sometimes parents become very worried because their children no longer tell them what happened at school each day when they come home, whereas in previous years they had been eager to tell and be listened to. Such parents should not feel they have done something wrong when they receive a bare and uninformative answer to some question. It is quite right and natural for teenagers to erect an invisible notice saying, 'Private, Keep Out.' The inner space is that of conscious personal soulhood. That part of the whole human being, which is called astral body because of its origin in the world of stars, begins to approach and penetrate the physical and living etheric bodies with greater effect. From a purely earthly standpoint this new 'body' has been undergoing its embryonic stage and is now ready to be born.

This is the age when personal discovery of wider realms of experience, allied to the feeling of a growing idealism, calls forth the need for wider imaginative thinking. The history of the discovery of Southern Africa and the

Americas makes such a strong appeal in Class 7. The geography of the lands bordering the Atlantic Ocean in Class 7 will be complemented by that of the Indian and especially the Pacific Oceans in Class 8. (Schools in Australia, however, will naturally change the order of presentation.) Renaissance art and science make equally strong appeals. The corresponding elements in mathematical education need to be focused upon by the class teacher. Algebra provides a good example of this.

In the survey given in the early chapter 'What is mathematics?' the development from arithmetic through algebra to calculus and beyond was indicated. Algebra is often considered to be a more abstract, possibly duller or more boring discipline born out of arithmetic. In truth it is an activity requiring enhanced imagination, as qualitatively different from arithmetic as is the etheric from the physical body. In these terms, calculus' qualitative correlate would be the astral body. In the same way as the continued development of 'head, heart and hands'[1] is taking place in the young teenager, an overall development of algebra itself has three parts to it. Class 6 introduced the algebraic formula. Classes 7 and 8 introduce the algebraic equation and identity respectively. On closer inspection it is possible to observe the isomorphism

formula	—	head
equation	—	heart and lungs
identity	—	digestion and limbs

In a later chapter we may be tempted to posit some similar isomorphism regarding statistics, remembering the well-known threefoldness of 'lies, damned lies and statistics', but this may be going too far. All such trinities of real and not merely devised foundation are intimately related to the three soul activities of thinking, feeling and willing. The most fundamental of all is the Trinity of God the father, the Son and the Holy Spirit. It is in the teenage years that an understanding of this deepest of mysteries can develop. That neither human beings nor some wholly fortuitous combinations of atoms have been responsible for the creation of our world, but that some kind of Father Principle is at work, is obvious to everyone not completely indoctrinated with materialistic theory. The very existence of love in ourselves and others, a more conscious awareness of which appears in the teenager, can lead to the understanding of the word 'Christ', the Son principle – or whatever alternative word, as in non-Christian religions, may be preferred. To be able to act out of impulses drawn from realms higher than that of the personal self is a longing cherished, if only partly consciously, by the teenager. The Holy Spirit that can be active within each human individual is

Chapter 7: Arithmetic and algebra in classes 7 and 8

a reality (again some other words for 'holy spirit' may be preferred) which no positivist, reductionist or deterministic approach can ever hope to penetrate. The possibility of its existence is there in the young teenager. Without it there would be no idealism.

§2. Teaching algebra

The use of simple letters instead of whole words, and the combination of several such letters in a mathematical statement was introduced in Class 6. Such formulae have led human head (brain-bound) consciousness in recent times to coin such things as UNPROFOR, PAYE and IUDs, but their mathematical value lies in acknowledging the essential whilst dispensing with the inessential.

The next step in algebra, already lightly touched upon in Class 1, is to use letters to indicate an initially unknown quantity, which unlike appearance in a formula cannot be directly calculated without further thought. Statements incorporating these unknowns are called equations. So in Class 1 the child faced with $4 = 3 + x$ (x may be a piece of paper stuck over the hidden 1) has to picture what you have to do to 3 so as to end up with 4. Just as the Portugese, British, etc. explorers in new worlds began to carry European culture to other lands (Class 7 history lessons), so did the Arabs bring algebra to Europe across the Mediterranean Sea and the Bosphorus. The word 'algebra' is a shortening of the Arabic phrase 'Al jabr w'al muquabalah', which means 'The reunion and the opposition'. In '$4 = 3 + x$' the pieces of the puzzle are reunited, and in '$x = 1$' the unknown x stands opposite to the now known 1. The best practical aid for teaching algebraic equations is an old-fashioned pair of scales, for which some of the weights have been lost. With the class sitting round the teacher's table, upon which the well-polished brass antique is standing, ask one of the class to weigh a prepared object such as a bottle of ginger beer. (Tipple out some of it the night before so as to have an exact number of grams or ounces). Suppose we have weights of 1 Kg, 500 gm, 200 gm, 100 gm, 10 gm, 2 gm and 1 gm and the bottle of beer weighs 613 gm, confirmed by the weigher, assisted in manoeuvres by the suggestive utterances, not always polite, of surrounding peers. A second object weighing 1209 gm will require a little extra cunning by a second weigher.

Now you show the following: 7 matchboxes, partially filled with matches, together with a 2 gm weight, just balance the 100 gm weight. It is, alas, common practice with many factories not to fill the boxes; but this enables the teacher to add or subtract a few more matches from each box to give a whole number of gm weight. Then make a picture of the actual balancing scales.

Turning this into an algebraic statement (al jabr), we get

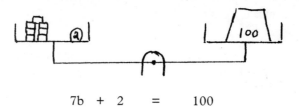

$$7b + 2 = 100$$

The secret of further procedure is always to maintain balancing scale pans. Remove 2 from each side. Here you indicate how a small piece could be sawn off the 100 gm, but not wishing to ruin the brass weight we will just imagine it.

$$7b = 98$$

The scales will still balance if we remove all but a seventh of what now lies on the imagined scale pans.

$b = 14$; so we finally know that each box of matches weighs 14 gm.

The three stages[2] in this whole process are
    1. percept   (the real pair of scales)
    2. mental picture   (the drawn sketch)
    3. concept   (the answer 14)

At this point the class can be given a set of equations like the following to solve:

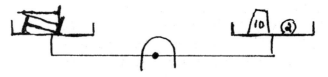

1. What does each nail weigh?

2. $9a = 117$
3. $5b + 4 = 39$
4. $10c = 84 + 3c$
5. $d + 170 = 9d + 4$
6. $25e + 13 = 200 + 14e$
7. $517 + 29f = 35f + 1$

8. $2g + 1\frac{1}{2} = 12 + \frac{1}{2}g$
9. $95h + 5 = 4h + 31$
10. $3 + 50i = 42 + 43i$
11. $j + 3 + j = 1 + 3j + 1$
12. $8^{3/4}k + {}^{5}/_{24} = 5^{5/6}k + 4^{3/8}$
13. $0.007L + 12.3 = 0.25L + 5.01$

Chapter 7: Arithmetic and algebra in classes 7 and 8

Answers: 2/7, 1, 1³/7, 4, 5, 5⁴/7, 7, 12, 13, 17, 20³/4, 30, 86

It will become important to show the class that this is not merely an intellectual game but will have practical consequences for solving real problems in life. As a quasi practical example we might describe a human situation like the following:

> Two parties of Arabs crossing a desert in opposite directions met halfway between two oases. Everyone in the first party of 7 people had 2 full bottles of water left, but in the second party of 5 people, one person had only an empty bottle and the other 4 only one full bottle each. What should the first party give the second party so that everyone in both parties could have equal rations?

(The last of the 5 Arabs on the right, who carried a full bottle, lagged behind and so does not appear in the picture.)

Let the number of bottles given be x.
The parties now have $14 - x$ and $4 + x$ bottles.

Sharing out,		$\dfrac{14 - x}{7} = \dfrac{4 + x}{5}$
Multiply both sides by 35		$5(14 - x) = 7(4 + x)$
		$70 - 5x = 28 + 7x$
Add 5x to both sides		$70 = 28 + 12x$
Subtract 28 from both sides		$42 = 12x$

Divide both sides by 12 $\qquad \dfrac{42}{12} = x$

So $\qquad x = \dfrac{7}{2} = 3\tfrac{1}{2}$

Three and a half bottles of water should be given. As a check, each Arab in the first party now has a ration of $\dfrac{10\tfrac{1}{2}}{7} = 1\tfrac{1}{2}$ bottles

and each Arab in the second party now has $\dfrac{7\tfrac{1}{2}}{5} = 1\tfrac{1}{2}$ bottles.

Of course, such a problem doesn't really require algebra. The total amount of water could be divided by the total number of Arabs and so on, but the *algebraic principle* is illustrated above. In fact every time a simple equation is used the problem could be solved by arithmetic alone. This will not be the case for quadratic and higher equations, which suit Class 9 and higher classes.

Negative signs have begun to appear and negative answers have now to be introduced. The best way to understand a negative number is through the experience of debt. If I have a balance of £50 in my bank and write out a cheque to someone for £70, then I shall find that my account is £20 'in the red'.

$$50 - 70 = -20$$

If I then receive a cheque for £80, the account will again be 'in the black'.

$$-20 + 80 = 60 \text{ or } +60.$$

An alternative introduction is by a picture of sets of stairs leading from the ground floor to both the upper floor and the basement.

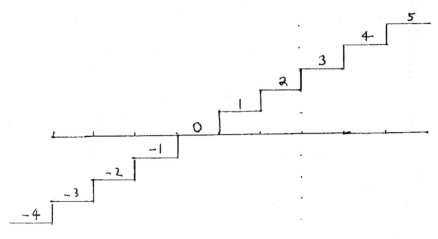

Chapter 7: Arithmetic and algebra in classes 7 and 8

Stand on step 3 and go down 7 steps. $3 - 7 = -4$
              -2 up 4 $-2 + 4 = 2$
              -1 down 2 $-1 - 2 = -3$
              -4 up 3 $-4 + 3 = -1$

This idea can also be turned into class movement. Have everyone in a circle facing in a clockwise direction. Take 3 steps forward, then 5 steps backwards! Then 2 backwards, followed by 6 forwards etc. A similar exercise with everyone standing behind their desks results from the instructions:
  'All face north!'
  'Turn clockwise through 3 right angles!'
  'Turn anti-clockwise through −2 right angles!' and so on.

Class 7 should not be feeling too adult to allow the immortal Mr. O'Grady to participate in these games, the last person standing being the one not falling a victim to the absence of this Irish gentleman's charms, and thus being declared the winner. Some will be caught out if in the midst of these rotations, when they happen to be facing West, the instruction 'O'Grady says face East!' is followed by 'All face East!'

How do negative numbers appear in practical life?
    Take the problem, 'At what temperature do Centigrade and Fahrenheit thermometers show the same reading?' The class should already have learnt from Class 6 Physics that the freezing and boiling temperatures for water are 0 and 100 Centigrade and 32 and 212 Fahrenheit. 100 gradations on the former equate with 180 gradations on the latter, but at freezing point the latter is 32 ahead. Let the temperature for equal thermometer readings be t°.

Then $$\frac{t}{100} = \frac{t-32}{180}$$

Multiply both sides by 900 $9t = 5(t - 32)$

$$9t = 5t - 160$$

Subtract 5t from both sides $4t = -160$

$$t = -40$$

So both thermometers agree at 40° below zero, and one thinks about northern Canada.

Brackets have also begun to appear. They were already introduced in Class 6 examples about animals in farmers' fields. Returning to the picture of the pair of scales, how may the following equation be visualised?
$$3(c - 4) = 2(5c + 19) - 8.$$

Ask the class! Someone will soon come up with weightless paper bags for brackets. The –8 must be something that pulls up on the scale pan instead of pushing down. Ah yes, a gas-filled balloon! ...but one which would just hold up an 8 gm weight, let's suppose. The picture becomes

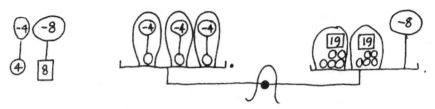

The letter **c** might stand for capsule.

Removing the bags or brackets,
$$3c - 12 = 10c + 38 - 8$$

Add 12 gm to the right hand pan and cut the three strings attached to the capsules on the left hand pan so that the three balloons fly off and the scales remain level.
$$3c = 10c + 38 - 8 + 12$$

Simplifying, $\qquad 3c = 10c + 42$

Remove 3c from
both sides $\qquad 0 = 7c + 42$

So the capsules themselves must be filled with gas!

Remove 42 from
both sides $\qquad -42 = 7c$

This means imagining a big balloon attached to the left scale pan.

Finally $\qquad -6 = c \qquad$ or looking at the picture from the back,
$\qquad\qquad\qquad c = -6$

Each capsule would therefore be able to hold up a 6 gm weight. One also notices that the paper bags must have been glued to the scale pans. An absurd example? – not at all, compared to some science fiction videos.

A point has been reached at which the mental pictures of scales, weight, balloons, etc can be left behind, with the one exception of the activity of balancing. We can now work with pure concepts, including that of breathing, which continually balances in-breath with out-breath. A further set of examples for Class 7 now follows.

Remove the brackets and simplify where necessary.
1. $6(9x + 8)$
2. $7(12 - 5x)$
3. $11(3x + 2) + 4(4x + 9)$

Solve the equations
4. $8a = 56$
5. $20b = 12 + 18b$
6. $9(3c + 1) = 25c + 13$
7. $6(5 + 4d) = 7(5 + 2d)$
8. $8(6e + 5) = 2(3e + 17) + 13(3e - 1) + 1$
9. $5(9f - 5) = 3(11f - 8) + 4(2f - 9)$
10. $12(4g - 0.9) + 0.34 = 4(5g + 0.15) + 7(3g - 0.8)$

Answers:
$-8^{3}/_{4}$, -6, $-^{1}/_{2}$, 0.78, 2, 6, 7, $49x + 58$, $54x + 48$, $84 - 35x$.

Two final steps remain before saying that every kind of simple equation has been practised. The first concerns fractions, e.g. solve

$$\frac{3p}{8} + \frac{5}{12}(2p - 7) = \frac{p + 2}{6} + {}^{3}/_{4}$$

Always remembering that you can do anything whatever to the left hand side of the equation, provided that the same is done to the right hand side, thus preserving the balance, multiply every term by the lowest number into which all the denominators go, i.e. 24.

$$9p + 10(2p - 7) = 4(p + 2) + 18$$
$$9p + 20p - 70 = 4p + 8 + 18$$
$$29p - 70 = 4p + 26$$

Add 70 to both sides
$$29p = 4p + 96$$

Subtract 4p from both sides
$$25p = 96$$

$$p = \frac{96}{25} = 3\frac{21}{25} \quad \text{or } 3.84$$

The last step concerns the *multiplication* of signs. A return to the pictorial is always better than trying to teach logic directly. Whereas the *combination* of positive and negative terms has been pictured by a set of steps going upstairs from ground level and a set of steps going down to the basement, or by analogy with bank accounts, a different picture is now required. This will reinforce what the legs have learnt by dealing with Mr. O'Grady. A story of the following kind might be told.

Once four young people decided to go down to the sea to bathe. They set off in an old car and drove without incident down a steep hill to the coast. After an enjoyable splash and swim they set off back home. Halfway up the hill the car began to shudder, eventually stopping. The four occupants got out and the car bonnet ('hood' in American language) was lifted, accompanied by an enormous cloud of steam and vapour. On closer inspection they wondered if the car would be able to 'make it' and each expressed his or her opinion.

'It is possible,' said the first, a sanguine optimist.

'It is not possible,' said the second, a melancholic, of course.

'It is impossible,' said the third, a firm choleric.

After a while the phlegmatic member of the quartet, who became a lawyer in later life, pronounced

'It is not impossible.'

Translating these remarks into algebraic sign language, we obtain

+ + = +		+ times + is +
− + = −	or	− times + is −
+ − = −		+ times − is −
− − = +		− times − is +

Although the class is now fully equipped to solve any simple equation, it is essential that the *practical* application of what has been learnt to real situations in life is demonstrated and that the girls and boys work at many examples of this. Probably the best examples a teacher can bring concern the element of time.

Chapter 7: Arithmetic and algebra in classes 7 and 8

A visit to a factory will help the class appreciate the importance of the moving parts of machinery, synchronising to handle the products at precisely the right moments. Automation and the saving of human labour entirely depend on this. The problem of effecting such synchronicity depends upon the ability to find the answer to a question like 'At exactly what time between 3 p.m. and 4 p.m. does the hour hand of the clock lie underneath the minute hand?'

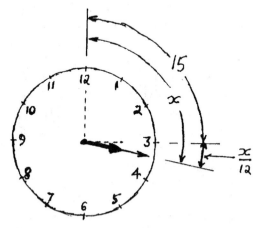

Ask the class to guess the answer and write down their guesses on the board. There will be much fiddling with wrist watches (except for the poor children who only possess digital ones!) However, you can confidently say that all their answers are wrong.

The first step necessary is one of modesty: 'I do not know what the answer is.' Translated into algebraic language, this becomes: 'Let the time be x minutes past three.' Since 3 o'clock the minute hand has turned through an angle of x divisions (minutes). Discuss how much faster the minute hand travels compared with the hour hand. Having agreed on the number 12, it is clear that the hour hand has turned through only $x/12$ divisions in the time it took the minute hand to turn through x divisions. The two hands were 15 divisions apart at 3 o'clock. The amount turned through by the minute hand can now be expressed in two different ways. So the reunion (al jabr) can be stated as

$$x = 15 + x/12 \qquad \text{———— (i)}$$

Multiply each term by 12, so preserving the balance of the two sides.
$$12x = 180 + x$$
Subtract x from both sides.
$$11x = 180$$

125

Divide both sides by 11.

$$x = 16^4/_{11} \qquad \text{------- (ii)}$$

This is the opposition of unknown to known (al muquabalah). The answer is therefore $16^4/_{11}$ minutes past 3.

The hardest part of such problems is achieving stage (i). Moving out of the physical and pictorial into the purely conceptual in this way, is what causes boys' and girls' feelings of helplessness and even fear. Once achieved, the path from (i) to (ii) is relatively easy. At this point a feeling of false pride can well up – a child can think she has finished the problem. But no, she has to return to the pictorial, and finally to the physical situation, and state the actual time on the clock. There are thus two temptations. One is to succumb to fear (to Ahriman in anthroposophical terminology) and the other is to succumb to pride (to Lucifer). Ahriman always tries to prevent us leaving the world of the senses for ideal and spiritual realms, whilst Lucifer would have us remain in the latter and not descend to the earthly and practical world. The central part of solving the problem is purely mathematical and non-material. It can remind us of the bliss of being asleep, free of the worries and tribulations of daily existence. The solution of the whole problem can remind us too, of the fairy story of Rumplestiltskin, who turned straw into gold during the night for the miller's daughter whilst she slept. That is only one element of the story, but the isomorphism will be clear. Fairy stories contain many elements of wisdom if we could but decipher them, yet to do so requires the soul's feeling and willing lieutenants to aid its thinking lieutenant, whilst its captain the ego looks towards the genius in us for guidance.

§3. Equations and problems they solve

There follows a set of questions suitable for Class 7 algebra, also drawn from topics not only found in arithmetic lessons but in geometry, physics and other lessons.

1. Solve the equation $\frac{x}{7} = 3$

2. Solve $\frac{3x}{4} - 2 = 5^1/_2$

3. Solve $x = 9 + x/_5$

Chapter 7: Arithmetic and algebra in classes 7 and 8

4. Solve $\quad 1 + \dfrac{2x+3}{6} = \dfrac{x}{8} - \dfrac{x-11}{3}$

5. What time exactly is shown on clock A?
6.   "   "   clock B?

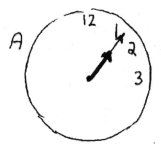 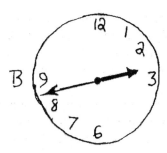

7. Solve the equation $\quad \dfrac{5(2t+3t)}{6} - \dfrac{3(5t-1)}{4} = \dfrac{2t+5}{3} - 2^{1}/_{12}$

8. The biggest angle of a triangle is 27 more than the next biggest angle and 48 more than the smallest angle of the triangle. How big is the biggest angle?

9. A slower train left Paddington at 10 a.m. travelling all the way at 40 m.p.h. A faster train left Paddington at 10:30 a.m. travelling all the way at 70 m.p.h. When did the faster overtake the slower train?

10. Where (how far from Paddington) did this happen?

11. On a hot summer day the Fahrenheit temperature reading was 56° higher than the Centigrade thermometer reading. What was the actual Centigrade temperature? Use the formula $F = \dfrac{9c}{5} + 32$.

12. The hypotenuse of a right-angled triangular wedge has to be made 2 cm longer than the base of the wedge, which is 10 cm high. What must the length of the hypotenuse be?

13. Check your answer to question 4 by substituting that answer for x separately in both sides of the equation and working each out. What is the result each time?

14. Try to solve the equation $3 - \dfrac{x}{10} + \dfrac{7-x}{5} = 5 - \dfrac{3}{10}(x + 2)$.

    If you can't, try x = 2. What does each side check out to?

15. Also try x = 3, x = 8 and x = 0. What conclusions do you reach?

16. I can row at 12 m.p.h. in still water. In a river flowing at constant speed I find that to row upstream 2 miles and then at once row back downstream to my starting point takes me altogether $22\tfrac{1}{2}$ minutes. How fast must the river be flowing?

17. A belt 90 cm long altogether passes round two equal pulleys. The pulley centres are 23 cm apart. What is the diameter of each pulley? (Use π = 22/7)

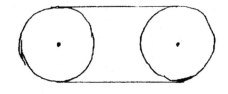

18. If p is equal to both 13g + 19 and 4(g + 25), what value has p?

Answers: $1^{1/3}$, $2^{5/6}$, $3^{4/5}$, 4, 4, $(5^{5/11})$, 10, $11^{1/4}$, 11.10, 14, $(16^{4/11})$, 21, 26, 30, $46^{2/3}$, 85, 136. Those in brackets are not the final answers.

Teachers should note that in questions 14 and 15, all four values of x give exact checks, so all four are possible answers. In fact any value given to x will work. The mystery will be cleared up in Class 8, for actually the given equation is an identity in disguise.

Many questions in the set above are on the difficult side, excellent for the cleverer half of the class. For the less able children, more questions like the first half dozen should be made up. Up to a week's work in main lesson is indicated by the selection of questions written above.

§4. Identities

By Class 8 any short cuts in doing otherwise tedious calculations are much appreciated by the class. At the age of 13 to 14 there is much interest in handy gadgets like mobile phones, tape recorders, microwave ovens, and the like, but it can be extremely unhelpful to young folk of this age (or younger) to allow them to use hand calculators (or computers) for arithmetic questions set to them. That will come a year later when they and their maths teachers can be sure that facility in all the ordinary numerical processes has been

Chapter 7: Arithmetic and algebra in classes 7 and 8

brought to a satisfactory pitch and that they know why these processes work. Much more valuable is mental and written practice of taking numerical short cuts. So one might begin a maths lesson by giving the class ten minutes or so to do all they can from the following list, any conceivable short cut being allowed. Do in any order you like.

1. 848 x 25
2. 102107000 ÷ 125
3. 15 x 9 x 6
4. 63 + 988 + 37
5. 8 x 13 x 9 x 0 x 7
6. 748 + 75 – 648
7. 79 x 87 – 85 x 79
8. $1^{7/10}$ x $6^{3/7}$ + $1^{7/10}$ x $3^{4/7}$
9. 62 x 62 – 58 x 58
10. $(7^{1/2})^2 – (6^{1/2})^2$
11. $3/4$ of $4/5$ of $5/6$ of $6/7$ …… of $16/17$ of $17/18$
12. $19^{3/5}$ x 2.75 + $2^{3/4}$ x 80.4

The methods used to get quick answers will indicate general laws of so doing, which are expressible as algebraic identities. It would be good to do several sets of such numerical questions before stating the laws and their names.

For the set above

1. 848 x 25 = 848 x $\frac{100}{4}$ = 21200 on cancelling.

2. 102107000 ÷ 125 = 102107000 x $\frac{8}{1000}$ = 816856

They both give rise to the *commutative and associative laws of multiplication*.
i.e.   a x b ≡ b x a   and   a x (b x c) ≡ (a x b) x c
or simply   ab ≡ ba   and   a(bc) ≡ (ab)c

So does question 3, for it is easier to multiply 15 first by 6 and the result by 9, i.e. 90 x 9 = 810

Question 4 illustrates the *commutative and associative laws of addition*, for it is easier to add 63 and 37 first.   100 + 988 = 1088.

Question 5 illustrates the *nought law*. The presence of zero anywhere in a multiplication makes the answer zero.

Teaching mathematics

Question 6 is like question 4, i.e. 748 − 648 + 75 = 100 + 75 = 175, the two laws being **a + b ≡ b + a** and **a + (b+c) ≡ (a+b) + c**. These letters can, of course, take negative as well as positive values.

Questions 7 and 8 involve the *distributive law* as well as laws already stated. So

$$79 \times 87 - 85 \times 79$$
$$= 87 \times 79 - 85 \times 79$$
$$= (87 - 85) \times 79$$
$$= 2 \times 79$$
$$= 158$$

and

$$1^{7}/_{10} \times 6^{3}/_{7} \times 1^{7}/_{10} \times 3^{4}/_{7}$$
$$= 1^{7}/_{10} \times (6^{3}/_{7} + 3^{4}/_{7})$$
$$= 1^{7}/_{10} \times 10$$
$$= 17$$

The law in symbols is a(b + c) ≡ ab + ac, which naturally can be written backwards.

The identity symbol ≡ means that the result is true no matter what numerical values any of the letters have. This is not so with equations where the symbol = is used; in all the equations earlier in this chapter only one numerical value of the letter was correct, saving the one exception of question 14 of the previous set, when the proper form is

$$3 - \frac{x}{10} + \frac{7-x}{5} \equiv 5 - \frac{3}{10}(x+2)$$

i.e. using ≡ and not = .

Identities produce immediate short cut results; they are of the nature of will.

Questions 9 and 10 depend on being able to do a long multiplication sum in algebra. Using the normal arithmetical lay-out to multiply (x − y) by (x + y).

$$\begin{array}{r} x - y \\ \underline{x + y} \\ x^2 - xy \\ \underline{ xy - y^2} \\ x^2 - y^2 \end{array}$$

The xy terms combine to dissolve each other. The result, written backwards, is x² − y² ≡ (x − y)(x + y), the most useful identity in the whole of algebra.

Hence 62 × 62 − 58 × 58 = 4 × 120 = 480 and $7^{1}/_{2}{}^{2} - 6^{1}/_{2}{}^{2}$ = 1 × 14 = 14.

Question 11 involves cancelling right through, exemplifying the associative and distributive laws of multiplication, leaving $^{3}/_{18} = ^{1}/_{6}$.

Question 12 needs the distributive law, giving
$$2.75 (19.6 + 80.4) = 2.75 \times 100 = 275.$$

Other useful identities are

$(x + y)^2 \equiv x^2 + 2xy + y^2,$ $\qquad x^3 + y^3 \equiv (x + y)(x^2 - xy + y^2),$
$(x + y)^3 \equiv x^3 + 3x^2y + 3xy^2 + y^3,$ $\qquad x^3 - y^3 \equiv (x - y)(x^2 + xy + y^2).$

These, however, belong properly to Class 9 in connection with the binomial theorem. But clever Class Eighters might enjoy them.

From the important $x^2 - y^2 \equiv (x - y)(x + y)$, we can deduce that
$(x + a)(x - a) - (x + a + 1)(x - a - 1) \equiv x^2 - a^2 - x^2 + (a + 1)^2$
$\equiv 2a + 1$

Suppose $x = 7$ and 'a' successively takes the values 0, 1, 2, 3...

Then
$\quad 7 \times 7 - 8 \times 6 = 1$
$\quad 8 \times 6 - 9 \times 5 = 3$
$\quad 9 \times 5 - 10 \times 4 = 5$
$\quad 10 \times 4 - 11 \times 3 = 7$

Herein lies the explanation of the discoveries made in Class 3.

Why not do that bit of Class 3 work again with Class 8?

§5. Areas and volumes

Class 7 is the age to calculate areas of all kinds. In geometry the theorem of Pythagoras can become a culmination of this. To begin with, calculating the areas of rectangles and the total area of the faces of a rectangular box is a revision and extension of what was learnt in Class 3.

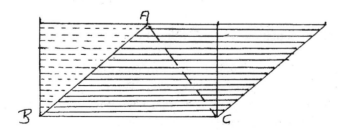

Often a teacher has a pile of exercise or main lesson books on her table. By shearing them and observing that the edges of all the pages remain visible and undistorted, the class can appreciate the area of a parallelogram as base times height.

By using a diagonal to divide the parallelogram in half, the area of a triangle ABC is established as ½ base x height.

Before showing how to calculate the area of a circle, the relationship between the sizes of its diameter and circumference has to be established. There are two places in the Old Testament[3] where the circumference is described as 6 times the radius or 3 times the diameter. That this is very roughly true can be seen from the familiar regular hexagon construction learnt in Class 5. But the arcs are longer than the sides, so the rough '3 times' has to be replaced by '3 and a bit times.' What the bit is can only be found experimentally in Class 7.

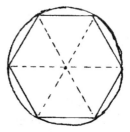

For this take a big ball of string or thread and wrap it round a large cylindrical tin a hundred times, say. Then, having carefully marked the beginning of the first and the end of the 100th wind, unwrap the whole and measure its length. Suppose this is 62.832 m and the diameter of the tin is 20 cm. Dividing we get '3.1416 times'.[2] The true value (called π) is 3.141592 of which 3.14 is often sufficient for calculations. The figures in the decimal places never recur in the same order, however. π is a transcendental number about which they will only learn in Class 12. The class could be told however, that to work out π completely, one has to calculate the endless fraction sum
$$4 (1 - 1/3 + 1/5 - 1/7 + 1/9 - 1/11 + \ldots \text{ forever}).$$

A good approximation to π is 22/7 or 3¹/₇, for this is 3.1̇42857̇.

To find the area of a circle one has to introduce the very first glimmer of integral calculus – again something they will only learn in Class 12. But these 'light touch glimmerings' are of extraordinary importance educationally. Cut up a circle into 6 equal sectors and rearrange.

This the class can do too – a revision of Class 5 geometry. Then cut each piece in half and rearrange these 12 sectors. Half the circumference appears on top, the other half below.

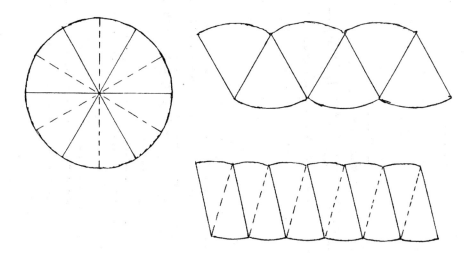

Let the more able and accurate children try a rearrangement of 24 sets, too. The whole shape becomes more and more like a parallelogram – indeed the further one goes the more like a rectangle it will become. Now imagine the circle cut up into 768 pieces. The rearrangement's border will look like this (with a very slight wobble on top and bottom).

$$\tfrac{1}{2}C = \pi r$$
$$r \qquad\qquad\qquad r$$
$$\tfrac{1}{2}C = \pi r$$

So the area $= \pi r \times r = \pi r^2$

Here is a selection of examples on areas for Class 7. Find the area in each case, except for nos. 7 and 16.

1. A rectangle 33 cm long and 12 cm wide.
2. A square whose side is $3^{1}/_{2}$ inches.
3. A triangle 3.6 cm high whose base is 3.7 cm.

4.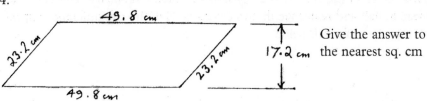

Give the answer to the nearest sq. cm

5. A circle whose diameter is 42 feet. (Use π = 22/7)

6. A circle whose radius is 5.2 cm (Take π as 3.14 and give the answer to 2 decimal places)

7. Express 0.01374 to (i) 3 d.p., (ii) 3 s.f.

8. The total of the areas of the faces of a box measuring 7" by 8" by 9"

9. The total of the areas of the faces of this prism.

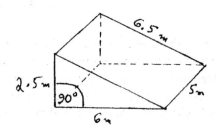

10. The centres of the arcs stand at the corners of a square. Give the answer to 3 s.f., using π = 3.14

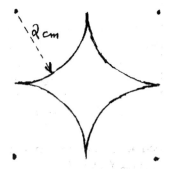

11. A closed cylindrical box formed by taking a strip of cardboard 57.4 cm long and 9 cm wide, then bending and joining the ends to make a cylinder and finally adding two circular pieces. (Answer to nearest sq. cm.)

12.

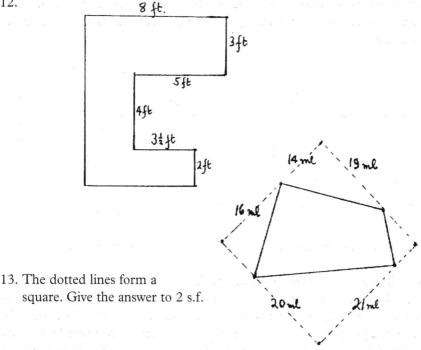

13. The dotted lines form a square. Give the answer to 2 s.f.

14. A sphere of radius 0.032". Use the formula $A = 4\pi r^2$ and give the answer to 3 d.p.

15. A book measures 13" by 8" and contains 300 leaves. What is the total possible area of writing space to the nearest square yard?

16. What radius must a circle have if the circle's area is the same as a long thin rectangle 377 cm long and $3^{1}/_{3}$ cm wide?

Answers (with units omitted) 0.013, 0.0137, 0.014, 3.43, 6.66, $12^{1}/_{4}$, 20, 48, 49, 84.95, 90, 382, 396, 427.5, 857, 1041, 1386.

Just as in Classes 1 to 3, through freehand drawing and modelling, the children were led to experience first 1, then 2 and finally 3 dimensions of space, a similar progression occurs in Classes 6 to 8, but now with mathematical awareness and accuracy. Area calculation in Class 7 leads to volume calculation in Class 8. The representation of 3 dimensional forms in perspective will be left to chapter 9, but a very good simple representation is by 'cabinet perspective', much better than 'turret perspective' (known in German as 'Kavalier Perspektiv'), as the two representations below of cubes will confirm.

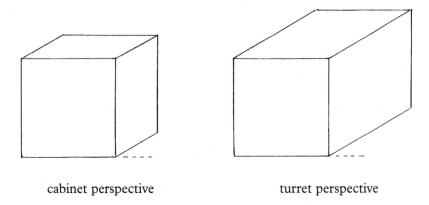

cabinet perspective   turret perspective

In both cases the dimension going backward is drawn at 30° to the horizontal, but whereas all the dimensions are represented on the same scale in the second drawing, the backward scale is halved in the first. The name for the second perspective originates from drawing castles, the name for the first coming from the design of cabinets and other wooden furniture made by joiners. It is interesting that Steiner recommended the second representation for Class 8; one can only presume that cabinet perspective was developed in England and was not used in German-speaking countries.

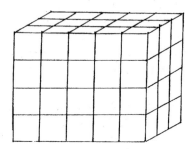

The volume of a 3 cm by 4 cm by 5 cm rectangular block as 60 cm³ will present little difficulty to the weakest children, but it is good for the whole class to draw one accurate cabinet perspective of such a solid and discuss the various ways in which its centimetre cube blocks can be counted.

The next kind of solid to consider is one which has a uniform cross-section and where the volume is obtained by multiplying the area of the cross-section by the depth perpendicular to it. For the first, purely rectangular-type solid below, this method is easily understood and is extended for the second solid, a cylinder.

Chapter 7: Arithmetic and algebra in classes 7 and 8

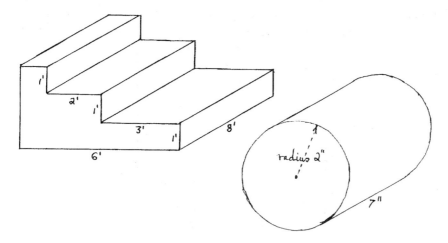

Instead of cutting up the set of steps into 3 blocks and adding their volumes, which it is good to do as a first check, it is simpler to find the area of the end and multiply by the depth.

$$(6 \times 1 + 3 \times 1 + 1 \times 1)8 = 10 \times 8 = 80 \text{ ft}^3$$

Similarly the volume of the cylinder = $(\pi \times 2^2)\,7 = {}^{22}/_7 \times 4 \times 7 = 88 \text{in}^3$.

Finally, when all the points of the boundary of a plane area are joined to a point outside its plane, a pyramidal or conical solid is formed. The simplest case arises by joining the corners of a horizontal square to a point vertically above one of those corners. For 3 identical solids of this kind can be fitted together to form a cube. This may be demonstrated by cardboard or paper models or by slicing up a clay cube. In a drawing it means joining any point of a cube (A below) to the 4 other points it is not already joined to. The 3 identical pyramids are A(EFGH), A(HDCG) and A(BCGF). If these are coloured respectively red, yellow and blue, then

    AE, EF and EH   will be   red   lines,
    AD, DC and DH   "   yellow   "
    AB, BC and BF   "   blue   "
    AH and HG   "   orange "
    AF and FG   "   violet   "
    AC and CG   "   green   "
    and AG   "   a grey line.

Each of the 3 pyramids has a volume of $^1/_3$ that of the cube = $^1/_3$ base area × height. Just as a parallelogram was considered earlier as a sheared rectangle, so can any pyramid be regarded as a sheared special pyramid, and it becomes fairly easy to see that the volume of any pyramid or cone = $^1/_3$ base area × height.

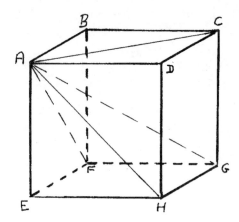

For very many solids with holes in them, the use of the identities already developed make volume calculation much easier. Cylindrical hollow pipes show a telling example of this. Consider a hollow pipe 3.8m long which has an external diameter of 8.8 cm and a bore (internal diameter) of 7.4 cm.

Its volume is that of the complete cylinder less the volume of the hole in it $= \pi \times 4.4^2 \times 3.8 - \pi \times 3.7^2 \times 3.8$, which using both the distributive law and the 'difference of two squares' identity,

$$= 3.8\ \pi\ (4.4^2 - 3.7^2)$$
$$= 3.8 \times 3.14 \times 0.7 \times 8.1, \text{ a far easier calculation.}$$

If we also know the density (gm/cm)of the material used, multiplying the previous answer by this figure will give the pipe's weight. If we also know the cost of the material in pence per gm, the price of the pipe can be ascertained. From this we could also work out the cost of laying an oil pipeline across the country, given the necessarily larger labour and installation costs. Such a calculation might occupy a Class 8 and its teacher half an hour or more of main lesson and the class could then copy the board work into their books afterwards – having contributed fully to the written work on the board. Larger calculations of this kind, in which there can be a contribution from everyone present, are very worthwhile at this age.

A selection of examples on volumes for Class 8 follows:

1. A rectangular box measures $3^{3/4}$" by $2^{1/2}$" by $1^{3/5}$". What is its volume?
2. The depth of a square metal plate of side 19 cm is 0.8 cm. Find its volume to the nearest c.c.

Chapter 7: Arithmetic and algebra in classes 7 and 8

3. The density of lead is 11.34 gm per c.c. Find the weight of a solid spherical ball of lead 10 cm in diameter in kg to 1 d.p. Use $\pi = 22/7$ and the formula $V = 4/3 \pi r^3$.

4. Calculate the volume in cubic feet of the greatest possible amount of water in this swimming pool.

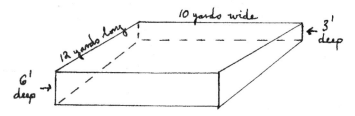

5. How many litres will this trough hold? Each semicircle has a radius of 30 cm and the length of the trough is 2 m. Give the answer to the nearest litre.

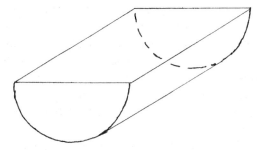

6. The volume of a pyramid is 528 cubic metres. It has a square base of length 12 metres. How high is the pyramid?

7. Find the weight to 3 s.f. of a hollow copper pipe which is 10 cm long and whose inner and outer radii are 0.7 cm and 1.05 cm. The copper weighs 9 gm/cm³.

8. A box of weight 110 gm is filled with 200 glass prisms, when the total weight then becomes 2 kilograms. Each prism has an isosceles right-angled triangle cross-section, the equal sides being 3 cm long. A cubic centimetre of glass weighs 3 grams. How long is each prism?

9. Two solid metal spheres, one of platinum and the other of silver, have radii in the ratio of 4 to 5 respectively. Platinum is twice as heavy as silver. Show that the spheres must have almost the same weights and calculate

the percentage of weight of the lighter sphere by which the heavier one exceeds it.

10. The plan view of 6 cones sitting on the base of a rectangular box is shown. The 6 apexes just touch the box's top lid. Show that the ratio of the total volume of the 6 cones to the remaining space in the box is approximately 5 to 14.

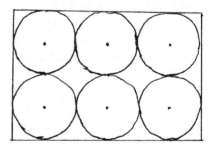

Answers: 2.4, 5.9, 7, 11, 15, 173, 283, 289, 4860

Many of the questions above will be difficult for the weaker children in the class. In composing daily sets of questions for the whole class, therefore, simpler examples of each type of problem need to be evolved and the earlier questions in each set left free of weight and density. In the morning following any set, however, the weaker ones will watch the teacher going over some of the harder questions which the quicker members of the class failed to answer correctly. They will learn from that, and need never feel left behind, or cut off from the world which the brighter ones are exploring.

So the following questions could precede the questions with the same question numbers above, and still more intermediate or simpler questions could be composed. How many must always depend upon the particular class being taught – and this is why textbooks are unsatisfactory. It is the individual teacher's careful preparation the evening before the lesson which is of paramount importance.

1. A box measures 9" by 5" by 4". What is its volume?

2. What is the volume in c.c. of this thin square plate? Give a decimal answer.

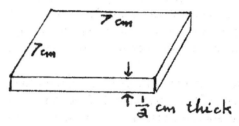

3. A cubic centimetre of gold weighs 19.3 grams. Find the weight of a block of gold 3 cm long, 2 cm wide and 1 cm high.

4. How many cubic feet must there be in a cubic yard?

5. A cylindrical beaker holds some juice which is 7" deep. The rim of the juice is a circle of radius 1". Use $\pi = 22/7$ to say how many cubic inches of juice there are in the beaker.

6. A pyramid is 9m high and has a square base of side 5m. What is its volume?

7. A piece of piping 8 yards long weighs 52 lb. How heavy will a piece of the same piping 14 yards long weigh?

8. What is the weight of this glass prism? (3 gm for every cubic centimetre)

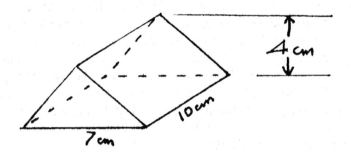

9. The metal 'invar' is 8 times heavier than water. Which is heavier, a cube of invar with each edge 5 cm or a litre of water?

10. A cone has a radius of 2 cm and a height of 6 cm. Use $\pi = 3.14$ to find its volume.

Answers (in order for a change): 180.3 cm, 24.5 c.c., 115.8 gm, 27, 22, 75 m³, 91 lb, 420 gm, the same, 25.12 cm³.

§6. Other arithmetical work including powers and square roots for Class 7

The 'simple interest' money problems introduced in Class 6 can be extended to 'compound interest' in Class 7 (for just 3 years, say) and then in Class 8 to the matter of mortgages. I have rarely met such indignation as a Class 8 can reveal when it becomes clear to them just how much one actually pays out to a building society or bank over the course of many years in order to purchase a house. 'There is something criminally wrong with our economic system!' – and one must admit that they are basically right about this. Once again, half an hour or more spent on such a topic has much social value, as in the example at the end of §5.

The topic of ratio and proportion needs dealing with in these two classes, but this will be dealt with in the next chapter in connection with geometrical properties. One can, however, extend the work done in Class 5 on 'rule of three' or 'unitary method' to ratio methods in arithmetic.

Frequent revision of basic arithmetic, including long multiplication and division with integers, fractions and decimals, needs to continue – especially in the shorter practice periods (minimum 2 per week, better 3). The demand for 'educational excellence' made by government and industry includes fostering the ability to deal with significant figures, decimal places and estimates of answers to problems before detail is worked out. These matters are ones with which children in Classes 7 and 8 should certainly be familiar.

Angle and length calculations in geometrical figures, e.g. those including circles, need practice in the 2 or 3 weekly ¾ hour slots, but these will again be dealt with in the next chapter.

There is also the matter of the powers and roots of numbers, which are needed in Class 7. Only positive powers (or indices) need introduction here.

So $3^6 = 3 \times 3 \times 3 \times 3 \times 3 \times 3 = 729$,

$(2^{1/2})^3 = {}^5/_2 \times {}^5/_2 \times {}^5/_2 = {}^{125}/_8 = 15 \, {}^5/_8$

and $(0.05)^4 = 0.00000625.$

Few people bother with the method for obtaining the square roots of general numbers today since they are immediately obtained from hand calculators. It is therefore interesting to know that in the first Waldorf school in Stuttgart, Rudolf Steiner was of the firm view that not only was it beneficial for Class 7 to learn the method, but that by Class 8 the class should also learn why the method works. Since 1919-25, when Steiner was frequently active in the classrooms of that school, some people have tended to forget the high demands Steiner made of the girls and boys in them – according to their age,

Chapter 7: Arithmetic and algebra in classes 7 and 8

of course. As an example let us take the square root of 143641. Mark it off in pairs from the decimal point and find the highest number whose square root does not exceed the one or two figures in the first column. So we get the number 3.

```
                     3    7    9
                   14   36   41
        3 x 3       9
                    5   36
       67 x 7       4   69
                        67 4 1
      749 x 9           67 4 1
```

Multiply the number 3 by itself and subtract from 14. Bring down the next pair of numbers next to it (5 36). Then double the answer so far written above the line (2 x 3 = 6) and ask the question, 'Sixty-what' times the same 'what' has to be as high as possible but less than 536? What is 'what'? It is 7. Do the multiplication and subtract, giving 67. Bring down the next pair (6741). The answer written so far is 37. Double it and ask the 'what' question. 749 x 9 = 6741 shows that the exact square root of 143641 is 379.

The teacher can easily make up similar questions by squaring the answer he wants. But why does the above extraordinary procedure work?

$$(a + b + c)^2 \equiv (a + b + c)$$
$$\equiv a^2 + b^2 + c^2 + 2ab + 2ac + 2bc$$
$$\equiv a^2 + b(2a + b) + c(2a + 2b + c)$$

So $\sqrt{a + b(2a + b) + c(2a + 2b + c)} \equiv a + b + c$

This is the first tasting of identities, the subject to be taught in Class 8. Whether one should already use 3 lines or keep to the familiar 2 lines of the equal sign is up to the teacher.

On carefully examining the identity, its left hand side is telling us to do exactly the complicated process we adopted. The 2s refer to the doublings. The identity is the source of all the instructions and can be extended to as many terms in the first bracket as wished, even an endless set of terms (numbers), as in the case for $\sqrt{2}$, but that is something which belongs to Class 9, where irrationality is not only a ripe mathematical topic but also describes the state of mind out of which the actions of the members of that class often seem to issue – very understandable in their difficult yet enjoyable task of finding a quite new relationship to the world.

Teaching mathematics

The more varied and complex mathematics becomes as the boys and girls become older, the more necessary it will be for the teacher to work out intermediary steps in development. Some of these will be indicated in further sections of this chapter.

Finally some practice in ratio and proportion in Class 7, good for its own sake in arithmetic, will help prepare the ground for dealing with similar triangles and enlargements in geometry, in Class 8 or 9. This is an extension of the work on unitary method (rule of three) in Class 5. Recalling the problem in Chapter 4-§5, 'If 12 pencils cost £3.48, what will 7 pencils cost?', this can be tackled in a new way. The number of pencils required in the second part of the sentence may be expressed as a fraction of those mentioned in the first part, i.e. 7/12. The same fraction or ratio 7:12 applies to the cost required compared to the original amount of money mentioned.

The ratios of the numbers of pencils is in proportion to the ratios of the amounts of money.

So $\quad \dfrac{\text{Cost}}{£3.48} = \dfrac{7}{12} \quad$ or Cost $= \dfrac{7}{12}$ of £3.48 = £2.03.

Another question on this topic has to do with sharing a given amount among a group in proportional parts. Suppose a tin of grass seed is equivalent to 60 handfuls of seed and is to be spread evenly over 3 lawns whose areas are 30, 45 and 105 square yards. The proportion 30:45:105 is the same as 2:3:7.

$\qquad 2 + 3 + 7 = 12$ and $60 \div 12 = 5$

So the lawns will receive respectively 5 x 2, 5 x 3 and 5 x 7, i.e. 10, 15 and 35 handfuls of seed.

Further exercises for Class 7:

1. Calculate 3^2, 2^3 and 3^3
2. What is the difference, if any, between $(7^3 - 3^5)$ and 10^2?
3. Calculate $(1^{2/3})^2$
4. Calculate π^2 correct to 2 decimal places, given that $\pi = 3.1415926536...$
5. Calculate $(5^3)^2$ and 5^6.
6. Calculate $(2^2)^4$ and $(2^4)^2$.
7. What new number law do you learn after doing the last two questions?
8. Calculate $6^5 \div 6^3$, then write the answer to $12^{37} \div 12^{35}$ at once.
9. What is $13^{14} \div 13^{14}$? So what is 23^0?
10. What are the square roots of 81, 8100 and 196?
11. Express 74529 in prime factors. Hence work out the square root of 74529.

Chapter 7: Arithmetic and algebra in classes 7 and 8

12. Calculate the square root of 841.
13.   "   "   664225.
14.   "   "   345.96.

15. The total area of all the faces of a cube is 235.8774 cm. What is the length of the cube edge to (i) 2 d.p., (ii) 2 s.f.?

16. A legacy of £2050 is shared between 2 people in the proportion of 2:3. What does each one receive?

17. Four people invest £2000, £4000, £5000, and £7000 in a business, and a year later the business makes a net profit of £2412 which is distributed to the investors. How much should each of the 4 investors receive?

18. A farm has an arable acreage of 713 consisting of 5 fields where each field has an area twice as big as the next smaller field. What are the acreages of the largest and smallest fields?

19. Between them 3 bottles hold 2 litres of water. Their capacities are in the proportion of 2:6:7. How many grams of water, to the nearest gram, does the smallest bottle contain?

20. A row of 18 square slabs placed edge to edge in a long line occupy an area of 7m². What smaller area would 12 of them take up? What is the slab width in cm correct to 1 d.p.?

21. The rate of interest remains at 12% per annum whilst £625 is invested in a bank over a 2 year period. Calculate the amount of money withdrawable at the end of that time.

22. What is the compound interest on £400 after 3 years at 15%?

23. The capital for a business is provided by three people who contribute $2600, $3900 and $6500. After tax deduction and money ploughed back into the business the profit one year is $1230. What should each of the three receive?

24. By examining factors find the cube root of $456533 \, x^3 \, y^6$ if $x = 2$ and $y = 5$.

Answers: 0, 1, 1, 2⁷/₉, 4²/₃, 6.27, 6.3, 8, 9, 9, 9.87, 14, 18.6, 23, 27, 29, 36, 62.4, 90, 144, 208.35, 246, 256, 267, 268, 273, 368, 369, 536, 615, 670, 815, 815, 820, 938, 1230, 3850, 15625.

§7. Simultaneous Equations; also the dissolution of brackets (Class 8 topics)

Although graphical work will be dealt with in another chapter, it will enrich students' power to think if we help them solve simultaneous equations without the aid of the picture of intersecting lines.

These equations should also remain linear at this age. Nor is it helpful to introduce 'unequations' (inequalities). The point here is that a question should have one definite answer, not two or more possible answers, nor a range of answers. Only when the astral body has been fully born (Class 9) do multiple answers to questions make inner sense to a young person. We know the havoc that can be caused in children when the authorities of mother and father are in conflict. It is when puberty has been passed that the existence of various answers to a life problem, many of them quite tenable, can be experienced and understood. Although linear simultaneous questions provide two answers, these are actually the distinct single answers to two distinct though related problems.

Let us take a practical case. Suppose a wall has to be built consisting of two types of brickwork, pillars and lower sections. The whole wall has to be 47 feet long and three pillar widths together have to be just 6 inches more than a single lower section. The rough design in which there are 7 pillars is:

What width must each pillar and each lower section have? As with simple equations, we admit that we do not know. Translated into algebra, let each pillar width be p feet and each section width be q feet.

The reunions ('al jabrs') of the separate pieces of information give

$$7p + 6q = 47 \quad \text{———— (i)}$$
$$3p - q = 1/2 \quad \text{———— (ii), as } 6" = 1/2'.$$

Treat these as two separate pairs of scales. Multiplying the quantities on the second pair by 6, we obtain

$$18p - 6q = 3$$

Chapter 7: Arithmetic and algebra in classes 7 and 8

Combining these quantities with those in (i), the letter q will vanish.
$$25p = 50$$
$$p = 2$$

Substituting this value in (i),
$$14 + 6q = 47$$
$$6q = 33$$
$$q = {}^{33}/_6 = {}^{11}/_2 = 5{}^1/_2$$

So each pillar has to be 2 feet wide and each lower section 5 feet 6 inches wide.

An alternative solution to finding the value of q is obtained by saying 'Multiply (i) by 3 and (ii) by 7,' meaning multiply the parts of each equation by 3 and 7.
$$21p + 18q = 141$$
$$21p - 7q = 31{}^1/_2$$

Now subtract
$$25q = 137{}^1/_2$$
$$q = \frac{275}{2 \times 25} = \frac{11}{2} = 5{}^1/_2$$

The dissolution of sets of brackets is also a good exercise in Class 8.

Facility in manipulating complicated formulations with several numbers and/or variables strengthens one's algebraic muscles rather as five-fingers exercises do for the budding pianist. This is a process known as simplification

For example,
$$7 - \{ 9 + [6 - (4 - 1)] - [(12 - 3) + 8] \}$$
$$= 7 - \{ + [6 - 3] - [9 + 8] \}$$
$$= 7 - \{ 9 + 3 - 17 \}$$
$$= 7 - \{ -5 \}$$
$$= 7 + 5$$
$$= 12$$

The innermost brackets are dissolved first.

Again
$$[4 (3x + 2y - 6z) - 7 (4x + 5y - 1)] - [3 (8 - 9y) + 5(x - 5z) - 31]$$
$$= [12x + 8y - 24z - 28x - 35y + 7] - [24 - 27y + 5x - 25z - 31]$$
$$= [-16x - 27y - 24z - 7] - [-7 - 27y + 5x - 25z]$$
$$= -16x - 27y - 24z - 7 + 7 + 27y - 5x + 25z$$
$$= -21x + z$$

On the other hand a quick overview of $a - (b - (c - (d - (e - (f - (g - h))))))$ shows the whole expression must be the same as
$$a - b + c - d + e - f + g - h.$$
and it would be tedious to remove brackets pair by pair in this case.

Exercises in the above topics complete this section. Solve the simultaneous equations
1. $5x - 2y = 31$ with $3x + 2y = 25$.
2. $6a + 7b = 46$ with $a + 7b = 31$.
3. $8p + 4q = 44$ with $3p + 2q = 17$.
4. $6h - 4k = 48 = 7h - 10k$.

The three below can be done by trial and error.
5. Two numbers add up to 17 but differ by 5. What are they?
6. Two numbers multiply to make 48, but add up to 19. What are they?
7. A pair of successive whole numbers multiply to make 552. What are they?

8. A silver collection following a concert produced lots of seven-sided coins. When these were sorted out into heaps, a quantity of one kind together with a different quantity of the other kind were worth a £10 note. Had these two quantities been reversed, however, this total would have been worth £2.40 more. What were the two quantities?

9. A dressmaker exhibits a row of differently coloured blouses and slacks along her 3 metre wall. 8 blouses and 5 pairs of slacks just fill up the space, but had she had 7 blouses and 6 pairs of slacks she would have had 5 cm spare. Assuming that the blouses are all of the same width and also the slacks take up equal but different spaces along the wall, how wide is each blouse and each pair of slacks?

10. Viewed from the earth the planet Saturn each year moves forward along the zodiac and then makes a smaller retrograde (backward) movement. After 7 forward and 6 backward steps it reaches a position in quadrature (90°) to its original position, whereas after 9 forward and 8 backward steps it is 6° short of a trine (120°) from its starting point. How many degrees of arc along the zodiac does the forward and also the backward step comprise?

11. From a heliocentric perspective,[5] Jupiter's peripheral movement is 6.3 times slower than that of Mars. Indeed Jupiter takes about 10 years longer (actually 3645 days) than Mars to move right round the zodiac.

How many days does it take (i) Mars, (ii) Jupiter to do complete revolutions? Express each answer also to the nearest year.

12. Simplify 17 + 8(10 – 9) – 3[5 – (4 – 6)].

13. Simplify
    7[x(2x – 5) – 2x(3x – 4)] – 3[5(x + 1) – 2(3 – x)] + 4x[3(x + 4) + 4(x – 3)].

14. What values of L and m make m – L = –26, and make the expression
    3[7(L – 2m) – 1] + 4[5 – 2(2L + m)]– 4m nothing at all?

Answers: 1, 1½, 2, 2, 3, 3, 3, 3, 4, 4, 5, 6, 6, 7, 9, 11, 12, 12, 16, 18, 20, 23, 24, 25, 29, 688, 4333.

Nicolaus Copernicus, inaugurator of heliocentric perspective

Teaching mathematics

§8. A further possible topic in Class 8

Since the class teacher's task in history lessons in this class is to bring history up to the present day, part of that task must be to refer to the scientific and technological advances through the whole twentieth century. Whilst lessons in the operation of computers do not belong to this class, a basic *survey* of what they do and how their arithmetical units operate *does* belong here. A visit to the computer laboratory used by Classes 11 and 12, where members of the top classes could give a demonstration, would be very helpful. This could be followed by arithmetical practice in the use of number systems and especially of the binary system made use of in computers because of the 'on' and 'off' positions of switches in electric circuits and their equivalents in electronics.

Ask the class to examine these 3 simple little sums, clearly incorrect *without* change of figures. You might give the class a clue by saying it has something to do with what they learnt in Class 3!

```
    52              372             2 3
  - 26            + 145             x 5
    23              166            11 1
                    725
```

The spacing of the figures in the third sum should give the game away. For in each sum the columns are not those of hundreds, tens and units. The subtraction sum has to do with weeks and days, a base 7 number system since the figure 7 never appears (1 week 0 days would appear instead). The addition sum becomes correct when its columns are labelled bushels, gallons and pints, a base 8 system, and the multiplication sum becomes correct when thought of as the combined weight of 5 small children each weighing 2 stone 3 pounds, a base 14 system.

After further practice with bases 7 and 8 in all four rules you could go straight to base 2, in which only figures 0 and 1 appear, corresponding to 'off' and 'on' in electrical circuits. Translations from binary to denary (ordinary base 10) language and vice versa are also good exercises. So the computer multiplies 23 by 5 as follows. Repeatedly dividing by 2 and leaving the remainders untouched to start with,

```
   2) 23           2) 5         Hence 23₁₀ = 10111₂
   2) 11   1       2) 21
   2)  5   1          10        and 5₁₀    = 101₂
   2)  2   1
       1   0
```

Hence $23_{10} = 10111_2$

and $5_{10} = 101_2$

Chapter 7: Arithmetic and algebra in classes 7 and 8

The long multiplication is therefore

```
   10111
 x   101
   10111
  10111
 1110011
```

To translate back into denary, start on the left, double and add the next digit and repeat as follows   1110011

3
7
14
28
57
115

which as expected is 23 x 5. This is a good illustration of how terribly laborious the method employed by calculation computers is compared with our usual human method. On the other hand, of course, the computer operates so rapidly once the problem is entered, so that in *complicated* cases the computed answer is obtained in a tiny fraction of the time it would take us to work it out.

Some further examples in binary notation for the class may be designed as follows.

1. Add 10101, 1101 and 11001
2. Subtract 11100 from 101110
3. Multiply 10011 by 111
4. Divide 1011011 by 111
5. Express each of these four answers in ordinary denary language.
6. Express 63_{10} in binary language.

Answers: 1101, 10010, 111011, 111111, 10000101 and 13, 18, 59, 133.

Chapter 8:
Geometry in Classes 7 and 8 (ages 12 to 14)

§1. Dimensional Development

Several examples of three stages have come to the fore in previous chapters. Class 1 arithmetic had the developmental stages of demonstration, imagination and computation. Class 6 learned three stages in the use of money together with the three corresponding virtues stimulated by them. Then through Classes 6, 7 and 8, three stages in algebraic development were described – closely linked to thinking, feeling and willing approaches to the subject. Attention has also been drawn to the three stages in the acquisition of any new knowledge – perception, mental picturing and concept.

> This 'threefolding' quality may also be discovered in the pages of many books on education. Jean Piaget[1] for example has described three stages through which the young child approaches arithmetic:
>
> (i) composition of multiplications of relationships
>
> (ii) a sequence of equivalences where two successive transformations are reducible to a single one,
>
> (iii) generalisation – passing from an intuitive relationship between two objects to an operational relationship between many, completing the grouping of multiplications of asymmetrical relations.
>
> Once this terminology has been understood, we can recognize it as a description of a fluid 'threeness' of developmental stages.

Now space also has three dimensions. The first thing a child in Class 1 is led to experience is the vertical direction related to the spine. In standing and in making his first chalk line on the blackboard he has a conscious thinking experience. The vertical plane containing this 'spine line' and the line running straight ahead of us from the eyes, also has to do with consciousness and thinking. The eyes always focus on objects lying in this plane, whether higher up or lower down, when we are in a normal standing position. The sightlines of the two eyes cross at the point of focus. An element of will is always present in this, for the ciliary muscles of the eye control the focusing (except when watching TV, when the cameras do it all for us and contribute to the laziness developed in box-addicts.[2])

The will line goes directly forwards and backwards. It is often along this direction that our conscious actions proceed. Perpendicular to it is the will plane containing our shoulders, sideways stretched arms and our face. This is what we carry as we move forward.

The feeling plane, on the other hand, is horizontal. Often when our arms and hands move up or down to make gestures as we speak, it is our feelings rather than our thoughts which are being expressed. The French have developed this to a fine art, using wrists, shoulders and eyebrows in subtle ways (whereas the English are still famous for the 'stiff upper lip'). The feeling line in us is the one going horizontally from left to right. Sometimes we can feel our left as protective and our right as aggressive, which is an echo of the shield and sword stance adopted by knights of old. The dimensions of space are therefore anchored in our own bodily experience; but they can also be abstracted from it. Any three lines mutually at right angles can then serve as the x, y and z axes in analytical geometry.

Just as during Classes 1, 2 and 3 the child's work with form in drawing and modelling changes from 1 to 2 to 3 dimensions respectively, a similar progression takes place through Classes 6, 7 and 8 – but now with geometrical exactitude. From the one dimensional measurement of angle and length in Class 6 we move on to the experience of area in Class 7, which has a much greater affinity to feelings. A line drawing of a scene in nature or of a person appeals far less to our feelings than does a painting in which the various areas of colour impinge upon, blend into or contrast with other areas.[3] Geometrical area has already been experienced in a feeling way in Class 5 and can be taken a step further in Class 6 using Perigal's dissection of the Pythagorean square, through which the proposition becomes a little more accessible to thinking. Only when the 5 numbers shown are replaced by different colours, however, will we feel the tone of truth in what our thinking discovers.

Chapter 8: Geometry in classes 7 and 8

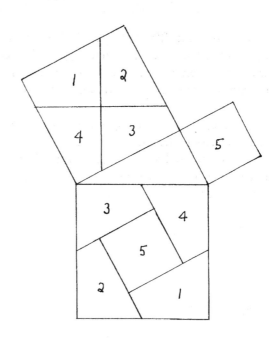

Note that the sloping lines in the lowest square pass through middle points of its sides and run parallel to the sloping sides of the right triangle.

In the highest square the interior lines pass through the centre of it (where diagonals will cross) and run parallel and perpendicular to the hypotenuse.

The notebooks of Leonardo da Vinci show the figure below many times. His feelings must have been aroused strongly by the remarkable fact that the areas of the two 'lunes' add up to the area of the right-angled triangle. Why this is so belongs to Class 8 geometry.[4] The centres of the three semi-circular arcs lie at the middle points of the sides of the tirangle.

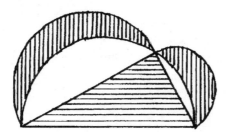

The figure also gives a faint impression of a ship whose sails have unfurled in the wind.

When we reach Class 8 and deal with 3-dimensional forms we move into the domain of will. The actual modelling and construction of the spatial objects will be at least as important as finding ways of drawing them. Yet not *only* making and drawing should take place in these classes. The thinking has to penetrate and apply the geometrical laws to be discovered in them. Both cabinet and orthogonal projection belong to Class 8, as well as true perspective drawing. The latter needs freehand practice in art lessons, but an exact geometrically constructed example follows in which only one circle and two supplementary arcs are used in addition to straight lines. Some of the reasons justifying the constructions employed will come later in this chapter.

In this beginning of a perspective view of a bridge over a river a scaffolding of construction lines has been left visible.

This only looks right if the eye is placed about 8 cm (= circle radius) exactly in front of the centre of the circle – which represents the edge of the cone of vision.

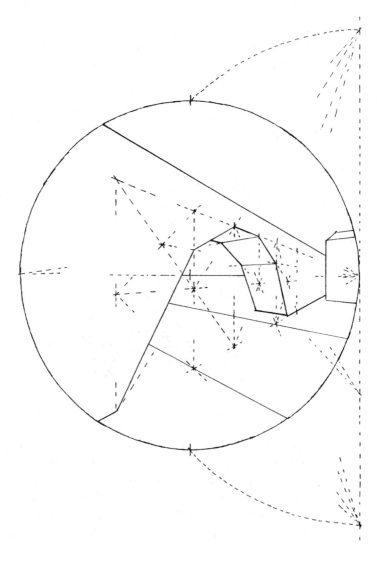

§2. Class 7 Geometry

After the basic introduction of geometrical proofs in Class 6, culminating in tests for finding congruent triangles, we could proceed without more ado to the central task in Class 7 of proving and applying the theorem of Pythagoras.

In his books on the Elements of geometry, poor old Euclid gave a long and tedious proof which the author remembers having to learn by heart at age 11 or 12. It is much better to use the far simpler original method of Pythagoras himself, which he demonstrated with a square wooden frame and four coloured congruent tiles in the shape of right-angled triangles. The pair of sides forming the right angle had their lengths such that their sum was equal to the side of the square. The arrangement is shown on the left. Geometrically we mark off four points on the sides of the square corners in a cyclic order.

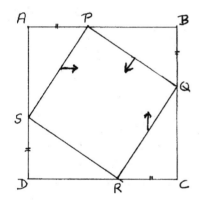
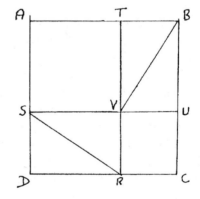

Thus AP = BQ = CR = DS. It follows that PB = QC = RD = SA. Because there are 4 right angles, the 4 triangles must be congruent (2 sides and the included angle).

From this it follows that PQ = QR = RS = SP.

Also $A\hat{S}P$ = 180° − $S\hat{A}P$ − $A\hat{P}S$ (angles of triangle)
              = 90° − $A\hat{P}S$
              = 90° − $D\hat{S}R$ from the congruent triangles.

Hence $P\hat{S}R = 180° - A\hat{S}P - D\hat{S}R$ (adjacent angles)
              $= 90°$

So each angle of PQRS is a right angle. The figure is a square. On the right ABCD is drawn again. R and S are as before. T and U are chosen so that BT = RC and CU = DS. TR crosses SU at V. B and V, also R and S, are joined.

It is easy to prove that there are again 4 congruent triangles which are congruent to the first 4. The change from left to right drawings can be illustrated by tile movements. SDR does not move. PBQ slides down to position SVR, RCQ ascends to VUB and APS moves to the right to TBV. Arrows indicate movements.

Appropriate colouring of the 4 movable triangles will naturally enhance the drawings made by the class. The proof is completed by observing the parts of the figure ABCD in the two drawings which are *not* coloured. On the left is the square on the hypotenuse, whereas on the right are the squares on the other two sides. Hence etc. Since the length of AP can be chosen arbitrarily, the theorem is true for all shapes of right-angled triangles.

It is now essential to use the result to solve practical problems. In fact *whenever* the value of lengths are required in structures basically consisting of perpendicular lines but having a line sloping in relation to them, the theorem is vital. Let us introduce an instance which shows its practical value but has its humorous side, too.

Two villages lie on mountain slopes separated by a precipitous valley. Travelling by road between them is a very long and dangerous journey via the valley below. The village elders decide to construct a bridge. By means of a lasso, first one then several ropes together connect the village terrains from A to B. Using more ropes a long and strong platform shaped from the wood from the highest trees on the mountain slopes of one village is slid across into position over the fixed ropes, bolted and concreted down at A and B. This is fine though a little nerve-racking for pedestrians since, besides the height and unprotected sides, the bridge is apt to sag and bounce under the heavier villagers. Somebody then has the bright idea of erecting uprights in the middle of the bridge near the edges, joined by a cross piece above, and then using sloping beams as illustrated. The problem is how long to make them.

You can ask the class about this. It is not very wise to put a long beam leaning beyond an upright and saw off the end. Possible disastrous consequences could be listed. A scale drawing of the bridge could be made, of course, and it would be a good exercise to get everyone in the class to do so. This would lead to a useful disagreement about the correct answer.

Chapter 8: Geometry in classes 7 and 8

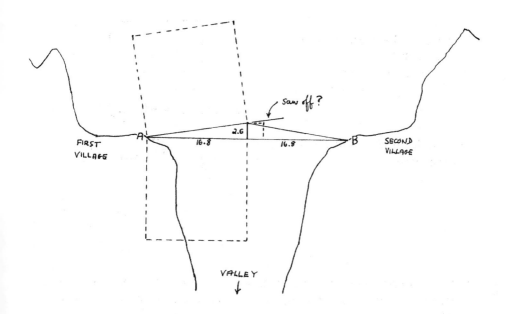

Let us suppose that the length of the horizontal bridge is 33.6 m and that an upright is 2.6 m high. The only way to obtain the exact answer is to imagine three squares, one on the bridge, one hanging below it partly into the mountain side and one sticking out into space. To these extraordinary additions to the architecture the theorem of Pythagoras is applied.

Half the bridge length is 16.8 m and $16.8^2 = 282.24$ m² is the area of the bottom square.

$2.6^2 = 6.76$ m² is the area of the smallest square.

Pythagoras's theorem tells us to add the answers...

$\underline{289.00}$ m² is therefore the area of the biggest square.

The sloping piece has a length of $\sqrt{289} = 17$ m exactly. In engineering practice these squares are forgotten and people simply use the formula $\sqrt{a^2 + b^2}$, but the experience of how this formula was discovered in the first place is very important educationally.

Navigation problems can also be solved in this way. Suppose a ship near the equator sails 37 miles from P to Q, and it is found by observing the sun's position and the time on the clock that the ship is 35 miles further east than before. How far north has it sailed?

The area of the smallest square
$$= 37^2 - 35^2$$
$$= 1369 - 1225$$
$$= 144 \text{ square miles}$$

So, PR, the distance sailed north
= 12 miles.

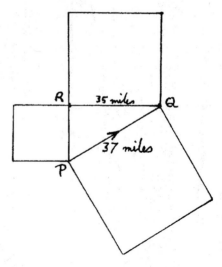

Examples of problems involving Pythagoras' theorem will follow later, but it may help the class relax at the end of a morning's difficult written assignment to tell the old Red Indian story of the chief who lived in a big white wigwam and had two wives, but felt he needed a change. One day on hearing of the imminent visit of another chief, together with Hilary, that second chief's only wife, he quickly arranged hospitality. He bade *his* two wives sit on buffalo skins and spread out a hippopotamus skin for the wife of his guest. When his guests arrived, the host was enchanted with Hilary and after a long palaver, during which many pipes of peace were smoked, the two chiefs agreed to exchange wives. For it was asserted that *the squaw on the hippopotamus was worth the sum of the squaws on the other two hides!*

Lest the story subsequently reach the ears of mothers alert for any sign of male chauvinism in the school, a sequel to the tale had better be attempted, too.

The chief who now had two wives had always regarded himself as a superior being because one of his ancestors in the distant past had been king of East Anglia in far-off England. It was because of his Angle blood that he named the tallest mountain in his domain High Tor after a peak in Derbyshire. It was there, too, that he had positioned his regal, lofty and exclusive camp. To punish him for this dreadful *a(l)ttitude*, and particularly for his disdain for womens' rights and freedom, the two wives planned a fitting revenge for his appallingly base line of behavior. They took it in turns to make such a noise each night that he could not sleep and he soon became a physical wreck. Meanwhile the first chief's wife made a rule (news of which filtered through to Washington D.C. a couple of centuries later) forbidding all smoking in the white wigwam. A week later the first chief, his nerves shattered, went to tell his fellow chief the sad story. In reply his sleep-starved friend could only voice a weary 'Ah!' on the mountain air. As his wives declared later, the *airy Ah of a wrecked Angle is the product of the base line and High-T – or altitude.*

Well, I did say 'attempted'!

Going from the ridiculous to the sublime, large-scale drawings illustrating the metamorphosis of the Pythagorean theorem's figure can be composed as shown.

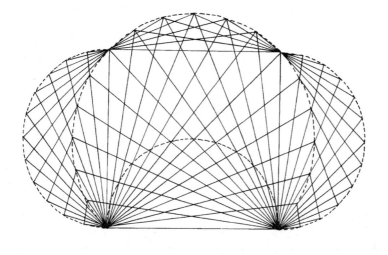

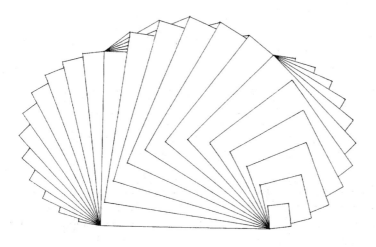

One drawing is reminiscent of ladies' fans or spread-out hands of cards. What is remarkable perhaps is the way the corners of squares move along circular areas. Choosing a sequence of colours can heighten the effect. Notice that parts of some squares appear in several places.

The main area theorem in Class 7 apart from that of Pythagoras concerns the general triangle. This has already been worked with in chapter 8, but can now be stated more precisely as:

'The area of a triangle is half the product of the length of any side, and the perpendicular distance from it of the opposite corner of the triangle.' Sometimes the perpendicular lies outside the triangle.

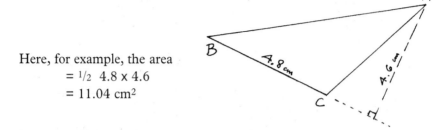

Here, for example, the area
= ½ 4.8 × 4.6
= 11.04 cm²

This theorem in conjunction with the construction of a parallel line enables a triangle equal in area to a general quadrilateral to be constructed. So given a quadrilateral PQRS, complete parallelogram QPRX using the two arcs to find X. Then QX cuts SR produced at T, and PST is the triangle wanted.

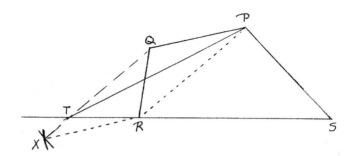

The 2 dotted lines PR and RX are not needed in the construction. That the construction achieves the desired result is because triangles PQR and PTR are equal in area (they have a common base PR whilst Q and T have equal perpendicular distances to it).

Chapter 8: Geometry in classes 7 and 8

The classification of four sided figures and their properties is more complicated than that for triangles. Leaving aside re-entrant shapes like arrow heads, the principal types of quadrilateral can be obtained by transforming a square. First rectangles and rhombi can be constructed, then parallelograms. Further modifications give trapeziums and kites. Each time the main properties could be determined and listed. For example, a rhombus is a quadrilateral with all its sides equal, a kite is a quadrilateral with 2 distinct pairs of adjacent sides equal and an isosceles trapezium is a quadrilateral with one pair of opposite sides parallel and the other two sides equal but not parallel.

Each of them has other properties too. In the cases of rhombus and kite the diagonals are perpendicular, but in isosceles trapeziums the diagonals are equal in length.

§3. Geometrical Examples for Class 7

1. Find the hypotenuse of a right-angled triangle if the other two sides are (i) 3" and 4", (ii) 14 cm and 48 cm.

2. Find the shortest side of a right-angled triangle if the other two sides are (i) 15 ft and 17 ft, (ii) 3.5 m and 3.7 m.

3. What kind of quadrilateral is ABCD? Why?

   Calculate the lengths of AC and CD. Then calculate the area of ABCD.

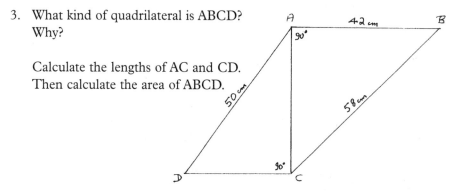

4. A rectangular field measures 90 yd by 60 yd. To walk from one corner to the opposite one, how many yd to the nearest yard would you save if you walked a diagonal instead of round two edges?

5. How high above the ground is the roof of this building?

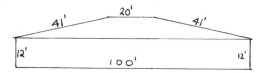

163

6. The diagonals of a rhombus are 18" and 14". Calculate the perimeter of the rhombus in feet and inches correct to the nearest $^1/_{10}$".

7. A ship travelled 126 miles eastwards along the equator and then 32 miles due north. How far from its starting point was it then?

8. KLMN is a kite in which KL = 12 cm and KN = 25 cm.

   The angles at K and M are also right angles.

   Calculate each of the diagonals LN and KM correct to 1 d.p.

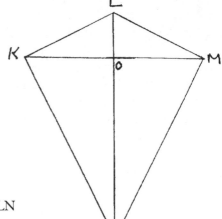

9. Name the most general kind of quadrilateral which is both
   (i) a kite and a parallelogram,
   (ii) a parallelogram and an isosceles trapezium,
   (iii) the first answer and the second answer.

10. Construct a convex pentagon PQRST in which each side is 7 cm, the angle at O is 120° and the angle at P is 90°. By constructing lines through T and R parallel to SP and SQ respectively, find a triangle SUV having the same area as the pentagon. Measure the length of UV.

11. A television mast for a transmitter is 84 m high. The top is anchored by a set of wire ropes just 1 m longer. How far from the bottom of the mast must they be fixed?

12. Draw a triangle OAB in which OA = AB = 2 cm and OÂB is a right angle. Then construct points C, D, E, ... I, so that CBO, DCD, EDO ... are all right angles and BC = CD = DE = ... = HI = 2 cm, so obtaining the beginning of a spiral. What is the length of OI? Can you prove what the length should be? Do the points B, O and I lie on a straight line?

13. Construct 24 equally spaced points on a circle of radius 6 cm and label them 0 to 23. Remembering the 2 times table, join point 1 to point 2, point 2 to point 4, point 3 to point 6, and so on. Points 24 and 26 will be the same as points 0 and 2. Stop when point 23 has been joined to point 46. Where have you seen before the curve which comes in the drawing?

14. Try the last question again but use the 3 times table instead.

15. Etc. Make further discoveries of curves in this way but don't use big numbers – you could try $1^1/_2$ or $1^1/_3$ if you wish.

16 Etc. Suppose one end of the moving line goes clockwise and the other end goes anticlockwise. What happens then?

Answers and notes:

1. 5" and 50 cm
2. 8 ft and 1.2 m

The identity $(a^2 + b^2)^2 \equiv (a^2 - b^2)^2 + (2ab)^2$ enables a teacher to make up as many 'whole number' right angled triangles as required for further examples. A different shape emerges whenever a and b have no common factor or when they are not both odd numbers. Thus

a	b	$a^2 + b^2$	$a^2 - b^2$	$2ab$
2	1	5	3	4
3	2	13	12	5
4	1	17	15	8
4	3	25	7	24
5	2	29	21	20
5	4	41	9	40
6	1	37	35	12
6	5	61	11	60
7	2	53	45	28

The last three columns give the 3 sides of triangles. Doubling the last row gives 106 90 56
So if the class is given 106 and 56 as two sides it won't be difficult to obtain the square root of 8100.

3. A trapezium, since the equal alternate angles make AB parallel to DC.
   AC = $\sqrt{58^2 - 42^2}$ = $\sqrt{1600}$ = 40 cm and DC = 30 cm.
   Area ABCD = $\frac{1}{2}$ 40 x 42 + $\frac{1}{2}$ 40 x 30 = 1440cm^2

4. The diagonal = $\sqrt{11700}$ = 108 yd, so saving = 42 yd.

5. $\frac{1}{2}$ (100 – 20) = 40 so we have triangles 41, 9, 40 as on the list above. The height is thus 12 + 9 = 21'.

6. Each side = $\sqrt{9^2 + 7^2}$ = $\sqrt{130}$ = 11.40", so perimeter = 45.6".

7. 130 miles.

8. LN = $\sqrt{144 + 225}$ = 19.2 cm.
   The area of triangle LMN = $\frac{1}{2}$ LM x MN and also $\frac{1}{2}$ LN x OM.
   So OM = $\frac{12 \times 25}{19.2}$ and KM = 2 OM = 31.2 cm.

9. Rhombus, rectangle and square.

10. UV is about 13.7 cm.

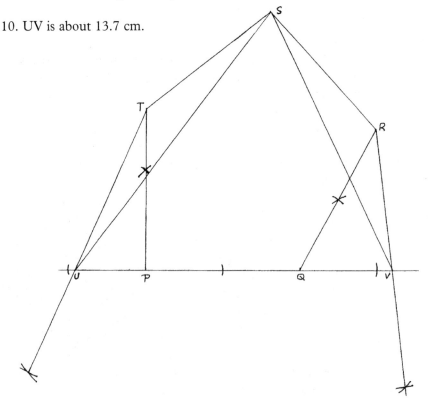

Chapter 8: Geometry in classes 7 and 8

11. $\sqrt{85^2 - 84^2} = \sqrt{169} = 13$ m

12. OI = exactly 6 cm. This is the result of repeated application of Pythagoras' theorem.

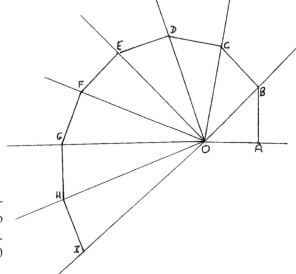

OB = $\sqrt{8}$
OC = $\sqrt{12}$
OD = $\sqrt{16}$
....
OI = $\sqrt{36}$

B, O and I are not in line. Actually $B\hat{O}I$ = 178.3°. Incidentally, $A\hat{O}G$ = 183.6°. Quick, accurate children could be asked to develop this further. Then OX would be 10 cm exactly.

13. The curve is seen on the top of the coffee or tea in a cup. Strictly the curve arises when a light source is immediately above point O and the cylindrical inside of the cup reflects its light. However, the darker part of the drawing corresponds to the lighter part of what the cup shows. The law of reflection of light (equal angles of incidence and reflection) can be seen with the lines drawn. But these are thought-out lines. Thinking itself, which is different from observing finished thoughts, is an activity of the same nature as that of light.

14. (half size)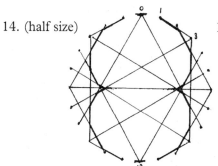

This is a 2-cusped curve. For a factor of 4 there would be 3 cusps.

15. (half size)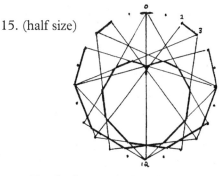

For the factor 1½ there is a loop (node) in addition to a cusp

167

16. When the factor is negative, i.e. ends of lines moving in opposite directions, no curve can be seen within the circle. All lines have to be continued outwards and then outward-pointing cusps are revealed. A good pupil will begin to discover how many cusps, nodes, etc. arise according to the factor, whether positive or negative, integral or fractional.

There is almost no end to the drawing exercises which can be chosen in Class 7. Curves which arise as envelopes – of circles as well as of straight lines – have a particular attraction at this age. This fact is closely related to the strong interest girls and boys at the gateway to puberty have for the shaping forces in the world, whether of oceans and rivers in geography, or of new civilisations brought about by explorers and those who followed them, or of good hygiene in their own bodies.

Two final examples close this section. Class 7 chemistry includes work on forming and dissolving crystals. Here is a triangle geometrically dissolving. Reduction takes place with 1 cm steps along edges. After 8 stirs, behold! It has gone.

Lessons in cookery also belong to this age. Here is a dumpling formed by an envelope of circles whose centres lie on a fixed circle and which touch a fixed straight line.

It looks a bit rubbery. Maybe Mr. Michelin cooked it. What would happen if the line were higher? Or touched the circle of dots? Or went outside them? Here is another discovery-type exercise for the class.

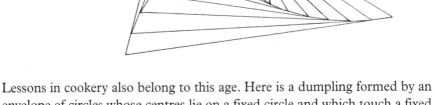

§4. Class 8 Geometry (i) loci

Whereas the envelope has been the means to form curves in Class 7, the curve appearing without more ado, it is the locus to which attention will be directed in Class 8. The sequence of adjacent dots will need joining up with some artistic skill to exhibit the curve.

At puberty boys have a tendency to think that a job can be done in any old way provided it is done. This is partly because they have not yet come to terms with their longer limbs and new need for balance. With girls it is different. Doing the job tends to have less importance than the style in which it is attempted. Practising and understanding the formation of a locus helps restore equilibrium in both cases. Also awareness of the efforts and tendencies of the other sex helps both boys and girls – yet another example of the value of co-education.

The most important locus of all is the circle. Ask a class to mark a point somewhere in the middle of the paper and then to measure carefully 8 cm away from it in various directions. Let them do it as many as 50 times, marking the end of the length each time with another dot. The circle will gradually reveal its presence and the girls will on the whole want to circumscribe the dots with a beautiful coloured curve, which they will work to make as perfect as possible. Many boys will prefer to go on to 100 dots. I once knew two boys in a Class 8 in an English Waldorf school go further, to over 200 dots. It became a game between them to see who could produce the most dots. Subsequently one of them became a physics professor in a university and the other a violinist leading an orchestra on the European continent.

Next day the class can write down the exact statement that the locus of points lying equidistant from a fixed point is a circle. Then at once ask about its 3 dimensional equivalent and they will obtain the definition of a sphere.

The properties of a circle now need to be discovered. Already some drawings and calculations in earlier classes have touched upon them, e.g. angles in the same segment have appeared to be equal. There are two ways to establish this property. First a more mobile method could be used.

Let A, P, B and C be any points on a circle. We want to show that $\alpha = \beta$. Let P^1 be the middle point of arc BP. Construct A^1 and C^1 so that arc AA^1 = arc CC^1 = arc PP^1. Now imagine APC is a rigid 'wishbone' that can slide inside the circle. Because of the equal arcs shown in the first drawing, as P slides into position P^1, so do A and C slide into positions A^1 and C^1. This could be demonstrated by a movable 'wishbone' on the blackboard.

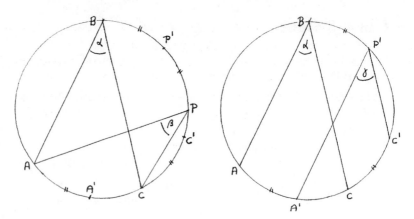

In the second drawing it is clear that because of the symmetry of the circle and the lines across it to the ends of equal arcs, AB is parallel to $A^1 P^1$ and BC is parallel to $P^1 C^1$. The practice in Classes 1 to 3 of 'symmetrical drawing' has come to fruition in a new way. Since angles between pairs of lines which are parallel as in the second drawing are equal, $\alpha = \gamma$. By the sliding movement, $\beta = \alpha$. Hence $\alpha = \beta$.

The second method lies in first proving that the angle at the centre of a circle is twice the angle at the circumference. It involves three cases, depending upon where B is in relation to A, C, and centre O.

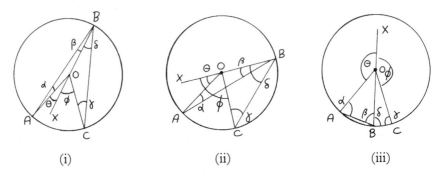

(i)   (ii)   (iii)

The proof is much easier to follow, of course, if the various pairs of equal angles are coloured.

AOB is an isosceles triangle $\Rightarrow \alpha = \beta$ and $\theta = \alpha + \beta = 2\beta$. Similarly $\phi = 2\delta$. Add the results for (i) and (iii) and subtract them for (ii). $\hat{AOC} = 2 \hat{ABC}$, but in (iii) $\hat{AOC}$ is a reflex angle.

    Since any angle in a segment of a circle is half the angle at the centre, *angles in the same segment are equal.*

Other well known angle properties follow from these results, e.g.
a) the opposite angles of a cyclic quadrilateral add up to 180°,
b) the exterior angle of a cyclic quadrilateral is equal to the opposite interior angle.

So in the figure below it follows from these properties that $\alpha = 45°$
$\beta = \gamma = 135°$

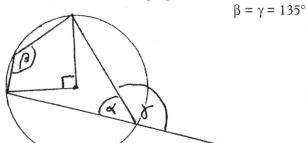

A set of examples on circles for the class to do will follow in the next section of the chapter, as well as further examples of loci, a few of which will be looked at next. Two straight line loci are (i) of a point moving so that its distance from one fixed point is equal to its distance from a second fixed point, (ii) the same except that fixed points are replaced by fixed lines.

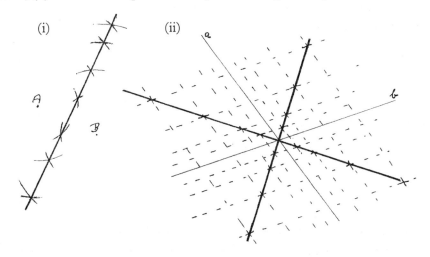

In (i), crossing points of equal radius arcs from A and B determine the locus and this drawing will at once remind the class of the construction of the middle point of a line learnt in Class 6. In (ii), dotted lines distant 0.5, 1, 2, 3.5 cm from both a and b are drawn. A good exercise is to prove that the two lines forming the complete locus are perpendicular. (Congruent triangles will have to be used.)

Consider the locus of a point moving such that the sum of its distances from two fixed points is always the same. Demonstrate this with a loop of fine cord hanging from two drawing pins A and B on the board. Pull the cord tight by means of a piece of chalk C *inside* the loop and slide the chalk over blackboard and cord simultaneously. The class can then make their own experiments, obtaining several results by changing the positions of the pins.

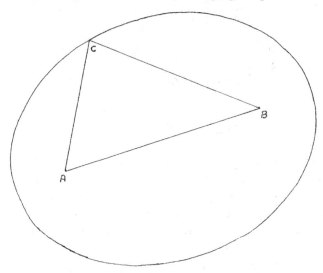

Alternatively the pins can remain fixed and the cord length changed. A series of ellipses will then emerge. This is also a preview of Class 9 and Class 10 work, when instead of a locus of constant sum of distances from A and B, constant differences, products and quotients will be investigated.

Further loci for Class 8 can be found in the moving parts of machinery, for example what happens with particular points on the connecting rod in a reciprocating steam engine (an engine studied and experimented with in Class 8 Physics)? A question almost always answered wrongly is 'A ladder leaning almost vertically against a wall slips along smooth ground until it lies flat. What locus would a girl or boy sitting half way up the ladder experience before getting a sore behind?'

The error arises through picturing the ladder's envelope, which is actually a complicated curve – part of a 4-cusped shape suitable for investigation in Class 12. It is a good exercise to prove that the locus is a quadrant of a circle.

Also what would happen if you sat on various other rungs of the ladder? Quadrants of what sort of curves would result?

Four positions of the sloping ladder are shown here, together with initial and final positions.

Chapter 8: Geometry in classes 7 and 8

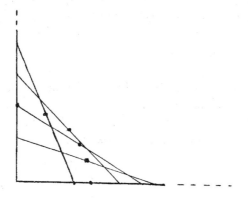

§5. Class 8 geometry (ii) solids

The cube, which is the metric means for volume calculation, has already been referred to in Chapter 7. All its faces and also all its corners are congruent. It is the most familiar regular solid. There are four other regular solids and a very good pictorial introduction to them all is found in Plato's 'Timaeus'. This can be slightly simplified as follows.

When God wished to create our home in the world, he first made the element of *fire*. To do this he used the simplest regular solid, the tetrahedron, which translated means four faces. (The easiest view of it is obtained by a repetition of the beginning of the very first compass-drawing in Class 5.) God next created the element of *air*, for which he used the next simplest regular solid with triangular faces, the octahedron. (Again the easiest view is obtained from just 2 circles passing through each other's centre). Finally, to complete God's creation of the whole fluid domain, the least simple regular solid composed of triangular faces, the icosahedron (20 faces), was used. This enabled *water* to be created.

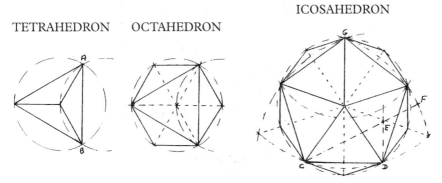

TETRAHEDRON   OCTAHEDRON   ICOSAHEDRON

173

The edge length in each (orthogonal projection) view is the same. So CD = AB. In the third drawing DE = ½CD, DE is perpendicular to CD, EF = DE, the large arcs centred at C, D and G have radius CF and the smaller arc centred at G has radius CD.)

No further regular solid composed of triangular faces is possible (3, 4, and 5 edges meeting at each corner describes the solids above, but 6 would give rise to a flat and infinite triangular honeycomb), so God used square faces, giving a hexahedron or cube in creating the *earth* element.

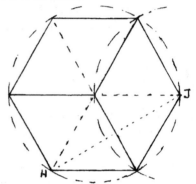

(Here again the 2 circle scaffolding is used, but with a larger radius to maintain the same true edge length as before. HJ is the true length of a diagonal of a square.)

CUBE OR HEXAHEDRON

No further regular solid composed of squares is possible (4 edges meeting at each corner would give rise to a flat and infinite square honeycomb) and God used pentagonal faces, giving a dodecahedron in creating the *life* element or essence. So this was also called the *quintessence*.

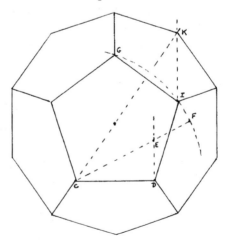

DODECAHEDRON

Chapter 8: Geometry in classes 7 and 8

(The pentagon and its centre are constructed in the same way as the icosahedron. K is the point of intersection of the vertical through I and the continuation of the radius through C. Dodeca means 12.)

There are no more regular solids. (To have 4 pentagons meeting at each corner is impossible – they would overlap. If hexagons are tried, 3 edges per corner would give rise to a flat and infinite hexagonal honeycomb – the real honeycomb of bees. To have polygons of more than 6 edges meeting with 3 edges at a corner is again impossible – they would overlap). So there are only five regular (or Platonic) solids. God's creation of all the elements or essences needed to build our home in the universe is now complete.

Although the stories of the Old Testament and Greek mythology belong to younger age groups and the teenager's interest is directed towards mastering the material world, the fact that this description of the Creation comes from the renowned Plato causes them to listen attentively. The very word 'quintessence' awakens special interest, for despite the materialistic views of the world they meet so often among peers or media, they are likely to be aware that there is more to the universe than the solid, liquid and gaseous state of matter and the energies manifested through nuclear fission and fusion.

Regrettably, this cannot be said for some modern commentators on Ancient Greek ideas about the world of nature.[5]

Having drawn views of the 5 regular Platonic solids it now becomes important to make them. Construction of the nets drawn on cardboard or cartridge paper now follows.

FIRE (3 flaps) F4, V4, E6   AIR (5 flaps) F8, V6, E12

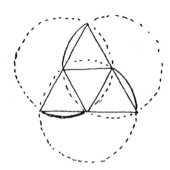
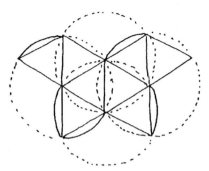

Tetrahedron   Octahedron

175

WATER (11 flaps)

F20, V12, E30

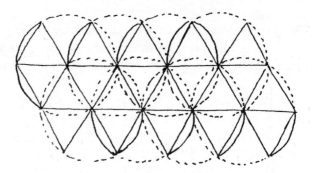

Icosahedron

EARTH (7 flaps)

F6, V8, E12

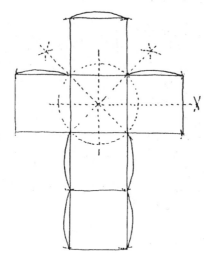

Cube or Hexahedron

QUINTESSENCE (ETHER)
(10 flaps for half the net)

F12, V20, E30

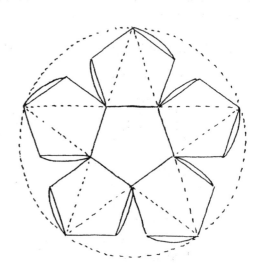

Dodecahedron

F, V & E stand for the number of faces, vertices and edges. It will be noticed that in the 3 higher drawings we are once more using the constructions first carried out in Class 5. The shapes of the nets are themselves suggestive of the corresponding elements. Bonfires have a triangular flame shape. Next we see something like a bird in the air, then waves of water. Then comes a cross like that on which the earth's saviour was crucified, and finally something which resembles the living human form. This last drawing only serves for half the solid; a copy of it upside down, joined to the first half above its left hand, is needed for the whole dodecahedron.

When the astronomer Johann Kepler became aware of the 5 solids and what Plato had said of them, he became very enthusiastic, not only making many models of them, but painting their faces or making sketches upon them. An example of the latter is shown below. For him the quintessence was bound up with sun, moon and stars, whilst gathering fruit and crops depicted the life of the earth.

Class 8 pupils will also want to paint their models and then hang mobiles of them from the classroom ceiling.

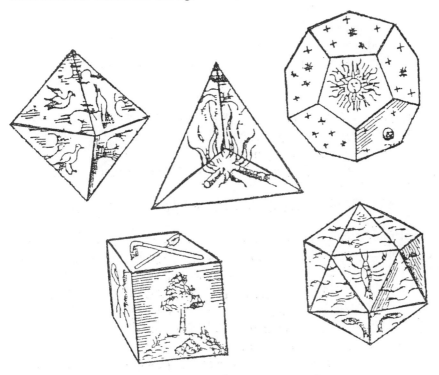

The solids can be made in other ways, too. It is particularly good to model them in clay, either completely formed by bare hands or assisted by pressing down with a flat piece of wood on the raw clay lump and then rotating and repeating. Three of the solids are easily made by stitching together the ends of milk straws, the other two (cube and dodecahedron) requiring supporting stays to preserve their shape.

The number of faces, edges and vertices will have been counted on each model. Already some of the children will have observed that these numbers show that (i) cube and octahedron, (ii) icosahedron and dodecahedron are pairs of opposite or complementary shapes. This will be gone into at a much deeper level in Classes 10 and 11 when Projective Geometry and its Principle of Duality is developed.

The same counting process can be applied to any 3D shape composed of plane faces, straight edges and vertices.[6] So a list can be compiled, for example:

Name	Faces	Edges	Vertices
Cube	6	12	8
Tetrahedron	4	6	4
Dodecahedron	12	30	20
Triangular prism	5	9	6
Hexagonal pyramid	7	12	7

An excellent task for homework is to find and add 5 more examples to the list and then discover the formula which always relates F, E, and V, picking one or two more examples to verify the discovery. It may even be that one or two bright pupils will be able to prove the truth of the result, which is that
$$F + V = E + 2,$$
first discovered by the Swiss mathematician Euler.

The phenomenon of shearing was used in Class 7 to obtain the areas of parallelograms and triangles, and in Class 8 to obtain the volumes of pyramids and cones. Another transformation in geometry is that of enlargement (or dilatation). These two transformations, together with others like translation, belong to a whole class of transformations called homologies, whose proper place in an educational curriculum is with Classes 10 and 11, where matrices will also be introduced.

However, following the work on ratio and proportion in Class 7 arithmetic, simple examples on similar figures would be suitable for Class 8 geometry. When a geometrical figure is enlarged or reduced in size but not in shape, every length receives the same proportional increase or decrease. This is called the scale factor, which will be denoted here by s. Suppose a triangle is photographed and an enlargement is made…

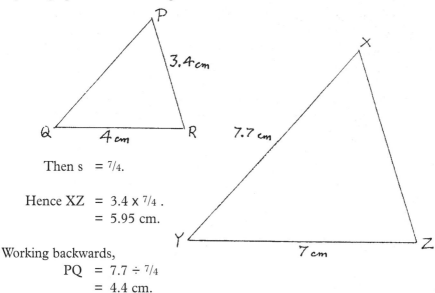

Then s = 7/4.

Hence XZ = 3.4 x 7/4 .
       = 5.95 cm.

Working backwards,
   PQ = 7.7 ÷ 7/4
      = 4.4 cm.

The next figure shows two right angles and hence a pair of similar triangles. The scale factor = $\frac{17 + 8.5}{17}$ = $\frac{3}{2}$.

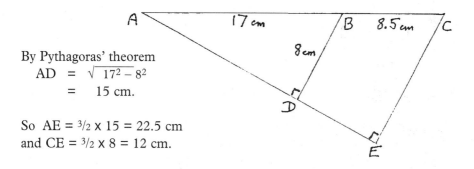

By Pythagoras' theorem
   AD = $\sqrt{17^2 - 8^2}$
      = 15 cm.

So AE = 3/2 x 15 = 22.5 cm
and CE = 3/2 x 8 = 12 cm.

Notice that area ABD = 1/2 15 x 8 = 60 cm^2
and area ACE = 1/2 22.5 x 12 = 135 cm^2.

The area scale factor is therefore s^2.
(3/2 x 3/2 = 9/4 = 2 1/4)

Teaching mathematics

No treatment of figures involving pentagons would be complete without reference to the golden ratio. Although this is much more appropriate for higher classes than Class 8, a little foretaste can whet appetites for future work. First let us find an easier way to construct regular pentagons than the one given earlier, which is strictly exact in pure geometry. Engineers do not bother with such constructions. They use trial and error methods – and often achieve greater physical exactitude thereby. The following method can be applied to drawing *any* regular polygon.

Guess the compass radius needed to step round a circle in 5 equal steps. An error will appear on completion of the 5th step. Guess a fifth of this error and modify the radius guessed by this amount. Do again and if necessary repeat the process a third time (or even a fourth). Satisfaction is soon achieved.

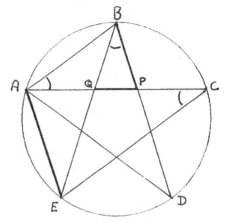

The faint-hearted can, of course, use a protractor, marking out angles of 72° round the centre.

It is easy to prove that the angles marked are equal (for equal arcs of a circle subtend equal angles at the circumference, as was shown earlier). Symmetry then shows that the 3 triangles PAB, QBP and ACE all have the same isosceles shape. Properties of similar triangles can now be used since the proportions of lengths of these 3 triangles must be the same.

Taking the larger pair of triangles, $\dfrac{AP}{PB} = \dfrac{AC}{AE}$

Since PB = PC and AE = AB = AP, $\dfrac{AP}{PC} = \dfrac{AC}{AP}$.

So, looking along AC, $\dfrac{\text{major part (AP)}}{\text{minor part (PC)}} = \dfrac{\text{whole (AC)}}{\text{major part (AP)}}$.

Chapter 8: Geometry in classes 7 and 8

This ratio is called *the golden ratio*. It is the scale factor in enlarging the smaller into the larger triangle. This has considerable significance in architecture, painting and music.[7] P is called the golden mean of the interval AC. It is easy to prove that Q is also the golden mean of interval AP. If the pentagon-pentagram figure is developed further, golden ratios abound all over it.

What is the numerical value of the golden ratio? Its exact value cannot be understood before Class 9, when quadratic equations are dealt with, but Class 8 can measure pairs of lengths as well as they can and then do a long division sum. They should get 1.62 to 3 s.f. There is a lovely 'magic' way of obtaining it, however. Here is a good 'discovery' situation. Choose any two whole numbers. Add them. Then add either of the numbers to the answer. Then add the last answer to the new answer. Repeat ad lib, say for a column of 12 numbers, as shown.

```
    3
    7                        1.618
   10              487 ) 788
   17                    487
   27                   3010
   44                   2922
   71                    880
  115                    487
  186                   3930
  301                   3896
  487                     34
  788
```

Now divide the last number by the one before it

Always the same answer comes, no matter which numbers you start with. 1.618 is the correct value of the golden ratio to 4 s.f.

The reason for this cannot be grasped before Class 11, when the concept of 'limit' is taught.

§6. Geometrical examples for Class 8

Calculate the angles marked with Greek letters in the figures below.

1.   2.   3.   4.

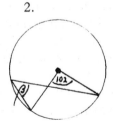
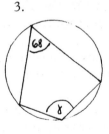
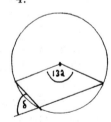

5. A goat is tethered by a rope fixed to a ring which can slide along a horizontal rail near the ground. The rope is 3 m long and the rail 10 m long. Using a scale of 1 cm per m draw accurately the area of grass the goat will eventually consume. Calculate this area to 3 s.f.

6. Two pins are fixed to the flat surface of a board. A 30-60-90 set square is pushed between them and moved about in all possible ways without either pin losing contact with it. What loci do the set square corners make whilst the 2 edges of the particular corner are touching the pins?

7. Draw a line, l, across the paper 3 cm from the bottom. Mark a point P, 8 cm from the bottom of the paper and halfway between the left and right edges. Mark a series of points 1cm apart along l and join each one to P, extending each joining line outwards in both directions. Along each one mark a further series of points 1 cm apart, beginning with the point on l. Join up relevant points by smooth curves to show the loci of points on lines through P whose distance from their intersection points with l is constant. These curves are called conchoids.

8. Construct the 3 lines which are the loci of points equidistant from the 3 corners of a triangle ABC, 2 at a time, where AB = 4", BC = 5" and CA = 6". Label the point where the 3 lines meet O, the circumcentre. What special function for the triangle does O have?

9. Repeat the last question except that the loci have to be equidistant from the 3 sides of triangle ABC and the point where the 3 lines meet inside the triangle is I, the incentre. What special function does I have?

10. With the same triangle as before, draw the locus of a point P moving so that AP remains always perpendicular to BC. Draw two other loci where

BP ⊥ AC and CP ⊥ AB. Label the point of intersection of the 3 lines this time H, the orthocentre.

11. Cut out a cardboard triangle of the same dimensions as before and experiment to find where you can balance the triangle on your compass point. Then draw the 3 lines through the balancing point G and through each corner across to the opposite side. What do you notice? G is called the centroid or centre of gravity of the triangle.

12. A human being has many centres. Which of the points G, H, I and O do you feel is analagous to the heart centre, the centre of the observing head, the centre of weight and the centre of uprightness in the human being?

13. Copy this drawing (the actual measurements are not important). Then join AC and BD. What do you notice? Would this always be true, no matter where the lines APB and CQD are drawn? Why? (Hint: join PQ)

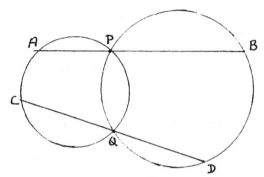

14. The line DC touches the circle centred at O at T. B is anywhere on the circle on the opposite side of TA to C.

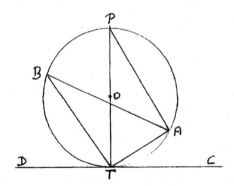

(i) Prove that PÂT = 90°
(ii) Using the symmetry of circle tangent about PT, prove that AT̂C = AP̂T.
(iii) Prove that AT̂C = AB̂T.

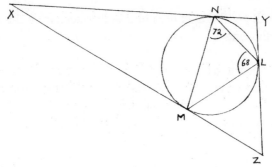

15. Using the result of question 14, i.e. that 'the angle between a tangent and a chord is equal to the angle in the opposite segment', calculate the 3 angles of triangle XYZ, which touches the circle at L, M and N.

16. The quadrilateral ABCD touches the circle at E, F, G and H. BF = 15 cm, FC = 53 cm, AH = 16 cm, HD = 15 cm.

    Calculate the lengths of AB and DC. What type of quadrilateral is ABCD?

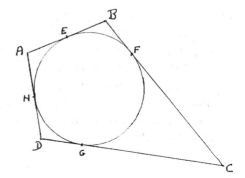

17. A regular dodecagon forms the base of a vertical column, towards the top of which a pyramid is mounted whose sloping faces meet the column's vertical faces in the edge of another regular dodecagon. How many edges has the whole integrated solid? Verify Euler's law for it.

18. If the column above were based on a polygon of n sides, write down the algebraic expressions for F, E and V and again verify Euler's law.

19. Calculate the volume of a regular octahedron of edge 4 cm correct to 3 s.f.

20. Draw an orthogonal projection of a regular octahedron in which one vertex is right in front of the opposite vertex. Can you see how to fill the whole of space with touching octahedra and tetrahedra so that no part of space is left out?

21. Sketch the solid called a cuboctahedron by cutting off all the corners of a cube by cuts passing through the centres of the edges meeting in their corners. What are the values of F, E and V?

22. If you carry out the same corner-cutting-off process with a tetrahedron, what do you end up with?

23. Make a simple orthogonal view of an octahedron, using a circle of radius 5 cm to begin the construction. Mark off 9 more points on the lines as shown, where lengths a = 5.35cm, and lengths b = 3.09 cm. These points are golden means of the 9 lines. Join the new points to make triangles in the 4 spaces, using a new colour, red say. By drawing 6 more red lines joining the new points, a new view of another regular solid is obtained. Which? (To help the teacher, all the 'red' lines are shown dotted.)

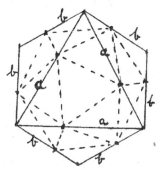

24. Make a simple orthogonal view of a dodecahedron. Using a new colour draw edges of a cube whose corners fit into those of the dodecahedron. How many such cubes are possible?

25. Show that if 8 is chosen for the first number and 2 is chosen for the second number in the continuous addition leading towards the golden ratio, the decimal obtained by dividing the number by the one before is exactly 1.1618 at one stage. How many numbers have had to be written down altogether at that point?

Numerical answers are in this set:
5, 12, 13, 13, 24, 30.2, 31, 36, 44, 47, 48, 51, 88.3, 66, 68, 100, 112.

Comments on other questions:

6. arcs of circles.

8. to 12. O is the centre of the circle through the corners and I is the centre of the circle touching the sides. The lines through G cut the sides in half.

G corresponds to the centre of weight   (physical body)
I   "   "   "   heart   (etheric body)
O   "   "   "   centre of observation   (astral body)
H   "   "   "   centre of uprightness   (ego)

but the words in brackets are not for the class, of course. The 4 triangle centres (there are several more not mentioned here) are shown in the drawing completing this section. Notice the important 'spine' line through 3 of them and how I, like the human heart, is not on this central line.

13. AC is always parallel to BD because of equal angles in the figure.

14. $P\hat{A}T = 1/2 \ P\hat{O}T$.

18. $E = 4n$, $F = 2n + 1$ and so is V.

20 and 22. These are best understood by using clay models. The set of 25 questions above is not intended as a set to be given to Class 8 on some particular day, nor as a revision set, but to show the variety possible. Class teachers should compose their own questions according to circumstances and the abilities of those they are teaching.

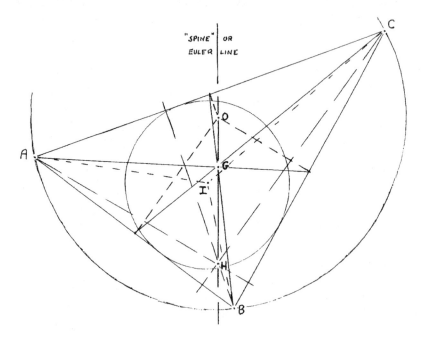

Chapter 8: Geometry in classes 7 and 8

§7. Perspective Drawing

In Class 7 the teaching of history has reached forward to the time of the great discoveries of the New World, and the Renaissance of art and learning. The fifteenth century saw the dawn of a new age which subsequently developed into our modern scientific age. Before that time perspective was altogether lacking in the art of painting; the portraits by Giotto, for example, have flat backgrounds of a beautiful gold. Then, through people like Alberti and Leonardo da Vinci, the whole science of perspective burst into the art of painting. It is entirely fitting that Class 7 should begin to learn perspective technique, first through freehand drawing. To begin with this will consist simply of depicting parallel lines as lines meeting on the horizon and vertical lines remaining vertical in the picture. This entails making objects shorter in height as one goes further forward into the scene being sketched. Hence the term 'foreshortening'. There is no need in Classes 7 or 8 to draw other than horizontally observed views. Perspective views looking up at 60 degrees to the horizonal at skyscrapers, or at a similar angle downwards from an aeroplane will be developed in Class 10.

Before going on from freehand to exact geometrical perspectives it is good to work at simple 2 dimensional configurations. Already in Class 2 such a configuration was drawn freehand; here it is developed exactly, and then extended a few more steps in the drawing on the left.

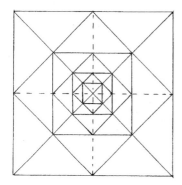
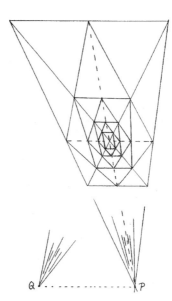

The four sets of parallel lines could be continued inwards, but would soon become difficult or impossible to draw.

In the drawing on the right the first figure drawn is a trapezium, not a square. Two intermediate drawings could have been shown, beginning with a rectangle and then an isosceles trapezium. It would be good for the class to do both of these, too. The horizontal parallels appear again, although the distances between them are much more varied. To get the second (downward) dotted line it is necessary to extend the left and right sides of the trapezium downwards to meet (at P). Then it will be found that all 'downward' lines pass through P if they are extended. Even more remarkable will be the discovery that what were once 45 degree lines would, if extended, meet in Q, level with P. Also the complementary set of 45 degree lines if extended would meet in R (not shown above) as far to P's right as Q is to its left.

The first drawing shows 2 sets of squares; the intermediate drawings would show (i) a set of rectangles and a set of rhombi,
(ii) a set of isosceles trapezia and a set of kites
and the second drawing shows a set of trapezia and a set of quadrilaterals.

Ask the class if the second drawing reminds them of anything. 'It's a bit like a window.' 'Going into a sloping cave.' 'Alright,' you say, 'How about turning your drawings upside down?'

Perhaps the penny will begin to drop for two or three pupils, but to ensure that all pennies drop, start the next drawing upside down with a horizontal dotted line RQ and draw any suitable quadrilateral, choosing the lowest point first.

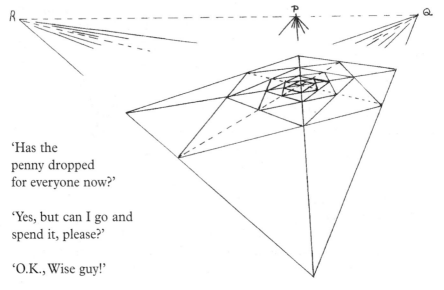

'Has the penny dropped for everyone now?'

'Yes, but can I go and spend it, please?'

'O.K., Wise guy!'

'Hey, I know what it is. It's looking at the first drawing of squares from the side!'

Fine. They all pick up drawings and squint at them from various perspectives. Finally you ask what the line RPQ really is. 'The horizon!' A good exercise you can set the class after this is to draw a chess board in perspective, colouring alternate squares black (they begin to love black at puberty).

The next step is to move into 3D and bring in vertical lines. So a rectangular building with a pyramidic roof could be drawn (drawing on left). But how is a cube to be drawn in perspective?

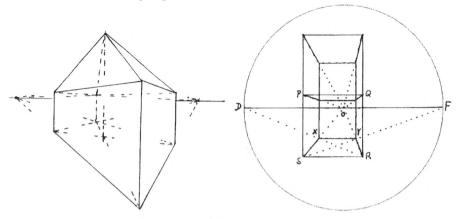

On the right two equal transparent cubes stacked facing the observer are shown. This is the simplest case. First of all the cone of vision has to be indicated. Place your eye right above the centre of the circle at a distance from it equal to the radius. It would be as well to redraw with a much bigger radius than shown to avoid eye strain. You will then be aware that objects outside the circle are indistinct – actually outside the cone joining eye to circle – but play fair! The focus of your sight must be the circle centre – wandering eyeballs are not allowed. The reason why the drawing on the left looks wrong is that your eyes are too far away from it. (Put an eye nearer and squint at it for a moment – then it looks right.) For every perspective drawing there is one and only one place from which to look at it properly. Hence the way people move backwards and forwards in art galleries (at least one hopes they all know why they are doing this); sometimes the proper viewpoint is to the side, or above or below the picture.

The points D and F are called distance points; they are equidistant from the centre of vision. First the square PQRS is drawn wherever one wishes. Since D and F lie in perpendicular directions for the eye, the actual angles $F\hat{S}R$ and $D\hat{R}S$ are 45°. Also the actual angles $O\hat{R}S$ and $O\hat{S}R$ are 90°. It is clear that the dotted lines complete the actual square RSXY. The drawing of perspective cubes is, however, probably better left to Class 8.

Before drawing a perspective cube in general position we need to know how a circle looks drawn in perspective. Suppose this circle is on the ground. Let us divide the cone of vision boundary into 12 equal parts, something which every member of the class has become expert in since Class 5.

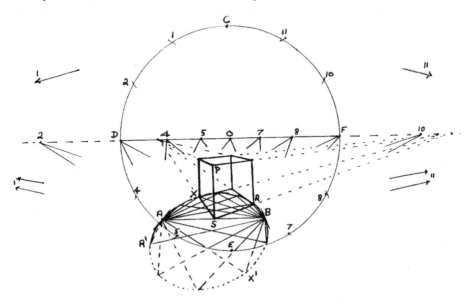

As before D and F are the distance points, C is above and E is below. S is chosen anywhere as before, but now point A, B and P are taken at equal distances from S. The numbered points round the circle are put in line with C and the numbers transferred to where the joining lines would cross the horizon. Diametrically opposite points on the cone of visions are, of course, perpendicular lines for the eye. Take 5 and 11. So the points 5 and 11 on the horizon must also lie in perpendicular directions for the eye. Join both these points to both A and B. The intersections of these joining lines are found at R and R^1. In the same way 2 and 8 give rise to X and X^1. All points like the Xs and Rs must lie on the perspective view of a circle because angles in a semicircle are right angles and AR is perspectively perpendicular to RB, etc. The actual centre of the perspective circle is S.

Hence the actual SR and SX are equal to SP. The points 2, 5, 8 and 11 on the cone of vision circle form quadrants of it. Again the right angles are preserved. Hence the figure shown is a cube in perspective.

Chapter 8: Geometry in classes 7 and 8

The above reasoning may be too difficult for most of Class 8, although most of them could carry out the practical constructions. 'All will become clear to you in the upper school!' the perplexed class teacher will assert – and in this particular case he would be quite justified. For we are here beginning to touch on two subjects which belong to Classes 9, 10 and 11.

One is the subject of conic sections which forms a large part of a Class 9 main lesson. Although an ellipse has resulted in the drawing above, had A and B been placed further away from S and the cube made larger, a parabola or hyperbola could easily result. When you stand inside a large circle drawn on the ground, your horizontal perspective view of the circle is always hyperbolic. The second subject, begun in Class 10 and continued right through to Class 12, is projective geometry. It is important not to begin this subject before puberty has reached its nadir. (Experienced teachers of adolescents will know what that means.) It will become a wonderful means of helping adolescents up out of it, and of supporting the emerging idealism with which their own inner selves can bless them. But the task before the time of deep puberty is first to help children experience the earthly and practical domain. The danger of too early an awareness of the non-metrical qualities of projective geometry, before measure and weight have been mastered, is that airy-fairy ideas could be promoted so that feet lose their wish to remain on the earth. However, as is the case at every age, a gentle preview of what is to come later, given with a light touch, can be very helpful.

A final exercise, good for both Class 8 and Class 9, is the construction of shadows. Given the position of the sun, where does the shadow of an object lie? Let us take some vertical posts.

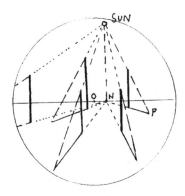

Let N be the foot of a perpendicular from the sun's position in the drawing to the position of the horizon. Imagine you are lying on the ground with your head in line with the top of a post and the sun, e.g. at P. A few moments' thought will convince you that the construction employed is correct. Now here is an interesting case. Observe the shadows below and determine exactly where the sun is shining.

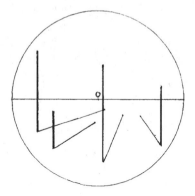

If the top of each post is joined to the end of the shadow of that post, as was done in the previous drawing, it will be found that the extensions of the joins all pass through a point well below the horizon. How can that be the position of the sun in the picture? In fact it is the position of the shadow of your own eye. The sun is actually behind you in line with your eye and its shadow.

It will be noticed that the four shadow lines meet, when extended on the horizon, in the point previously labelled N.

The bare bones of perspective pictures have been drawn in all the pictures in this section. What is needed now is some artistic skill to put real flesh on them. A line of trees of roughly the same actual height,[8] hills, human or animal figures, clouds, architectural details of buildings – these would complete the task of perspective representation. At the close of lessons on the subject, teacher and class might well contemplate a large print of Leonardo's 'Last Supper'. What a wonderfully balanced composition it is. Immediately to Christ's left and right are the cholerics and melancholics. Beyond them, again three in each group, are the sanguines and the phlegmatics. Yet the centre of perspective, the point to which the ceiling beams converge is the point between the eyes, at the root of the nose, of the head of Christ.

Chapter 9:
Statistics and Graphs

§1. Their value and place in the world

We are all familiar with the fact that statistics can often reveal themselves as the worst kind of lies. Information is collected, analysed and displayed in such a way as to convince or at least suggest to the observer that a strong tendency (which had better not be ignored!) is developing in some situation affecting life. In commercial terms for instance, we had better 'get a move-on' so as not to be left out. Few statistics compiled today are without ultimate financial implications. Of those which are not, many can leave us with the feeling that they do not supply knowledge that can guide what is individual in us. It is a true feeling because the whole of statistics is based upon what is general. What is peculiar to an individual piece of data has to be ignored.

This does not mean that all statistics are unnecessary in striving for human progress. It is by discovering why and how they have the proclivity to deceive that we can find where they have real value. Statistical information is easy to display in graphical form, whether of the pie-chart or block diagram varieties, or of the kind where two rectangular axes enable the relationship of two different quantities to be ascertained – or apparently so.

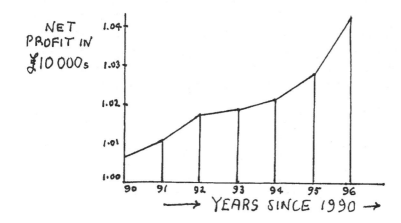

Teaching mathematics

The deception practised in the 'sales promotion chart' above is very obvious. In the fast pace of modern life the compiler assumes or hopes that the reader will have little time to examine the small print down the left-hand side.

Let us examine some population figures of a few years ago.

POPULATION DATA 1989

1. Estimate in millions in mid-1989 from U.N. and other official publications.
2. Rate of annual natural increase (birthrate minus death rate, per 1000 of population).
3. Life expectancy at birth in years.
4. Percentage of women, married or 'in union', of reproductive age, using
   (i) modern contraceptives (pill, I.U.D., etc),
   (ii) older contraceptive methods ('safe' times in the month, etc.)

	1.	2.	3.	4(i)	4(ii)
The Whole World	5234	1.8	63	46	7
Africa	646	2.9	51	11	4
Asia (excl. U.S.S.R.)	3061	1.9	62	48	5
North America	275	0.7	75	64	4
Latin America	438	2.1	66	46	9
Europe (excl. U.S.S.R.)	499	0.3	74	47	26
U.S.S.R.	289	1.0	69	?	?
Oceania(Australasia)	26	1.2	72	48	8

Data for the countries with the largest* populations within continents (*with two exceptions).

	1.	2.	3.	4(i)	4(ii)
Nigeria	115	2.9	47	1	4
Ethiopia	50	2.1	41	?	?
South Africa	39	2.6	63	45	3
Iraq *	18	3.8	66	12	2
Turkey	55	2.2	64	64	29
Iran	54	3.4	62	?	?
India	835	2.2	58	32	8
Pakistan + Bangladesh	225	2.8	53	13	17
Indonesia	185	2.0	56	44	4
China	1104	1.4	66	73	1
Japan	123	0.5	78	60	4

Chapter 9: Statistics and graphs

	1.	2.	3.	4(i)	4(ii)
Australia	17	0.8	76	47	20
Canada	26	0.8	76	69	4
U.S.A.	249	0.7	75	63	5
Mexico	87	2.4	68	45	8
Brazil	147	2.0	65	56	9
Argentina	32	1.4	70	?	?
U.K.	57	0.2	75	75	8
France	56	0.4	76	51	24
Germany	78	0.0	75	68	10
Poland	38	0.6	71	26	49
Italy	58	0.0	74	32	46
Spain	39	0.3	76	38	21
Iceland *	0.3	1.0	78	?	?

It is interesting to try and explain the two largest figures and the two smallest figures in each list.

Where column 2 is concerned it is possible to calculate from it what the populations would be in the year 2000 *if* the rate did not change, a very questionable assumption. So the whole world would have 6320 million people and Iraq would have 27 200 000 people.

Already some predictions made at that time have proved to be quite wrong. Famines, the spread of AIDS and wars will make 1997 figures show new tendencies. Also, some figures are based upon random sampling and whilst this technique has been much improved in recent years, the way in which questions are formulated can condition the answers in the sampling.

What value have such figures? If they were related to more figures showing food consumption per individual, would that lead to a world effort to provide the undernourished with the food they need? If the annual amount of food wasted or thrown away in the U.S.A. were to be compared with the annual need for food in Ethiopia, say, would that really lead to action? And what are we to make of column 4(i)? We are not very good in this country at present in playing test matches or in the Olympics, so it may be a pleasant surprise to find that we were top of a world league in something. At 75% we were 2% ahead of China, and the rest of the field was well spread out behind. One wonders if we still hold the gold today or do we now have to be content with a bronze once again?

Teaching mathematics

Besides falsifications arising through the ways statistics are compiled and arranged, they can be very seriously flawed as guides to the future. Extrapolation in particular is a very dicey business. For example, look at this succession of numbers.

4 5 6 7 8 9

What number must come next? Did you say 10? I declare that 12 comes next. Prove it? Certainly! Just look at the differences between these numbers and then the differences between the differences, etc.

```
(4)    4   5   6   7   8   9   12   (26)
  (0)    1   1   1   1   1   3   (14)
  (1)    0   0   0   0   2   (11)
 (-1)    0   0   0   2   (9)   (25)
    (1)    0   0   2   (7)   (16)
   (-1)    0   2   (5)   (9)
              1   2   3   4   5
```

At the 7th level of number sequence – down in the depths, where the 'true causes of surface phenomena lie', you can see the natural sequence of integers. On the surface, beyond 12 comes 26. After that it is easy to calculate that 76 is the next number. In fact I could nominate any number I like to succeed any set of given numbers and justify my nomination. Nor need I just analyse differences between terms. I could use ratios or something more complicated. The base line (in the depths) could also be reversed in direction. To take another example, what numbers come next in the following population-type sequence? You may say that there are not enough numbers to make a judgment. But there *never are* with *any* set of discrete numbers, no matter how many you have.

2 1 3 6

Is this the beginning of a population explosion after a slight dip to start with? Proceeding as before we would obtain

```
   2   1   3   6   (9)   (12   (16)   (23)   (36)
    -1   2   3   (3)   (3)   (4)   (7)   (13)
       3   1   (0)   (0)   (1)   (3)   (6)
        -2  (-1)  (0)   (1)   (2)   (3)
```

196

Chapter 9: Statistics and graphs

The surface sequence certainly does begin to grow rapidly, but the law of succession could be quite different. Suppose we were to subtract 4 from each of the original four numbers and then examine the result

–2   –3   –1   2

Each number, when subtracted from the next number gives the next-but-one number. Thus –3 – (–2) = –1, and –1 – (–3) = +2.

Continuing the procedure we obtain

–2 –3 –1 2 3 1 –2 –3 –1 2 3 1 –2 –3 –1, a cyclic sequence.

Adding 4 to each one we get

2 1 3 6 7 5 2 1 3 6 7 5 2 1 3

So the population would be subject to a rhythmic variation in size, with highs and lows.[1] Is it at all possible, one might ask, that this is the sort of thing that may actually happen with world population? Nearing the year 2000 we obviously approach a high, even if the particular year of maximum population lies still further ahead.

Back in 800 to 1000 A.D. we seem to have had a low. What about still earlier times when no records were kept? Archeological expeditions have uncovered the remains of what were once vast or very large populations in now deserted forests or arid regions. Is such a rhythm conceivable? So much else in our lives is like this. For example we are very active for about 16 hours every day, then move into apparently inactive sleep for 8 hours. The transition is not abrupt. Between the two we live in the half-land of dreams. Also we are aware of increasing tiredness and reduced energy some time before making for bed. One thing is certain: statistics cannot answer the questions posed. For a very perceptive (and highly amusing) example of a very important question statistics cannot answer, read Soesman.[2]

Interpolation is a different matter and here the construction of graphs and the finding of approximate mathematical equations to describe them has immense technical value. Provided the upper and lower limits of the data figures are sufficiently reliable, the solutions to problems between them are fully justified.

Yet there are still pitfalls. Anyone who listens to shipping forecasts on the radio at a certain time of day may be intrigued to hear that whether the general weather is fine or not, the reports from coastal weather stations always seem to include falling atmospheric pressures. If a different time of listening were chosen, however, it would be found that most of these pressures would be rising. Whenever data is subject to daily or other periodic variation, this has to be taken into account before deductions can be made.

§2. Statistics and statistical graphs in education

It is essential that whatever data is studied in schools should be of real practical value and meaningful for the pupils. To ask a group of children to go and stand at a street corner with a notebook to record the number of vans, trucks, buses, private cars, etc. passing during a particular half hour is one of the most banal things a teacher can do. It is no better than the imposition upon children of set theory problems involving washing powder surveys, where the aim is to discover the relative popularity of 'Glooch', 'Poof' and the like. Fortunately, since the decline of the 'new maths' syndrome in more recent years, such tasks are slowly being withdrawn.

A preliminary stage to the collection and arrangement of data can occur naturally in the youngest school classes. The arrangement of nuts or stones in Class 1 arithmetic is a case in point. Classroom tasks also show such examples. When a child is asked to go and tidy up all the children's outdoor shoes along the wall, she might be asked to arrange them in order of size. The heights of the children are often marked on a vertical piece of paper on a wall. Books require arrangement according to size on various shelves. By Class 3, classification of vases, jugs etc according to water capacity is needed. Coinage is another example. In Class 5, pie charts were introduced and in Class 6 pictograms and block graphs.

The skill required later for work of a statistical character will owe much, however, to a thorough grounding in geometry and geometrical drawing. Here lies a significant difference between Waldorf schools and many if not most kinds of other schools. The time used in many schools on simple statistical work and its development, also early work on computers, is spent in Waldorf schools on geometry. Where computers belong in Waldorf education will be dealt with later.

Chapter 9: Statistics and graphs

Class 7 is a suitable time for a more focused introduction to statistical data, although in a main lesson in Physics in Class 6 some children may already have been given the task of recording the temperature (and possibly barometric pressure too) in the classroom at certain times each day. The varying climates of countries round the Atlantic Ocean will be studied in a geography main lesson and deductions from given statistical data will be of practical value. The algebra main lesson dealing with the solutions of equations will naturally lead to the drawing of graphs, especially once powers and roots of numbers have been worked with. Archimedes' principle, and hydraulic pressure as well as the atmospheric conditions needed to produce the condensation of water vapour belong to Class 7. It is important in holistic education that every subject is taught in relationship to others to which the class is being introduced in the current school year.

Arithmetical graphs (i.e. without algebra) are best introduced first. The natural unit along the horizontal axis (abscissa) is that of time, whilst the vertical direction (that of the ordinate) shows what takes place at particular times. Temperature charts showing what is happening to patients in a hospital during a day or successive days are of interest to Class 7 – again in relation to another main lesson, that of hygiene. Whilst some young people (without being too gender-specific!) may be more interested in the progress of their vital statistics and fluctuations in their weights, others may show interest in the weekly movements of their favourite football teams up and down the premier league. Many in the class will probably wish to keep themselves informed of the weekly progress of various hits in 'Top of the Pops'.

Turning to more serious music, the musical score will have become a quite familiar graph by this age. The singer or instrumentalist has to follow the ascents and descents of pitch, sometimes of a convex shape on the score (usually in a major key) and sometimes of a concave shape (minor). If one imagines the curves as belonging to a profile of hills that has to be traversed, labouring up a slope that gets increasingly steeper corresponds to a feeling of minor mood whilst a slope that becomes less steep as one ascends it corresponds to a major feeling in the hiker. The ordinates of such graphs measure frequency, again a topic met in the physics lessons of the class.

Here is an example from the beginning of a wonderful Handel song in A minor, which contains many ups and downs. Instead of the usual arrangement of notes in the treble clef, heights here are measured in tones and semi-tones above bottom C. Gaps occur where there are semi-quaver rests. The words of the song are:

Droop not young lover, pine not in sadness,
Sighs ne'er will move her,
Grief is but madness,
Love joys in glad ——— ness,
Tears are in vain.

Notice the minor arpeggio beginning (concave slope) and later the convex slope as a C major descent accompanies 'Love joys in gla...'

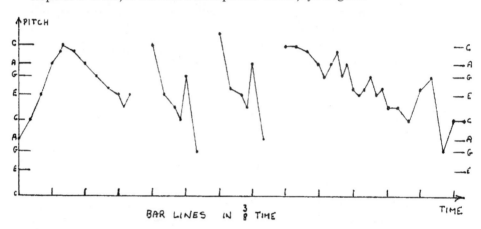

For those finding it hard to summon up a love for statistics, the advice given above is worthy of adoption. Instead of contemplating the tears which run down the human countenance, let us turn to those which fall from the skies. The geography of the Atlantic Ocean and the lands bordering it is a main lesson for Class 7, so the statistics of monthly rainfall in various ports on its shores should tell the class what kind of climate these places enjoy. This would become particularly clear if the average midday and midnight temperatures each month were included too, but in the table below latitudes give some help. The figures opposite show inches of rainfall correct to 1 d.p. Ask the class if they are able to pronounce the mysterious word in the middle of the top line!

The first four cities are on the west and the second four are on the east coast of the ocean. The remaining two belong to other oceans but are included to show extremes. Choosing appropriate scales, ordinates can be plotted for each month and joined by straight lines to give annual graphs for each place. A set of interesting questions can then be devised for the class to answer, e.g.:

- Which of the four seasons is wettest or driest in each place? Where would you like to go for a holiday and in which month?
- What clothing would you take with you? Why? What clothing would you take at the same time of year to the place on the list that seems opposite

Chapter 9: Statistics and graphs

PLACE	J	F	M	A	M	J	J	A	S	O	N	D	Total	Latitude
Buenos Aires	3.1	2.8	4.3	3.5	3.0	2.4	2.2	2.4	3.1	3.4	3.3	3.9	37.4	35°S
Caracas	.9	.4	.6	1.3	3.1	4.0	4.3	4.3	4.2	4.3	3.7	1.8	32.9	10°N
New Orleans	4.6	4.2	4.7	4.8	4.5	5.5	6.6	5.8	4.8	3.5	3.8	4.6	57.4	30°N
Hebron	.9	.7	.9	1.1	1.6	2.1	2.7	2.7	3.3	1.6	1.1	.6	57.4	58°N
Oslo	1.7	1.3	1.4	1.6	1.8	2.4	2.9	3.8	2.5	2.9	2.3	2.3	26.9	60°N
Funchal	2.5	2.9	3.1	1.3	.7	.2	0	0	1.0	3.0	3.5	3.3	21.5	33°N
Lagos	1.1	1.8	4.0	5.9	10.6	18.1	11.0	2.5	5.5	8.1	2.7	1.0	72.3	7°N
Cape Town	.6	.3	.7	1.9	3.1	3.3	3.5	2.6	1.7	1.2	.7	.4	20.0	34°S
Lima	0	0	0	0	.2	.2	.3	.3	.3	.1	.1	0	1.5	12°S
Singapore	9.9	6.8	7.6	7.4	6.8	6.8	6.7	7.7	7.0	8.2	10.0	10.1	95.0	2°N

Rainfall in inches

to the place you chose? How many times wetter is the wettest place on the list compared to the driest place?
- In which places would you expect the following foods to be found: sugar? walrus meat? rice? wheat? manioc? oranges and peaches?

Of course you would expect everyone to find the places in their atlases before tackling the graphs or the questions.

Many interesting statistical graphs can be studied in connection with (or as part of) the physics and chemistry main lessons. Comparisons of the coefficients of expansion for different metals or of specific heats of substances can be tabulated and graphed. The extraordinary behaviour of water (which is also the supremo in specific heats) as it is cooled from about 8°C down through zero can be followed by measuring its volume. The volume reaches a minimum around 4°C, increases a little as the temperature drops to zero, then shoots up as the water turns into ice. Once again the consequences for life on the earth, not only for humans but for fish in ponds, birds and plants give rise to discussion of the value of water's extraordinary perversity.

Class 8 can tackle subtler questions. The differences between mean, mode and median can be learnt. For example suppose the weights in stones of the crew of a rowing eight is as follows:

Cox	6
Stroke	11
No.7	15
No.6	16
No.5	18
No.4	15
No.3	14
No.2	11
Bow	11

A graph could be constructed showing the importance of placing the heaviest oarsmen in the middle of the boat. By adding the nine weights and dividing the total by 9 the average weight or *mean* is found (13 stone).

The *mode* is the commonest weight (11 stone). The *median* is the weight of the person who has 4 people lighter than him and 4 heavier than him in the boat, so the median is 14 stone.

A similar question could be devised for a female crew with the weights suitably reduced. Other questions concerning means, modes and medians

Chapter 9: Statistics and graphs

can be devised, for example having to do with clothing (hat sizes or the prices of swimwear) or farming (cows and their milk yield, or the harvesting of wheat grown under varied conditions in an agricultural research station). Good problems can be taken from industrial manufacturing – car performances (miles per gallon or litre), aeroplane safety records and so on. The information needed is much better found from newspapers and magazines than from textbooks. The punctuality records of members of the class might provide a useful problem in more than one way, and the regularity of attendance in the House of Commons by M.P.s might lead to interesting revelations.

§3. Algebraic graphs

The construction of graphs obeying pure mathematical equations is an entirely different business from those built on statistical data. The qualitative difference is analogous to that obtaining between the parallelograms of velocities and forces in mechanics.[3] In the former we are fully awake, fully conscious of every element in the geometrical process we are engaged in bringing about, but in the latter the empirical data has to be accepted without any participation by our thinking activity in creating the data substance.

The equation, subject of a lot of work in the algebra main lesson in Class 7, now receives pictorial expression. It is good to spend a little time in translating a simple equation into its geometrical form ('little' because equations which are not 'simple' in the technical sense are much more interesting). For example, take the simple equation

$$3(x - 1) = 3 - x$$

Two events (the left and right hand sides of the equation) in which the variable x has taken part are united (al jabr). Each side may be considered separately and its value (y) can be expressed as a formula. $y = 3(x - 1)$ and $y = 3 - x$ are these two formulae. The values of y in each case can be determined as x varies, and the results first tabulated and then graphed.

	x	−1	0	1	2	3
	x − 1	−2	−1	0	1	2
LEFT	y = 3(x − 1)	−6	−3	0	3	6
RIGHT	y = 3 − x	4	3	2	1	0

The sloping lines cross where x = 1.5, which is the solution to the equation (al muqua-balah).

The checking process in this case happens to give 1.5 also for both sides, the value of y at the crossing point.

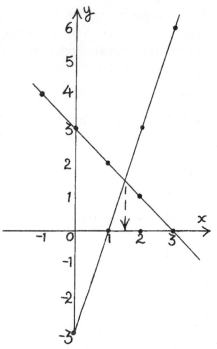

All simple equations give rise to straight line graphs and the points where graphs intersect provide solutions to equations of all kinds. This way of solving equations belongs more to Class 8 and higher classes, but it can be introduced for simple cases as above in Class 7. What is of more interest for Class 7 is the drawing of graphs from slightly more complicated formulae where x² or x³ appears or x appears underneath a fraction line.

An easy example, which already gives a beautiful curve, is y = 10 – x².

A table with x running from –4 through zero to +4 can be worked out, the class having to remember that
 – x – = +.

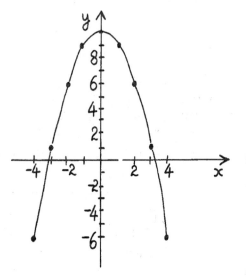

They will learn later in a Class 8 mechanics main lesson why the curve (a parabola) is made by any object thrown through the air.

Chapter 9: Statistics and graphs

As they draw a smooth curve in Class 7 it will remind them of playing tennis or any ball game. Notice that the horizontal and vertical scales need not be the same. Ask the cleverer ones to say exactly where the curve should cross the x – axis. The opportunity arises in graph work to get the weaker boys and girls to just deal with whole number values of x and later obtain answers for decimal values from their quicker peers. The girls will be interested to learn that one of the earliest professors of mathematics a few centuries ago discovered a curve which bears her name to this day, the 'Witch of Agnesi'. The boys, too, will want to find out what kind of curve must be concealed in the equation

$$y = \frac{10}{x^2 + 1}$$

The weaker ones will easily work out y for x values between –3 and +3. Extra points for small x values need calculating to ensure the smooth rounding at the curve top.

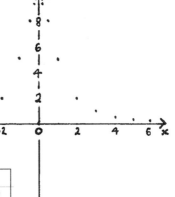

x	0	±1	±2	±3	±4	±5	±.5	±.2	±.1
y	10	5	2	1	.59	.38	8	9.62	9.9

What Professor Agnesi had in mind, of course, was the witches hat. The curve is the younger sister of what will become known in Class 11 as the 'normal curve of error' in relation to the theory of probability, but has the more complicated equation

$$y = e^{-x^2}$$

Other graphs with interesting forms come from the equations

$$y = \frac{4}{x} \quad \text{(a hyperbola)}, \qquad y = x^2 + \frac{1}{x} \quad \text{(a trident)},$$

$$y = \frac{x(x + 2)(x - 3)}{10} \quad \text{(a wavy curve) and}$$

$$y = \frac{x^2(16 - x^2)}{10}, \text{ which is a hill with two humps.}[4]

An easy example for those not yet confident is $y = x^2 + 1$, another parabola, but this time with a valley shape; it is best here to choose a smaller scale on the y-axis than on the x-axis.

Graph paper with cm and mm are alright for measuring cm to 1 d.p. but inches and tenths of an inch enable inches to 2 d.p. to be achieved. In this respect English measure leads to greater drawing accuracy than does Continental measure.

In Class 8 the algebraic solution of linear simultaneous equations can be followed by their graphical solution, perhaps in the following term. Having become convinced through practice that linear equations give straight lines, it is only necessary to plot 2 points in each line. Thus the problem of building the wall in Chapter 7 requires the point of intersection of $7x + 6y = 47$ and $3x - y = 1/2$.

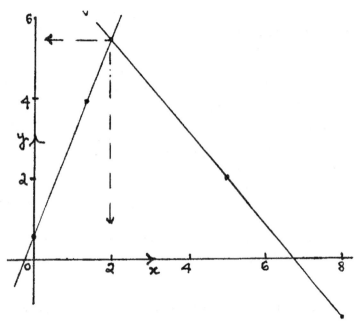

Choosing numbers which make for easy division, although any choice of x or y will do the job, for the first equation, when $y = 2$, $x = 5$; and when $x = 8$, $y = -1.5$; then for the second equation, when $y = 4$, $x = 1.5$; and when $x = 0$, $y = 0.5$.

The graphs cross where $x = 2$ and $y = 5.5$.

Chapter 9: Statistics and graphs

There are three questions concerning the teaching of graphical methods on which concluding comments need to be made:

1. Why should the teacher not go further in class 8 and show how to solve equations with more than one answer?
   This matter has already been dealt with to some extent. Class 9 will be the time for solving quadratic equations. It is at that age, after the 15th birthday, that the psyche of the young person is ready to understand that questions – also in life itself – can have more than one valid answer. It therefore makes sense to leave comparable mathematical questions to that time. However, every group of pupils has its own character, and a teacher may have good reason for showing how for example the equation $x(x - 2)(x - 5) = 5 - 3x$ has 3 possible answers.

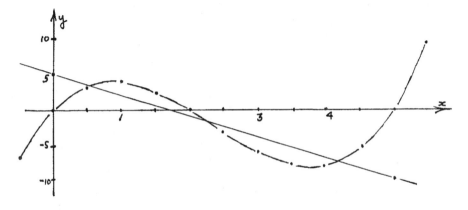

   The left hand side gives the curve plotted at 0.5 x-intervals and the right hand side is a straight line requiring only two points. There are 3 crossing points and therefore 3 answers.

2. Has not the time arrived when inequalities should be introduced, too?
   The same answer applies as above. In the middle period of growing up, the 7 to 14 period, children need authority in a firm but kind sense. They need definite and precise answers, not 'somewhat more than' or 'less than' or 'between this and that'. Understanding inequalities belongs to the next period of maturing.

3. Must we keep to rigid Cartesian co-ordinates in Class 8? The pair of perpendicular axes of measurement serve the adolescent at this time in helping her to become 'earth ripe'. Yet there is again no harm in

introducing bipolar co-ordinates if the occasion warrants it. Some pure geometry in this respect has already been proposed – using 2 pins and a cord to construct an ellipse. The sum of the distances from two points is constant for that curve. So one could develop measuring from 2 points instead of from 2 lines as in ordinary graphs. Instead of a constant sum a constant product could be used.

Take 2 fixed points 12 cm apart. Then find all the points such that the product of their distances from the 2 points is 36 sq.cm. The figure of 8 or lemniscate will appear. With a product less than 36, two ovals would appear, whilst with a product more than 36 a single oval would appear. Keen girls and boys with a flair for this work may gain much by embarking upon a discovery project of this nature. They will, however, meet this family of curves in more detail higher in the school. The curve here is half size.

36 = 6 x 6 = 9 x 4 =12 x 3 = 2.5 x 14.5 = 13 x 2.77 = 14 x 2.57
= 7.25 x 1.25 = 4 x 9 = 3 x 12 etc.

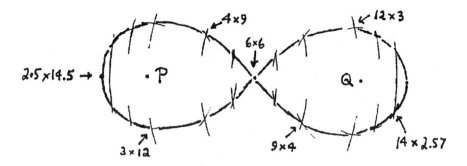

Compass construction (i.e. locus construction) has to be used if specially printed paper is not available. If the distances from P and Q are p and q, the bipolar equation is pq = 36.

Chapter 10:
A summary of a modern Waldorf Curriculum in Mathematics in the 7 to 14 age range

§1. The original curriculum 1919-1925 and subsequent development

The Waldorf school on the Uhlandshöhe (the mother school, as it became known subsequently) was established through the efforts of Emil Molt, head of the Waldorf-Astoria cigarette factory in Stuttgart. It was he who wished to have a school for the children of the workers in his factory and who bought an empty building, previously a restaurant, for this purpose. He invited Rudolf Steiner to address a crowded meeting of employees in the tobacco storeroom, resulting in great enthusiasm for the project. Two days later Steiner returned from a lecture given to workers at the Daimler works in the city and outlined the curriculum he had in mind for the school.

During these last 5 or 6 years of Steiner's life the whole span of children's and young people's education from kindergarten to university entrance was established in this school. Reference to the curriculum in Steiner's lectures and conferences are too numerous to list here, but one of the more important and only just recently published sets was *Three Lectures on the Curriculum*.[1] The most comprehensive and most useful detailed account of curricula in all subjects is that given by Karl Stockmeyer.[2] A shorter book by Caroline Von Heydebrandt on the whole curriculum[3] was based upon the written information submitted by the Waldorf School teachers to the local education department prior to an official government inspection of the school in those early years. The inspection took place at very short notice, however, so there are gaps in curriculum description and somewhat uninformative remarks such as 'In Class 8 mathematics should be continued both theoretically and practically.'

Naturally there have been changes and developments in the curriculum since those days three quarters of a century ago, but one thing has remained essentially the same: the relationship between (a) the phases and topics of the subjects introduced at each age of growing up with (b) the developing and changing nature of the human being itself at each of these ages. This is not merely a comparison of 7 year or 3 year periods, but each chronological year has its own quite particular needs. Many modern educationalists are prone to exaggerate the changes in the nature of childhood over the last seventy years or so. They point to the completely different conditions of life in the modern world, the advent of modern technology, the widespread break-up of family life and the much earlier onset of sexual maturity. People who actually teach children and young people in schools, however, know that this fundamental nature has changed very little. It is true, for example, that little children today have a much greater aptitude for using gadgetry. Knobs and switches present few problems to them. But this is nothing new. Children have always played with little objects in their surroundings. Once, very many of them knew how to obtain milk from the teats of a cow or goat. How many can do that effectively today? Physical sexual maturity may be a little earlier than it was 70 years ago, but have the statisticians taken full account of the differences between the original racial forbears of the children they sample? Sexual maturity in Mediterranean countries, Africa, India and the Caribbean has always been much earlier than in Western Europe, whilst in more northerly climes like Greenland or Siberia the age of physical sexual maturity is later. The infusion of many new British inhabitants from the old overseas Empire and their effect upon the native 'whites' contributes to such research results. But in any case physical maturation is only one part of becoming sexually mature or 'earth ripe'. Children need the love and understanding which each year of life requires, irrespective of whether their parents are married, divorced or even unknown. When technology (including television and tapes, computers and cars) is allowed too much influence upon the growing-up process, significant changes in child nature will come about, but they cannot just be designated as normal, healthy developments in human nature.

The fact that Waldorf School curricula bore many resemblances in the 1950s to those in the early 1920s led many educationalists, training college lecturers and others who do not work in school classrooms, to declare at that time that whilst Steiner schools had been well in advance of other schools in 1930, they were now lagging far behind. In 1990, however, when many schools and local education authorities were hard put to make sense of the

Chapter 10: Summary of mathematics curriculum in 7-14 age range

new ideas contained in the newly-launched English national curriculum, a paper was submitted to the D.E.S. showing how the Waldorf mathematics curriculum answered the majority of the national curriculum requirements. This was welcomed as a fine, informative example – a guideline to other schools on what could be done and how to respond.[4]

All the advances in modern technology are in fact dealt with in Waldorf schools. As petrol and diesel engines developed during the 20th century, so the physics and mechanics curriculum was expanded beyond the steam engine. Typing or stenography, taught in Waldorf schools since 1920, has led to the use of word processors in those lessons in more recent years. The full understanding of telegraph and telephone was regarded as essential in the 1920 Waldorf school. Television and modern communication networks, faxes and internet, computer programming – all these form part of the Waldorf curriculum today. But as always the question has to be asked, 'At *what age* is their introduction healthy and fitting for the chronological age of the students?' Similar curricular developments could be indicated in other subjects such as history, modern molecular biology and foreign languages, though it is worthwhile highlighting the fact that foreign languages have been taught from the age of five in all Waldorf schools since their inception nearly 80 years ago.

What then have been the developments in the mathematics curriculum? First it has to be emphasized that the principal discoveries in mathematics this century – the theories of relativity, quantum mechanics and the chaos theory – are unsuitable for teaching to children under 14 years of age. So too, is anything beyond the simplest kind of statistical analysis. All these things belong to education beyond the age of 14, and will be dealt with in detail in a sequel to the present book. They have their proper place in the education of teenagers from 15 to 18, when independent power of judgment, penetrative analytical faculties and the synthesising ability of human reason have been developed. It is in the third seven-year period of life that thinking really comes into its own.

The tendency to flood schools with computers has been firmly rejected by Waldorf schools. Only in the highest classes are they used and only in good computer laboratories, not in classrooms used for all the usual learning and social purposes. Even hand calculators are not in use before the latter half of Class 9 (age 15). Despite the continuous pressure from manufacturerers and the vigorous exhortations of Margaret Thatcher and her successors, the fact remains that any adult or young person requires little more than a month's training to master the operation of and programming technique needed for a computer. 'Computer literacy' is one of the most fat-headed terms devised in modern times. Home computers, like advanced washing machines, and TV

211

sets in bedrooms, lounges and (fairly soon now perhaps) in toilets, have become status symbols. Until quite recently I used to receive a letter each year requiring TV license payment, with a space in the bill for those without a set. There you were required to say *why the house did not have a TV set in operation!* (Of all the damn nerve!) I always wrote 'TV is shit', and now wonder if my annual use of this four letter word has helped bring about the current deletion of this space on the bill.

All this does not mean, however, that children are not being prepared for the time when they will use computers. Learning arithmetic and algebra and the logical skill in deductive geometry are basic preparations. The intense work on permutations, combinations and the binomial theorem in Class 9 carries this preparation further. Some simple work in set theory (one of the additions made to the maths curriculum of the 1920s) can be taught in Class 7. A simple example given in an earlier chapter was:

$$\{\text{rectangles}\} \cap \{\text{rhombi}\} = \{\text{squares}\}.$$

Number systems can also be introduced in the later Class Teacher years, when everyone in the class knows the multiplication tables in the ordinary denary system thoroughly. When hand calculators come into use in Class 9, the writing down of the sequence of buttons pressed in calculations forms the best preparation for computer programming. It must also be reported here that technical colleges in the neighborhood of some Waldorf schools in England have requested that program language should not be taught in schools, since their experience has been that students from all schools who enter their colleges 'programme literate' have to unlearn all they have learnt and start afresh, due to the ever advancing progress in new computer techniques.

Changes and developments in Waldorf mathematics teaching in the 7 to 14 age range over the years have largely concerned the elaboration of curriculum detail and the extension of 'discovery methods' of learning, although these were already present back in the 1920s. Relationships of mathematical topics to those in other subjects has always had high priority in the holistic education Waldorf schools sustain, but a stronger integration has been achieved over the last 20 to 30 years. Naturally the range of problem examples has widened as technology has advanced and the social conditions in countries in so many parts of the world have undergone change. Geometry teaching has been inspired by the research work in projective geometry achieved by followers of Steiner's work since his death. Examples are cited in the notes at the end of this book.[5] Here again, however, just as with computer technology and chaos theory, the question of when to teach these new aspects of geometry has first to be answered. Projective geometry is

Chapter 10: Summary of mathematics curriculum in 7-14 age range

eminently suited for the upper school. Only a few previews, so to speak, belong to younger classes.

The introduction of envelopes in Class 7 prior to loci in Class 8 is however, an important consequence of the results of this modern research.

§2. The main ingredients, class by class, of the curriculum in mathematics.

It is absolutely not my intention to say 'At this or that age or in this or that class thou shalt teach precisely what is required as hereunder!' Not only do classes of the same age vary in particular abilities and interests, but individual teachers have their own proclivities too. Conformation to norms laid down by the bureaucrats in education offices and enforced by authority of headmasters and headmistresses tends to bring about educational disease and death. Frequent conversation and debate by the teachers in a school and at least twice a year by teachers from many schools in conferences – once purely within a Waldorf context, and once in conferences for teachers from all kinds of schools both within and outside the maintained sector – achieve far more than bureacratic effluent. Mentoring of younger, inexperienced teachers by older experienced ones (not inspectors) in all subjects is becoming a strong aspect and asset of Waldorf schools.

Where a teacher feels that some of the topics suggested below belong to children older than the age indicated, he may well decide to postpone it for a year or so. But he should also realise the danger of having too much to include in a later year if a topic is omitted. Here and there it may be felt that some small topic could be omitted entirely. The individual teacher must in the end be left free to determine what it is best for him to teach his particular class. To reach the end of Class 8 with *crucial* gaps left in the children's mathematical development however, would be a very sorry state of affairs for the teachers of Class 9 to have to (try to) remedy.

Class 1 (6-7 year olds)

a) Experience of straight and curved lines – in bodily posture, by walking along them and through drawing them in colour on the blackboard and on large sheets of paper. Painting and modelling them are also possible.

b) Introduction to whole numbers, proceeding from a whole to its parts (e.g. breaking up a dead stick). Finding where they reveal themselves in the world.

c) Counting – first up to 10, then up to 20, later up to 100. Rhythmic counting using the voice in rhymes, then with straight number names; also through throwing and catching bean bags or balls and especially by using the fingers (and possibly toes, too) to count with. Jumping, skipping, singing, touching various parts of the body, closing the eyes and whispering or shouting, movement round a circle forwards and backwards – these are all further possibilities.

d) Estimating the size of collections, especially of shells, stones and nuts. Playing shop with these objects as currency. Arranging them in groups and patterns.

e) Experience of forms containing straight and curved lines (including letters of the alphabet) by arm movements, leg movements in going round them, finally concentrating on the writing of Roman numerals and later Arabic numerals.

f) Experience of the 4 rules and developing imagination for the invisible third number in each sum – helped both by using fingers and by arranging shells, etc.

g) A lot of mental arithmetic – both orally (e.g. giving answers to incidents in a story told by the teacher) and through writing down just the answers. Games with mental arithmetic.

h) Written arithmetic with the 4 rules, first by writing the results of physically perceptible demonstration-type sums, then going on to the imaginative type, and finally to the purely computational type of sums.

i) Drawing repeating patterns, first on a large scale, later on a small scale.

j) Symmetrical form drawing (but only with a vertical axis of reflection).

k) Free modelling of shapes including flat and curved surfaces.

l) Comparison of lengths and weights, but not by using rulers or pairs of scales, i.e. with the children using their own limbs and bodily strength, both individually and collectively. Skipping ropes and see-saws could be brought into play here.

m) Rhythmic learning by heart of the 2 times, 3 times and 10 times tables; also of number bonds up to a total of 20.

Chapter 10: Summary of mathematics curriculum in 7-14 age range

Class 2 (7-8 year olds)

a) Rhythmic learning by heart the rest of the multiplication tables (up to 12 times) and in many ways: 12 is *three* times 4, *three* 4s are 12, 4 into 12 goes *three*. Rhythmic clapping, speaking, etc of sequences, both forwards and backwards, of sequences like 3 6 9 12..., 7 13 19 25...

b) Intensive mental arithmetic, and practical problems where it has to be used. Use of the familiar terms 'a half of', 'a quarter of', 'the difference between'. Playing shop with money tokens.

c) Written arithmetic in units, tens, hundreds and thousands – with addition, subtraction, short multiplication and short division; all involving 'carrying'.

d) Simple money sums.

e) Development of symmetrical form drawing
    (i) using several shapes on the same paper with one vertical axis of symmetry,
    (ii) extension to horizontal plus vertical axes,
    (iii) with horizontal axis alone.

f) Freehand drawing of various symmetrical shapes – ovals, pentagons, pentagrams and interlacing figures.

g) Experience of the directions of space N, S, E & W.

h) Factor multiplication and division.

i) Predicting the rough answer to a sum before doing it.

j) Translating large numbers into words and vice versa.

Class 3 (8-9 year olds)

a) Long multiplication and long division, remainders of division, checking answers by the reverse process.

b) Estimating approximate answers to the nearest hundred or thousand.

c) Regular practice in oral and written mental arithmetic so that answers to simple sums like 9 × 8 or 'How many 6s in 42?' become instinctive, and 27 + 31 gives rise almost immediately to its answer.

d) The recognition of number patterns in various multiplication tables and in the whole rectangular array of the 144 answers in all the 12 tables.

e) Telling the time on clocks (both analogue and digital) and speeds on speedometers.

f) Musical notation (quavers, minims, etc) and getting the correct number of beats in a bar.

g) Measures of time, liquid capacity, length, rectangular area, weight and wealth, practical manual work (cupfuls of water in a bucketful, modelling buildings, etc. preceding numerical problems). Estimating results before confirmation by measurement and calculation.

h) Problems about measures written in words and sentences.

i) Shopping lists and money calculations. Obtaining the correct change.

j) Freehand drawing of more complicated line symmetries and rotational symmetries. Mirror picture games. Awareness of right angles (perpendicularity).

k) Experience of the directions upward-downward in relation to (i) North, South, East and West, (ii) forwards, backwards and sideways.

Class 4 (9-10 year olds)

a) The life of number. Factors and prime numbers.

b) Abundant, deficient and perfect numbers. The number 360.

c) Fractions – vulgar (ordinary) and improper – and mixed numbers. Reducing fractions to their lowest terms.

d) The four rules applied to fractions, but taken separately and not combined. Best order of introduction: of, times, divided by, plus, minus.

e) Decimals as a particular case of fractions. Extension of all processes with the four rules on whole numbers to decimal calculations.

f) Money calculations with decimal notation, including foreign currency. Finding costs from catalogues.

g) Decimals in the whole metric system. Using rulers to measure in various units. Estimation of distances and weights.

h) Learning to draw accurate freehand circles and dividing them by eye judgment into 12, 16 or 20 parts. Deriving regular figures like pentagon and hexagon from them.

i) Asymmetrical symmetries. Artistic and geometrical design.

Class 5 (10-11 year olds)

a) Going backwards mentally with arithmetical operations and finding simple ways of applying rules to one number to obtain another number.

b) Mixed calculations with fractions up to examples like $6^{1}/_{2} \div (8^{1}/_{2} - 6^{5}/_{8})$.

c) The conversion of fractions into decimals and vice versa.

d) The presence of zeros in multiplying and dividing (with decimals, too). Estimating results to the nearest unit or hundred, etc.

e) Practice in the 'rule of three' or unitary method, with practical problems involving length, money, etc.

f) Triangular and square numbers.

g) Pie charts. The division of a complete revolution into 360 parts. The use of protractors.

h) Understanding map references and the ability to read scales – also in electricity meters showing consumption.

i) Skill in the use of compasses & ruler. The 7 circle net and its developments. Large, coloured and accurate drawings exhibiting the relationships between triangles, quadrilaterals, polygons and circles.

j) Accurate drawing and cut-outs to appreciate Pythagoras' theorem, but without any theory.

k) The construction of simple line envelopes.

Class 6 (11–12 year olds)

a) Percentages. Their conversion into fractions and decimals and vice versa.

b) Profit and loss. Simple interest. The 3 uses of money (purchase, loan and gift).

c) Algebraic formulae, substitution of numbers in them, beginning with
$$I = \frac{PRT}{100}$$
and proceeding to other formulae in commerce, geometry, physics, etc.

d) The four rules illustrated in algebra.

e) Block graphs and pictograms.

f) Geometrical constructions: line and angle bisection, right angles, parallel lines, the construction of triangles.

g) Construction of regular polygons, using compasses, protractors or 'trial and error' methods.

h) The beginning of exact deductive geometry, especially that of the angles of a triangle adding up to 180° Many numerical problems on angle geometry.

i) Further large scale geometrical drawing, including linear and circular envelopes.

j) Congruent triangles and simple applications to proofs.

Class 7 (12–13 year olds)

a) Recurring decimals. Later on the value of π. Full understanding and comparison of decimal places and significant figures.

Chapter 10: Summary of mathematics curriculum in 7-14 age range

b) Simple equations, including brackets, fractions and negative numbers. Their practical application to solving problems.

c) Making and transforming formulae.

d) Calculation of the areas of figures bounded by straight lines and circular arcs.

e) Powers and roots of numbers. The exact evaluation of square roots.

f) Deduction of the theorem of Pythagoras. Its numerical application to problems in engineering, navigation, etc.

g) Types of quadrilateral and their symmetries, leading to simple set theory, and the intersection of sets.

h) Construction of triangles having the same area as polygons.

i) More advanced envelope constructions.

j) Compound interest.

k) Transformations of plane figures, especially from square to general quadrilateral, leading to simple perspective drawing.

l) Simple statistical data rendered in graphical form and deductions therefrom.

m) Algebraic graphs of straight lines and simple curves.

n) Ratio and proportion.

Class 8 (13–14 year olds)

a) Identities and their use in arithmetical short cuts. The commutative, associative and distributive laws in algebra. The factors of the difference between two squares and the application of this to practical problems.

b) Volumes of rectangular blocks, pyramids, prisms, cylinders and cones. Density and the weights of solid objects.

c) Simultaneous linear equations and problems.

d) The dissolution of complex brackets in algebraic expressions.

e) The construction of loci. Angle properties of the circle locus.

f) The construction of the 5 regular (Platonic) solids, and drawing orthogonal projections of them. Euler's Law. The golden ratio.

g) Properties of the main centres of a triangle.

h) Perspective drawing of cubes and 3D structures. The construction of shadows in perspective.

i) Further examinations of statistical data. Mean, mode and median.

j) Graphs of more complicated curves. The solution of linear simultaneous equations by graphs.

k) A brief look at balance sheets and mortgages.

l) Number systems. Binary arithmetic and a brief look at the arithmetical unit of a computer.

m) Similar figures, especially triangles.

§3. How much time needs to be allocated to mathematics in school and in homework?

In the original Waldorf school in Stuttgart the mathematics main lesson allocation was

>   1st to 5th school years : 12 weeks each,
>   6th to 8th school years : 10 weeks each.[6]

In addition, from the 6th school year onwards, one hour each week within the framework of main lessons other than mathematics was given for mathematics repetition and practice.

Chapter 10: Summary of mathematics curriculum in 7-14 age range

Since those days, 70 to 80 years ago, changes have been made. The most important reason for change in this country was the abandonment during the course of the 1950s of Saturday morning school. In addition to this, many Waldorf schools reduced the time allocated for main lesson from two hours to one hour fifty minutes or even less. Some compensation was made by adding, after the mid-morning break, two 40-minute 'extra main lessons' each week for Classes 1 to 6, and using them for mathematics when a main lesson block in mathematics was not current. For classes 6 to 8 three 'extra main lessons' were added. Other main lessons were then no longer obliged to include an hour a week for repetition and practice in mathematics. It is easy to calculate that these changes kept the total time in the year given to mathematics very nearly as much as originally. It is equivalent to 4 hours per week averaged over the whole school working year.

Another variation from the original timetable has been to have 12 weeks of mathematics main lesson per year for *every* class from 1 to 8, and have just two 'extra main lessons' for every class as well. The advantage of this is that a main lesson block of 4 weeks in each of 3 terms in the year can be taken in the subject.

It should also be remembered that, in holistic education, a little mathematics will frequently come into other main lessons, and vice versa.

To sum up, with the modern five day week the allocation is

1st to 5th school years : 12 weeks (3 x 4) each in main lesson blocks plus two 40-minute weekly periods,

6th to 8th school years : either as above or 10 weeks (2 x 5 or 3 + 3 + 4) in main lesson blocks, plus three 40-minute weekly periods.

Besides these 'contact' hours with the teacher the question arises about how much homework children should be expected to do. This is a question which applies to every subject taught. Up to the end of Class 5, any kind of formal homework is of very doubtful value. The important thing for children under the age of 12 is to go home after school and enjoy work and play in the house or in the fresh air outside, along with parents and/or siblings and friends. Some people assert that a particular value of homework is that it reduces the time children spend watching the box. Negative views of this kind contribute nothing to a positive nurturing of education.

However, suggestions can be made to children to do things at home on a voluntary basis, things which have a real appeal to the younger ones. 'Some of you might like to take your books home today and show your parents what you have done in school and then you could take the next page and make a lovely coloured picture of the story.' A foreign language teacher might suggest that some in the class might like to make a few simple pictures to do with words or phrases or simple sentences they remember in the new language. In the next lesson that teacher could tell those children who produced drawings how to write a few of the words they remembered below them. In a Class 3 a teacher could say 'If anyone would like to have a go at another of those discovery sums, where you choose your own number times itself to start with, I'd love to see what you've done when you come tomorrow.'

By Class 4 and Class 5 the children may well ask if they can take their books home to write or draw a bit more in them or perhaps add a poem they have come across – or even compose one. In mathematics a bright child may want to prove by listing factors and adding that 8128 is a perfect number.[7] Once compasses are in use in Class it will take very little encouragement for many to go home and return with most interesting geometrical drawings. The development of initiative born of enthusiasm in these years is of far greater educational value than a teacher setting a class formal homework. Some children will collect berries and leaves or mosses and shells and make an exhibition in an empty shoe box, then bring it to school in a botany or geography main lesson. How much better this is than having to react to 'Tonight you have all got to do this for homework....'!

When children have crossed the Rubicon of the 12th year, however, they require definite tasks set for homework. In Class 6 history they have left the age of Greece and its myths and learn about Roman civilisation, where precise instructions and orders were needed to build aqueducts, and clear procedures were required by senators. At the beginning of Class 6, after a meeting advising parents of what is afoot, half an hour's homework once a week can be required of the class. Parents could be asked to see that the time taken did not exceed an hour, but also that it was a quiet and concentrated half hour, uninterrupted by food or the sound of TV from the next room. During Class 6 homework can be gradually extended to half an hour a day for all five school days in the week. The daily homework ration can be increased to 45 minutes in Class 7 and to one hour in Class 8. Homework over the five days is often distributed in Waldorf school as follows: two days on main lesson work, one on each of two foreign languages and one on mathematics (or on English during a maths main lesson). In still higher classes the daily homework time will increase still further.

Chapter 10: Summary of mathematics curriculum in 7-14 age range

Whether written homework is done in exercise books or on A4 paper will depend on the subject and the teacher's own preference. The essential thing is that it be done neatly and with good handwriting, in ink. When the results of homework are offered to the teacher next day it is wise to refuse to accept anything not meeting these requirements. Parents and guardians need to be informed at once, as theirs is the responsibility to ensure legible, tidy and also punctual homework. It is not a teacher's responsibility to supervise what is done in the home.

When mathematical homework is set, it is best to set sufficient for the brightest in the class to occupy themselves for the whole time allocated. Weaker pupils can be told that they will not be expected to answer all the questions, but the class teacher will know what constitutes sufficient work from them, as will the pupils themselves in consequence of the teacher's subsequent comments to them.

Chapter 11:
Looking Forward – to the Upper School and beyond

§1. Upper School Work

Although, as we have already seen, it is the activity of thinking which becomes the soul captain's principal lieutenant in the third phase of growing up – roughly between the ages of 14 and 21 – all three parts of soul activity nevertheless develop strongly during this later phase. As the teenager's own astral body is born, he has to experience and overcome an inner soul chaos as he learns to look in a new way at everything in the world and in himself.

In mathematics as well as in other subjects, the Class Niner wants to experience everything afresh. He welcomes the change from having a class teacher to being taught each subject by someone who has worked to become an expert in it, assisted by the rigours of a university degree and life experience. Teachers in their twenties and thirties are often the best people to teach young people of Upper School age. The Class Niner wants to be shown anew how you do addition sums and long divisions for example, but now in a fully conscious way, grasping the reasons for each whim of written layout. No longer is the underlying aim to receive the teacher's tick at the end of one's calculations. The pupil wants to be able to know *himself* whether or not his answers are correct. The authority of the individual teacher is replaced by experience of, and guidance by the truth itself. Despite the obvious lies, half-truths, deceptions and hypocrisies in the world and in the young person's immediate environment, he wants above all to find those realms where he can assert and experience that *the world is true*.[1] As a young child he needed assurance that the world is fundamentally good. Between roughly 7 and 14 he needed confirmation that the world is beautiful. Already basically strengthened in will and feeling respectively, he now needs this third guarantee to help him find the earthly home for his own individuality.

The human individuality is neither male nor female and it is sickening that anti-sexist propagandists have no notion of the difference between contexts where 'he' and 'she' are used to distinguish between the sexes and contexts where 'he' is used in a general human sense. Perhaps they do not know what 'individuality' means. Presumably they would use 'it' as a pronoun for the human individual as such. Teenagers, however, in contrast to these adult 'its' are fully aware of the difference mentioned.

A recent directive to employees of the American Department of Agriculture's Research Service states that animals will continue to be known as bulls, cows, roosters, hens, etc., but people are people, not men or women. No sexist language will be permitted. It would be wrong to write that an 'employee is to use his personally owned vehicle.' The right thing to write would be that 'an employee is to use their personally owned vehicle.' This was reported in the Washington Post, Sept 1, 1996.

The only way to solve the problem would appear to be the complete jettisoning of the rules of grammar. In the final chapters the expressions 'boys or girls', 'girls or boys', 'young man or woman' and 'young women or men' have already been thrown overboard and the reader will be credited with the ability to distinguish between contexts in which the word 'he' is used.

'Thinking', said Rudolf Steiner, 'is the all-one being that permeates everything.'[2] There are four stages in the development and strengthening of the activity of thinking and they correspond in a remarkable way to the path running through Classes 9, 10, 11 and 12.

In **Class 9** the emphasis a teacher can lay is on *contrasts*. Awareness of contrasts leads to the consciousness in which thinking can grow. In art lessons the best medium is black (charcoal sticks or paint brushes) on white paper. The physics of electromagnetism will contrast the power unit of an electric train with that of the telephone ear-piece. The principle is the same in both, but the contrast in current is enormous.

The first could be described as allopathic electricity and the second as homeopathic electricity. Contrasts in other subjects are between drama and comedy, plate tectonics and volcanoes, Olympic gymnastics and country dancing. At the same time there are strong common elements. In mathematics there is the contrast between permutations and combinations, which is isomorphic to that between melody and harmony in music. In geometry the conic sections ellipse and hyperbola are contrasted, and comparison can be made between these and the respective form and function relationship between head and limbs. In addition there is the intermediate chest and rhythmic system, represented above by the parabola, so that the metamorphosis in both groups can be made apparent.

Chapter 11: Looking forward – to the upper school and beyond

In **Class 10**, pairs of contrasts and their inter-action carries the thinking awareness a stage further. Ancient history in this class culminates in a careful study of Greek civilisation and the Socratic dialogues. The Pythagorean-Platonic description of the four elements in terms of the two contrasts moist-dry and warm-cold is part of this, and much of the mathematics developed from this, described in Chapter 1, can be used. Geometric constructions of the four basic spirals (Archimedean, Equiangular, Reciprocal and Asymptotic Circle) illustrate the 4 progressions of numbers arising therefrom, and how they indicate a progression from material to noetic aspects of the world. It is *independent judgment* that evolves in Class 10. Perhaps the prime example of this is in trigonometry. To be able to stand far away from a mountain, take three measurements and then be able to calculate the mountain's height without becoming involved in climbing it, exemplifies the particular ingredient of human intelligence required to make an objective judgment unfettered by personal feelings of involvement – which would be difficult for Class Niners to achieve.

By **Class 11** the young people are ready to plunge into greatest detail in everything they study, whether it be the history of music (one of the main lessons they have), the story of Parzival and its significance, atomic theory, the theory of organic cellular structure, or computer technology. It is the year when *analysis* is the key word. So in mathematics differential calculus is introduced. Also in geometry the fundamental theorem of projective geometry is proved and made use of – the same kind of procedure towards smaller and finally infinitesimal parts is required to do this. At the same time the principle of duality shows how the importance of point-like entities must be complemented by the equally valid and important planar entities which structure and shape the plant and organic world as a whole. The intellect can become finely honed at this age as well as developing an awareness of the noetic dimensions of life.

The final school year **(Class 12)** gives the young people an opportunity to gather together the many results obtained through analysis and experience, and discover the higher unities as true progenitors. Intellect has prepared the ground for reason. Analysis gives way to *synthesis*. The many points of view which scientific and artistic work have revealed help to form the indispensable modesty and wonder which every student requires in beginning to build his own view of the nature both of the world in which he lives and of what being human really means. He becomes aware that he possesses a unique individuality and that it will suffer rust and tarnishing if he allows it to become infused with mere egotism. He will seek a higher synthesis of himself with the best that human society endeavours to achieve. So in physics Class 12 concentrates on understandinq the whole world of colour. The diverging scientific descriptions of Newton, Goethe, Ostwald and others have to be evaluated and their contributions to the whole subject synthesised, yet not fully determined – only adult life will provide the experiences needed to do that. Renaissance and modern painting, which together with architecture figure in another main lesson, will further succour such endeavours.

Class 12 mathematics is again concerned with synthesis. Differential calculus gives rise to integral calculus. Human reason can now grasp the chaos theory and fractals. Earthly geometry (what used to be called Euclidean geometry) is seen to be but a limited part of a Projective Euclidean (or parabolic) geometry, which is only one of a whole host of geometries, e.g. hyperbolic, elliptic and polar Euclidean geometries, all of which have their own forms of measurement, be it of distance or angle. Practice in working with money in three different ways back in Class 6 now grows into a deep study of economics; and the realisation dawns in Class 12 that the problems of world economy will never be solved until a far more holistic approach to them is made than the world has so far managed to evolve.[3]

A summary of the mathematics curriculum in Classes 9-12 now follows. Description of details, methods and examples must await a sequel to the present book.

Brief Summary of Main Topics in Mathematics

Class 9 – Revision and practice of everything learnt in earlier classes, followed by the introduction and practice of hand calculators.
– Permutations, combinations and the binomial theorem leading to (i) the solution of quadratic equations and problems, (ii) approximations. Further properties of the circle in relations to similar triangles.
– Sections of right circular cones, using plan and elevations, leading to properties of conic sections (eccentricity, focal properties). Other constructions of conic loci and envelopes; their graphs. Foreign currencies and rates of exchange. Discount and tax.

Class 10 – Trigonometry – the six ratios; the solution of right-angled triangles, then the general triangle using Sine and Cosine laws. Graphs. Surveying and the application of trigonometry to practical problems in navigation, civil engineering and astronomy.

Chapter 11: Looking forward – to the upper school and beyond

- Proficiency in the use of calculators. Writing down the program used following numerical calculations performed upon them.
- The four progressions of numbers, related spiral forms and geometrical homologies (translations and shears, enlargements and affinities, elations) following the projective proof of Desargue's Theorem.
- Fractional, negative and zero powers. The concept of logarithm.
- Some 'new maths' – Venn diagrams, inequalities and programming.

Class 11
- Matrices and their application to arithmetical computation and the algebra of projective geometry transformations. Vectors.
- The exponential theorem and series. Graphs of e^x and log x.
- Imaginary and complex numbers. The use of e and i in trigonometry. Latitude and longitude trigonometry.
- The differentiation of polynomials.
- The fundamental theorem in projective geometry and the consequent theorems of Pappus, Pascal and Brianchon. The principles of continuity and duality.
- Large scale drawings of curves and their duals. Practical constructions of reguli using long rods to illustrate the fundamental theorem. Simple computer programming.

Class 12
- Further differentiation and its application to turning points of graphs, kinematics and biological growth factors.
- Integration and its application to the calculation of areas and volumes. The theory of probability and its uses. Introduction to the theory of numbers.
- De Moivre's theorem. Transcendental and superimaginary numbers.
- The different geometrics (Euclidean, Elliptic, etc) and their measures. The construction of path curves and their manifestation in plants, animals and human beings.
- The beginnings of analytical geometry.
- A history of mathematical development through the ages.
- Computer oriented work on chaos theory and fractals.

It is important in these older classes just as in the younger classes that every student gains a clear impression of what all the above topics have to do with. The range of mathematical ability will now be much wider, of course, and the difference in difficulty of problems set for more able and less able students will become much greater. None the less the social value of keeping all school students of the same chronological age in the same main lesson block is far reaching. The whole class will experience together the basic qualities of the various topics and their relevance to a wide range of human activities in life – all this in perhaps the initial half hour each day. Then the individual work of students and group work of some of them will follow different directions, some manual, practical and artistic, others of an advanced mathematical, analytical and also synthesising character.

> In many British Waldorf schools the full curriculum has had to be curtailed for many years in Classes 11 and 12 because of the need to sit for state examinations. Despite the cramping effect on their education these restrictions have produced, Waldorf schools pupils have done well at G.C.S.E. and A levels in all subjects. In several other countries Waldorf school students from Class 12 have been accepted direct into universities without having to sit these examinations; and this is becoming increasingly possible as the capacity of these Waldorf students becomes more recognised. In addition to many countries on the continent this is happening in Australia and America and may soon happen in our own European off-shore islands, too. The detailed reports of teachers, along with the projects submitted by students – projects on all kinds of subjects and often of a very high standard – will, it is hoped, begin to persuade universities here to adopt similar procedures towards students which Waldorf schools recommend to them. Then the full Waldorf curriculum in Classes 11 and 12 can be resumed here as well.

As an example of Class 11 geometry, this section of the chapter will conclude with a drawing exercise which students found inspiring. It is the construction of the dual of a freely drawn curve inside a circle. The points on the curve give rise to lines outside the circle. They envelope a new curve. The circle is not drawn as a full line, because the actual circle of reciprocation has an imaginary radius (5i). The shapes of the curves call to mind a Christmas theme, so one year this was used as a Christmas card bearing the following verse.

Chapter 11: Looking forward – to the upper school and beyond

Gabriel hov'ring in moon sphere
Came to bless our Mary mild,
Who upon the earth-made crib
Will lay her blessed child.

Borne as from a dove the Grail
Shines into the chalice round.
Imbued by the sphere of archangels
May Christ-courage in us all be found.

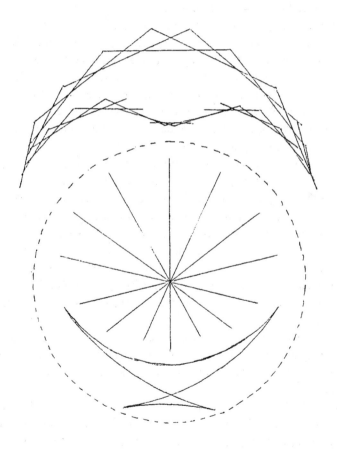

§2. Mathematics and Initiation

In Chapters 1 and 2 the nature of mathematics was described. Pure mathematics is a realm of pure truth. It can be distorted and defiled neither by the physical material world on the one hand nor by cynical or nihilistic criticism appearing in the consciousness of soul-deaf or spiritually blind people on the other hand. The way in which mathematical thinking has been employed in past ages to help reach deeper or more universal domains of existence, for example in the school of Pythagoras, was also indicated in the first chapter. Such contemplations enable us to broaden our vision and sense that we participate in a much more holistic world than we may have previously realised.

Yet, justifiably, many people retain a certain residual doubt about how healthy it is to bring the results of mathematics to bear upon practical life situations. If mathematical technology had not been developed to the level it reached earlier this century, we should not have had the atomic bomb. The computer, brainchild of mathematical geniuses, could become our master instead of our servant. The danger people can feel is that a heartless, completely logical activity born in human heads lacks the warmth and friendly intimacy which a truly human existence requires. Not only human society but the very earth with its fresh mountain air, its colourful plant covering and animal symphony, is endangered by mankind's preoccupation with mathematics and its application.

'No, no! You can't blame us for pollution, bombs, computer addiction and so on. That criticism must be addressed to physicists and other scientists,' may reply the pure mathematicians. In turn physicists, chemists etc. will pass on the blame to politicians, who in turn will cite the electorate who gave them or their opponents the powers of decision in the first place. A lot of ordinary people nowadays will voice doubt as to whether voting in elections decides anything and suggest that there are people and powers behind the scenes who make the real decisions, not discredited politicians, not tunnel-blind scientists, not even mathematicians living in cloud-cuckoo land.

The source of mathematics is, however, neither in the clouds nor in anything physical. Of its existence there can be no doubt. 'Today we know with absolute certainty that mathematical concepts are *free creations of the human mind.*' writes Unger.[4]

In the course given to scientists just referred to,[5] Steiner drew attention to the following. Consider our human breathing process. We breathe in life-giving oxygen. The lungs pass on its freshness and vitality to the arterial blood and also cleanse the venous blood of its carbon. We then breathe out carbon dioxide, which is not life-giving but death-giving. These things are essential for our existence upon the earth. Carbon is the simple chemical name for what was once known as the philosopher's stone. It has many forms. Coal, graphite and diamond are three of them.

But this whole process may be compared with what happens when we apply mathematics to the world of nature. We observe what occurs in the world outside us and take these perceptions into ourselves. Here we unite these perceptions with what we have constructed within our own souls – the edifice of mathematics. Then the pure mathematics is embodied within applied mathematics. We construct the laws of the world outside and apply them. In this manner the whole of modern technology arises and we rightly marvel at this achievement.

Yet we have to be cautious. The modern scientist of optics and chromatics will tell us that our experience of yellowness is simply that of light whose wavelength is 5875.6 Angstrom or 0.000058756 cm. This is fine for technology, but when you ponder these numbers you have to ask, 'Where then, has the radiance, the outward shining and joyful quality of yellowness gone to?' This vital essence of yellowness has in a certain sense had to be killed to allow the promotion of technical efficiency.

Perception of the world (all manner of sense perception – sound, smell, taste, etc as well as of light and colour) bring life into our whole being, just as oxygen does when we breathe in. Mathematics is like carbon. We unite it with our sense perceptions, permeate them with the mathematical and so evolve applied mathematics and proceed to practical control over the material world. But this is like carbon dioxide formation. We bring death to the previously life-giving freshness of perceived phenomena.

Surely this cannot be the whole story. The sequence ending in death is as inevitable as that our own lives have to end in death. Technology is essential for fully modern life. Yet may there not be some refinement in the middle of the process that enables us to end up with a new, revivified result? Steiner pointed to the wholly dark colour of many forms of carbon and also to the possibility of transforming the substance into wholly translucent diamond form. Modern technical advances enable the production of artificial diamonds through pressure and heat to be carried out relatively easily nowadays.

Suppose it were possible to transform the content of the mathematical so that a death-giving activity (when applied to physical sense perception) could become a new life-giving one, a resurrection. The great Christian ethic is the path from crucifixion to resurrection. Can the graphite-like mathematics be turned into a diamond-like mathematics, through which another kind of light can shine? It would not be an easy kind of light to gaze into. Diamonds, too, are difficult to look through, they have an extaordinarily high refractive index (2.417 compared to 1.333 for water and 1.5 for crown glass).

Pure mathematics is something virgin, freely creative in us. The question at stake is how and where it is applied. In its purely quantitative aspect it is entirely apposite for the material world. But it has a purely qualitative side as well. Familiarity with the qualitative aspect has been one of the aims of the mathematics teaching sketched in the previous chapters of this book, but the quantitative is equally important in preparing children for their future work in life. It is by working further at the qualitative within the mathematical that perceptions of wholly spiritual realms can be achieved (see Appendix). Such perceptions are unlike the normal subject-object confrontations we experience in ordinary life. In these new perceptions we find ourselves at one with what we perceive, we become active within what we experience, yet retain awareness that we remain individual selves – in contradiction to many practices of Eastern origin where the self dissolves into the universal spirit essence.

Let it not be imagined that success along the path being indicated leads to some new kind of algebra by which the activity of angels, archangels and all sorts of gods can be cognised and explained, or that the forms of Elohim or Devas, nymphs or satyrs can be geometrically determined. The actual mathematics undergoes a metamorphosis and becomes an inner faculty of orientation. In the physical world the law of separation and distinctness in space operates. If my friend chooses to sit on a particular chair at table for a meal, I must choose a different chair. Two humans cannot occupy the same space at the same time.

In real spiritual realms, on the other hand, the situation is completely different. Not only do many beings occupy the same space at the same time, but time is no longer a linear flow from past via present to future. Time there has 2 dimensions. The linear aspect we know in ordinary life is just one section cut in a vast canvas. Orientation in spiritual time is no less important than that in (spiritual) space.

A Steiner school in Australia regularly takes children of an appropriate age into part of the Great Australian Desert and deposits them there with food, drink, compass, clothing and canvas, leaving them to find their own way back to civilisation. Naturally provision is made for finding quickly anyone who gets lost. The skill of orientation thus developed is not unlike that which a transformed, qualitative mathematics renders in spiritual realms. For it is no longer mathematics in the way we normally understand the word.

§3. Astronomy

A brief survey of a curriculum in astronomy follows below. It is in keeping with the holistic integration of all subjects in a Steiner school. Whilst it is not part of the mathematics curriculum as such, there is naturally an overlap. Some of this has already been indicated and in higher classes the linking will become stronger. The reason for including this in the last chapter lies in the intimate relationship between the history of mankind's development and widening consciousness. A survey of this relationship will follow to conclude the chapter.

Class 1. Awareness of where the sun is whilst coming to school and whilst going home. The directions in which it rises and sets.

Class 2. The changing path of the sun (higher and lower zeniths) during the course of the year. The 4 seasons.

Class 3. The course of the moon. Its phases in relation to sunrise and sunset. Waxing and waning. When to plant seeds to obtain optimum germination.

Class 4. Eclipses. How to tell where the sun is below the horizon by looking at the moon's shape. Animal life and tides in relation to the moon's phases (e.g. the spawning of fish).

Class 5. The diurnal and annual movement of the Plough. The polestar. The relationship between mythologies and star constellations. The paths of sun and moon through the zodiac. Botany (analogies of form: simple Mercury path – monocotyledon; and Venus path – dicotyledon): flowers and geometry with compasses.

Class 6. Learning the main or great star constellations in the Northern or Southern hemisphere according to the school's latitudinal position. Construction of a simple cardboard planisphere to show the movements of the constellations learnt.

Class 7. The slow change of the Vernal point in the Zodiac. The planets, their revolution periods and angular sidereal movements. The telescope. Brightness, colour and moons of the planets. Geocentric and heliocentric conceptions. (In this class a whole main lesson block can be used to develop the subject of astronomy.)

Class 8.   The Milky Way, star clusters and variable stars. Shooting stars. The speed of light effects. Simple theory of distance calculations (sun, moon and planets; then 'light years'). The present limits of cosmos exploration by (i) astronauts, (ii) space probes. The relationship between the history of civilisations on earth and the occupancy by the vernal point of succeeding zodiacal constellations and their symbolism. (Parts of all this can be distributed among history, physics, geometry and geography main lesson blocks.)

In the upper (or high) school greater detail of astronomy is gone into and will include cosmogonies, parallax, red shifts, black holes, radio telescopes, the deficiencies of science fiction and the claims of astrology, path curve geometry and the exact scientific correspondence, between moon-planet conjunctions and oppositions and plant bud shapes (λ values). There will naturally be opportunities for individual project work where one or more aspects of the above can be targeted and possibly in wider contexts, e.g. embracing music, poetry, folklore, botany or zoology.

When they are old enough, walks into the countryside at night time far from the glare of street lights will be made in order to allow the young people to experience the starry dome of the heavens. Camping out, bivouacking and night orienteering will increase the intimacy of such experience. Visits to observatories can be arranged, too. Second-hand yet useful pictorial-diagrammatic representations of the stars can be studied in Classes 11 and 12 via videos, computer screens and visits to planetaria. As a balance to the achievements of modern technology, a class could learn to recite Walt Whitman's poem (from *Leaves of Grass and Democratic Vistas*):

> *When I heard the learn'd astronomer,*
> *When the proofs, the figures, were ranged*
> > *in columns before me,*
> *When I was shown the charts and diagrams, to add,*
> > *divide and measure them,*
> *When I, sitting, heard the astronomer where he*
> > *lectured with much applause in the lecture-room,*
> *How soon unaccountable I became tired and sick,*
> *Till rising and gliding out I wandered off by myself,*
> *In the mystical moist night-air, and from time to time,*
> *Looked up in perfect silence at the stars.*

Chapter 11: Looking forward – to the upper school and beyond

Over the ages our human understanding of the heavens has changed many times, but as far as what can be seen with our eyes is concerned, the arrangement of stars in the various constellations has undergone only a gradual change. If we were transported back to a time before ancient Egyptian civilisation, we would not recognise a plough shape in the Great Bear constellation. The excellent atlas by Readers Digest gives a good picture of these gradual changes. Yet an early Egyptian might well have referred to that position of the sky by the same name: Great Bear. For animal names for constellations were never given as a result of joining up numbered star points by lines on an imagined sketch – in the way shapes are fabricated as a (rather uninspiring kind of) game in some books produced for young children today. Constellation names arose in a quite different way. Shepherds lying down to sleep in the open fields with their sheep would often end their slumber with a dream. On awakening they would remember the different animals which had appeared in those dreams. At the same time, their eyes would open to behold the group of stars above them.

Recurrence of the kind of animals dreamt about, along with the same star groups they woke up to, led them to associate animal names with the corresponding constellations. This didn't simply happen with one or another shepherd. The experience was shared by many shepherds, both within particular tribes and between different ones; such experiences were confirmed by the priests or priest-kings and the constellation-names proclaimed in the language of the land. There was, in other words, a common kind of dream-perception which 'tuned in' to an actual quality of the star-groups.

That this could happen in those far off times was due to the quite different kind of consciousness people had. They were instinctively much more closely bound up with each other in their memories and habits, and lacked the individual or ego awareness common today, possessing instead an awareness of tribe and ancestors. It somewhat resembled what we can observe in animals as herd instinct. The inhabitants of a large area who spoke a common language shared a *group soul* from which they received direction, rather than acting as independent personalities. Another example drawn from the animal kingdom is that of a flight of birds. As they sweep across the sky, wheel, swoop and move in a new direction notice how the apparent leader of the flight gives way to the leadership of another bird and soon there is yet another leader. But there is no battle about which 'individual' shall lead, and the real driver or source of intelligence is the invisible group soul, within which all the separate birds are contained.

Distinct from the matter of naming star groups, and of their changing visible patterns over millennia, is the question of how people pictured the sun's *movement* in relation to the earth on which they lived. The following sketch comes from a cave drawing in what is now Iran dating from a period about 8000 years ago, and illustrates the kind of consciousness people had.

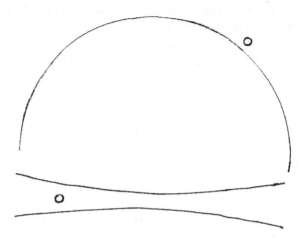

Two suns are depicted. On high, the daytime sun has passed the zenith and is beginning to sink towards the West. After setting, the sun proceeds through a tunnel. The lower sun shows the position shortly before dawn when a new 'launch' will take place. The half circle, however, has the shape of a skull bone and the tunnel, narrower in the middle, has the shape of a limb bone. The outside of the skull bone and the inside of the limb bone correspond. We can contemplate how our heads have a hard bone surrounding a soft space, while our limbs have soft flesh surrounding hard bones; and also that our thinking and our will are mainly focused on head and limbs respectively, revealing opposing qualities of light and dark, wakefulness and sleep. What we can think in clear thoughts today was, in the far distant past, sensed only dreamily, in a kind of intensely felt dream-thinking. This very different consciousness allowed people an intuitive grasp of their own bodily structure, right down to their bones, and of the contrasts between the more sleeping and more wakeful part of their own organism.

By the time Greek civilisation had become well established, consciousness had developed to the point of conceiving the earth to be in movement as well as the sun. The human legs lived in movement, so did the earth on which they rested. During a whole year the sun moved once round the complete zodiac whilst the earth (now experienced as a sphere) turned once right round its axis relative to the stars of the night and the sun of the day.

For Pythagoras (550 B.C.) the centre of all this movement was neither in the sun nor in the earth but lay in a point between the two. Hidden behind the sun and balancing our earth on this side lay 'anti-earth', through which departed souls passed when released from their tasks here. Dream consciousness had thus been replaced by one bearing a geometrical clarity. Earth and sun moved round a 'central fire', a balancing point, just as head activity and leg activity were balanced by a liberated limb activity – that of the arms, which expressed feeling life through gestures.

The development of pictures of the cosmos, especially those concerning the relationship of earth to the great life-giving sun, took different forms in different cultures. Even in the centuries of Greek culture, ideas about earth-sun relationships changed relatively quickly. By 280 BC Aristarchus had propounded an elementary heliocentric astronomy with the sun at the centre of the universe, yet by 150 A.D. Ptolemy's astronomy had placed the earth at the centre.

The coming of Christ to the earth confirmed for the early Christians that the earth was in fact the real centre, and geocentric astronomy was accepted as the truth for more than 1500 years afterwards. Planetary motions with their strange loop paths led to more complex systems of cycles and epicycles than those originating with Ptolemy, but the earth's central position was not doubted as the universe's physical centre. The Catholic Church of Rome continued to proclaim the earth as centre just as it proclaimed Rome as the centre of Christendom. During the dark and middle ages in Europe, Greek learning had been lost and forgotten – even the spherical nature of the earth ceased to be accepted as truth. The earth was imagined to be flat, and voyages out into the ocean towards the edge of the flat disc became too hazardous to even contemplate. Human consciousness had to await the next great leap in progress which took place in the Renaissance.

In less than a century Greek science, preserved in the interim in the Arab lands of Western Asia, e.g. in Baghdad, returned to Europe, albeit in an altered form. An artistic culture began to flourish, the great painters began to infuse new meaning and new beauty into Christianity and sailors crossed the oceans with great courage, showing by deeds that the flat earth picture was mere chimera. While the geocentric picture continued (indeed had been strengthened), there were people who never lost sight of the sun as a centre of light and life.

One of Copernicus' early achievements was to show scientifically that the earth is round and rotates on a North-South axis, thus complementing the voyages of discovery made by Vasco da Gama, Columbus and Co. Only on his death bed was the first copy of his book *Harmonices Mundi* placed into his hands. Copernicus had worked through the latter part of his life at the revolutionary idea that the sun was the true centre round which revolved the earth and the planets. Central to his argument was the fact that several of the complicated epicycles Ptolemy and his successors had had to employ could be completely removed from the astronomical picture. The Pope of that time was not opposed to Copernicus' ideas, indeed he evinced great interest, and there was a friendly relationship between them. There were critics in church circles and Martin Luther was particularly scornful, but the publication of the book in the mid sixteenth century was generally received with enthusiasm. Only some years later, under a new Pope, was strong opposition fostered – the book was placed on the index of forbidden writings. Many martyrs were burned at the stake, e.g. Giordano Bruno, for extolling the heliocentric conception.

This availed its opponents nothing however. Soon the sun as the centre of the whole system was universally accepted. Three hundred years later, as a result of telescope development and Newton's application of his gravitational theory to Kepler's laws, there came about another change to the human picture of the heavens. Whilst the sun remained the centre of the solar system of planets of which the earth was just one – and not a particularly significant one – no longer could the sun be regarded as the centre of the universe. It became just one among millions of suns, each having its own planetary dependents, all the suns (stars) making up the galaxy we know as the Milky Way. Then an increasing number of galaxies were recognised in other parts of the sky until the (for some people) depressing conclusion was reached in modern times that neither sun nor earth occupied universal seats of any importance.

The materialistic view of the heavens assumes that the physical phenomena observed are to be explained solely in terms of matter (solid, liquid and gaseous) and the mechanical, thermodynamical, electrical and nuclear activities at work within it. A less restricted view, however, which takes into account the presence of life, consciousness and individualities in the world (none of which materialism can explain) reaches not depressing but hopeful and heartening conclusions. For Rudolf Steiner the earth is the centre of the mineral world, the measuring centre of light and electro-magnetic effects, and the place where physical laws arising from our sense-perceptions are formulated. To imagine that similar cognitive activity takes place on Mars or on some planet of a star situated in Andromeda is mere scientific speculation. On the other hand our sun is for Steiner the centre of the etheric domain[6] in the world. We find him speaking of the earth as the centre of physical space and the sun as the centre of etheric space. When plants have germinated, they reach up from the physical earth foundation towards the sun-centre on which their very life depends. The flowers of the meadows do not simply open their petals in reaction to some photo-synthetic causality when the sun shines upon them. The opening out is rather a response to the life-filled warmth and light bestowed through the radiance of the sunshine.[7] Scientifically such considerations cannot be penetrated by point-centred Euclidean and Cartesian metrical concepts. They require the geometrical (and equally exact) concepts of a polar-Euclidean framework in which planes rather than points are the structuring elements.

Among the hosts of relativity ideas that can be applied to the earth-sun relationship against the backdrop of the starry worlds, Steiner singled out the following.[8]

The sun is shown moving along a lemniscatory screw followed by the earth. A side elevation would show the two of them moving in the same direction as more or less opposite points of a diameter of a circle, and this circle gradually changes its position. The general direction in which the sun is moving in relation to neighbouring stars and the galactic system as a whole was first determined in 1783 by Sir William Herschel. He called it the solar apex. Stars appear to move away from this apex and also to close in on the antipodal point called the antapex. Yet this apex, like everything else in the heavens, is also moving, albeit slowly. Steiner's picture also requires the point-plane polarity to be included. As shown the drawing is pointwise – one imagines points (sun and earth) moving tangentially along the curve. But planes are also moving (rotating) around the tangent at every point of the curve. No one to the author's knowledge has yet solved these difficult and complex mathematical problems (involving Einstein's general as well as special theory of relativity) which Steiner's whole conception requires.

The changing and developing human consciousness which has given birth to all the differing conceptions of what the true earth-sun relationship may be, appears to have come full circle in the course of two to three thousand years, returning in some respects to an awareness of the *qualitative* difference of sun movement relative to earth during day and night – circling above and tunnelling below, skull bone and limb bone – which people had in ancient Persia and Chaldea. Yet it was then a kind of dreaming. Real thinking in clear consciousness only began with the Greeks. Summing up the chief stages,

1. Pythagoras conceived of an ideal point between sun and earth, around which both revolved, a living central fire. He also referred to an anti-earth.
2. Aristarchus opted for the sun as centre.
3. Ptolemy opted for the earth as centre.
4. Copernicus again placed the sun in the centre.
5. Herschel and many other astronomers in the 19th century took account of the sun's movement in relation to the galaxy and to the stars as a whole.
6. In the early 20th century Einstein showed the need for an even greater relativistic approach, and Steiner proposed the lemniscatory screw picture with both sun and earth revolving round each other, yet with the former leading.
7. Exact confirmation of the relationship between cycles of living form in plants and the conjunctions of planets with sun and moon was provided by Lawrence Edwards.[9] Edwards demonstrated the need to develop holistic and not just materialistic thoughts about happenings in the universe.

The story is not ended. As new forms of consciousness develop, for example those described (in the Appendix) as Imagination, Inspiration and Intuition, so will the nature of sun-earth relativity become clearer, and, in those other realms of soul (feeling and will), hopefully lead to the healing and therapy our age needs. Just as each in-breath is followed by an out-breath, so has a similar rhythm become evident in the changes our astronomical picture underwent in the 7 steps above. What appears at an earlier stage and then disappears, reappears later, though in a new guise. Even a form of Pythagoras' 'anti-earth' has re-emerged since 1854, when the Danish astronomer Brorson discovered the *Gegenschein* (counterglow) – a faint oval patch of light in the sky, this time directly opposite to the sun. To see it, there must be neither moon nor artificial light-pollution anywhere about. Telescopic magnification reduces the oval glow, and the stronger the magnification the more the phenomenon is blotted out. Scientists were unable to propose any explanation before the 1960s. Even today there are only contradictory materialistic hypotheses.

The 'coming full circle' development of earth-sun relationship in astronomical conceptions during the period of nearly 2500 years between Pythagoras and Steiner is not just a path of repetitions. During a year the sun moves through all 12 zodiacal constellations and again its vernal point moves through all 12 during 25,920 years. There are certainly similarities between the initial and final positions wherever such cycles occur, but an advance of a different character has been made. The return appears at a higher level, rather like the Swiss Alpine railways climbing round and round through tunnel and viaduct as they leave one valley for another on the other side of intervening mountains. The same applies when the eye follows Steiner's sketch of the running lemniscate – a device used hundreds of times in old Bank of England pound notes, signed by chief cash officer K.O. Peppiatt. (Nowadays would-be forgers have to contend instead with scenes relating to Michael Faraday, Charles Dickens and George Stephenson). We cannot regard ourselves as *exactly* the same person one spring as we were in the spring of the previous year. 26 thousand years ago there were no Alps, Himalayas or Andes, even though birds had then recently begun to sing in deciduous woodland over the chalk strata where modern Surrey stands. (Birds had 'only just' evolved from reptiles.) The earth's axis ran through Africa, a continent which continuously faced the sun without any night. Rodents also began to appear in evolution, but as yet no apes. No skeletal remains of anything remotely human have been found from those far-off times, but if the bodily constitution of human beings was then somewhat similar to modern jelly fish, any such remains would be exceedingly unlikely to have survived the march of time. At any rate it seems indisputable that a real advance of human civilisation has taken place since the time when the sun's vernal point was last in the constellation of Pisces.

It was necessary for modern consciousness to lose all awareness of the deeds and lives of the gods as expressed in the cosmogony of Pythagorean times, an intrinsic part of the astronomy of those days. Embedded in this divine world, the people of those times could not yet attain the real freedom of independent, self-determining action and understanding, which has come within our grasp as a direct result of our loss of perception of the worlds of spirit. Yet from this point of deepest descent, we can begin to turn once more to a synthesizing view of the world and our place within it. Modern materialistic science wholly fails to understand life, the three human soul activities or the individuality in each one of us who controls them. Only an imaginative, holistic and essentially noetic approach can do so. The new science of the spirit, to the founding of which Rudolf Steiner dedicated his whole life, will enable mankind to reach much further into understanding, appreciating and co-creating with the active being-imbued world which the early Greeks knew as the world of the Gods, and the Norse peoples called Asgard. The 21st century needs this new science to guide human creative work for the future.

Such a new science needs to fertilise every subject and life activity. Yet it will be unable to evolve strongly or carry real conviction unless it can transform astronomy. Nothing is so impressive as the vastness and beauty of the stars experienced on a cloudless night. Unless that heavenly world which completely surrounds and contains us can be penetrated by the new science, all its efforts will be in vain. When a Walt Whitman no longer feels sick listening to astronomers and is able to unite what he hears from the new science with his experience of the 'mystical moist night air', then the perfect silence with which he looks up at the stars will begin to be slowly imbued with song.

We need to do two things. The first is to live with a modern consciousness into the whole manner in which, only 600 years ago, people pictured and imagined the nature of heavenly bodies. For them the moon was not simply the part-circular object they saw, but the visible reflector of sunlight which they experienced as marking the boundary of a great sphere centred in the earth. The sphere's essential content, as invisible to an observing eye as the air breathed out by a friend when in conversation with us, was felt to be everything that enables procreation and fertilisation to take place. Similarly the Mercury sphere made digestion possible, the Venus sphere anabolism, the Mars, Jupiter and Saturn spheres breathing, sense perception and thought-forming respectively. The heart's control over the blood pulsing through it was experienced as a gift of the sun sphere.

Just imagine what might happen to astronauts once it becomes possible for spacecraft to go out beyond the moon sphere. Will it be possible to conceive children out there? Beyond Mercury will digestion be possible? – perhaps not so crucial, since most food ingested by astronauts is already pre-digested and packed in toothpaste-like tubes, avoiding anti-gravitational problems in consumption. If breathing proves uncontrollable beyond Mars, no doubt artificial lungs, already long in hospital use, can be provided. If sense organs begin to fail beyond Jupiter, radio and television leads taped to suitable parts of the human skin might be the answer. It is unnecessary to see where you are going in a space craft anyway. Mechanical sensors as well as ground control look after all that. As for having thoughts beyond Saturn, no problem! The computers will deal with such things for you. Fitted pacemakers will similarly replace the heart's normal function when beyond the sun sphere.

So any volunteers for a long round trip to Uranus? On your return you would be assured of having a most remunerative interview with science fiction writers who could confirm with their own eyes and ears in observing you what non-human beings really look and sound like!

Chapter 11: Looking forward – to the upper school and beyond

On the other hand, to really live into the Imagination of these spheres whilst quietly contemplating our organic processes (there are many more not referred to above) can lead to an at-one-ness with the wandering, and later the fixed stars, that no future mechanical space travel could remotely approach.

Secondly we need to develop a new mathematical approach to the starry worlds. Pythagoras, Ptolemy and Co. dealt with angular measurements. Calculation of distances came much later. Distances of stars outside our solar system depend upon making assumptions about the speed of light effects. A 'light year' is a very convenient fiction, leading to quite fascinating mathematics. If we want to get nearer to reality, though, we need to understand the quite different kinds of measurement met in elliptic, hyperbolic and polar-Euclidian spaces. Without applying the first of these, Einstein could never have developed his theories of relativity. When it becomes clear how the last of these can be successfully applied to the *living* in contrast to the lifeless world, we shall be able to develop a new astronomy.

Only the marriage of these two needs, one Imaginative and one a transformed mathematical one – as outlined in the previous section of this chapter – will lead to the new astronomy.

Teachers of mathematics can do much to establish a basis in skill, purely mathematical imaginative ability, and the holistic approach to phenomena that can be taken up by their pupils at some point later, after (maybe long after) leaving school, should they so wish. For boys and girls to have pondered the issues described in this final section may at least allow them that freedom to reflect and research which we all desire in our inmost being. Only rarely will one of them seek a career in astronomy, but every single one of them will find moments in their future life when some question regarding the heavenly canopy of our earthly home awakens in their consciousness. The importance for life of such moments cannot be undervalued.

Such issues primarily concern teachers of the 14 to 18 age range, but teachers of younger classes need to know of their existence. To reiterate a principal theme of the earliest chapters of this book, anticipating with a light touch in a younger class something which will be developed more thoroughly in an older one is the stuff of which real education is made.

Appendix

More on Mathematics and Initiation

Whereas in the book about gaining knowledge of higher worlds[1] Steiner described the method which anyone can use to penetrate spiritual realms, he outlined a particular way in which a scientist can do this in the book *The Boundaries of Natural Science*.[2] The two boundaries are matter and consciousness. The first essential is a full familiarity with the spirit of mathematics; then a full working through of the book *The Philosophy of Freedom*, engaging one's clear thinking on every page and every line, like a musician reading a musical score. By this experience one gets to know oneself in part of the inner life not known before and thus develops pure sense-free thinking, beginning to reach way beyond the sense-free nature of the mathematical. One experiences directly what pure thinking activity is. This kind of thinking is not of the passive kind often applied in life, but is an active *willed* thinking. A capacity is acquired which is quite clearly *not produced by the brain*. It is a wholly spiritual activity sustained by itself and by nothing of a material or sense-transmitted character.

Yet at this point it becomes important to leave this capacity simmering on a back burner, so to speak. For on its own this is not enough to allow us to perceive the spiritual, even though we thereby become quite certain of its existence. We also need to actively surrender ourselves to the purely perceptual, to what is rendered by eye, ear, warmth, touch, etc., and to symbolic changes which we can form for ourselves. This path proceeds on a purely phenomenological course, in which the host of mental pictures and memory images which normally assert themselves in our thought processes have to be silenced by an effort of will. We live into the perceptual which then permeates us, and in consequence we acquire potent soul forces. A new and conscious experience of our constitution will follow this, an experience suffused by spiritual reality. This is a deeper, though in some ways similar, experience to what happens to a teenager at puberty. There the colours, sounds and warmth which reach him from the world at large bring about the sense of love. It is a mistake to suppose that love emerges from the sexual urge. The latter is a parallel psycho-somatic development whilst the former blossoms through the soul's irradiation by the spirit – the spirit which is active in both the cosmos and in the individual human being. When the sexual urge is not controlled by love in its most real and conscious character, the consequent problems – ones we are all too familiar with in our age – become ever more difficult, and subject to non-human and indeed evil influences. Love is the most conscious of all our feelings. It is a feeling inseparable from thinking. Shakespeare and others have alluded to the fact that the way to the heart is through the head.

Both soul activities reach their zenith in this union. This is why the third soul activity, that of will, can also unite with them and act at its most creative level.

Clear thinking on its own is unable to perceive anything wholly spiritual except itself. Feeling has to participate; and at this level of refinement there is an awareness of a feeling which is part of thinking and a thinking which is a part of feeling.

The experience of surrendering to spiritual reality is closely akin to a quality found in all great poetry. Contemplate, for example, these lines from T.S. Eliot.[3]

> *And the bird called, in response to*
> *The unheard music hidden in the shrubbery,*
> *And the unseen eyebeam crossed, for the roses*
> *Had the look of flowers that are looked at.*
> *There they were as our guests, accepted and accepting.*

How could one appreciate these lines without the active presence of human feeling? Just as the head is the focus of our thinking activity (although this activity is not confined to the head), so is feeling centred in our rhythmic system of heart and lungs.

The spiritual experience whose description in words[4] is being attempted here is what Steiner called *Imagination*.[5] Only through this do we acquire the second capacity needed, which enables the first capacity, the transformed diamond-like mathematical capacity left simmering on the back burner, to reveal a new power that Steiner called *Inspiration*. When these two capacities are united, genuine *Intuition* becomes active. Now the individual is at last able to be 'at one' with the world and its beings in a fully conscious way. Both matter and ordinary consciousness, like two imprisoning boundaries, are overcome.

Appendix

Very little of the content of this section concerns young people of school age. There will be a few in whom some of the questions touched upon will begin to form, and it is wisest to advise them to exercise patience and gather adult life experience outside the sphere of school, before attempting to fathom such matters. In face of a direct question, though, one needs to give one's own view honestly. In Steiner schools upper school pupils are naturally aware of some of the views (e.g. on reincarnation) promulgated by Steiner. If they find a library book or ask for the title of one, it often happens that on reading it they feel it is a bit beyond them and decide perhaps to put it aside for the present. As is to be expected, younger upper school pupils will jokingly refer to the dangers of being 'Steinerised', a healthy reaction to being educated in a Steiner school. No kind of proselytising takes place, however. The aim is to equip young people to meet life in whatever form it approaches them, or in whichever way they choose to investigate it, leaving them free to exercise their own will as adults in society at large.

Diagrammatically one may attempt to express the thoughts of this section as follows:

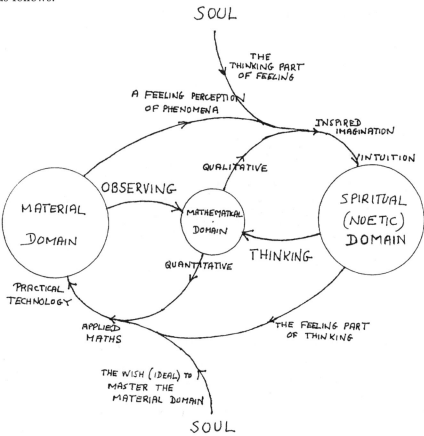

Note that
(i) Comprehensive though this may appear at first sight, it is constructed from a mathematical perspective in the first instance, so could only be one aspect of something more universal.
(ii) Material domain includes the physical (e.g. the distant stars which are physical though not necessarily material) and also the sense organs which belong to or penetrate our bodies.
(iii) No diagram of this kind can ever be satisfactory. The soul, for example, is put in two places somewhat like parts of the two branches of a hyperbola which meet asymptotically 'at infinity'. The best diagram showing the relationship of body, soul and spirit is contained in Steiner's course *Study of Man*.[6] Any diagram, however, can be little more than an aide-memoire. The real form and structure is continuously in movement and cannot be realised by lines drawn on paper. Such would also be the case were one to attempt to depict the human etheric body.
(iv) Intuition, like practical technology, is a deed. All the arrows indicate the presence of will.
(v) Readers familiar with the geometrical phenomena of Cassini's ovals (below) will notice a certain similarity of movement between tracing round such curves and following the arrows of will in the diagram above.

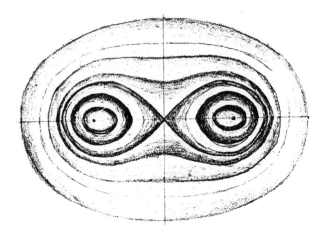

The larger ovals correspond to the 'feeling' connections of material and noetic domains and embrace practical technology and Intuition. The smaller (separated) ovals correspond to the separate applied cognitions relevant to the two domains. What, then, does the lemniscate correspond to? It is through observing our thinking that we obtain our first spiritual perception, i.e. we recognise that thinking is a spiritual activity. Continuing along the curve we experience how an essential difference between the noetic and the material is in the contrast of qualitative and quantitative.

(vi) An even more difficult meditative activity would be to reverse the lemniscatory direction and attempt to *think our observing*. This would involve not only knowing how each of our sense organs operates, but also thinking the creation of these sense organs. It would finally result in experiencing that matter and spirit are not just two mutually exclusive realms, but that these two are aspects of something even more comprehensive. Just as 'at rest' and 'in movement' is an important polarity in the Pythagorean description of mathematics, so when the 'even more comprehensive' is at rest we have matter and when it is in movement we have spirit.

(vii) Yet another aspect of the real movement and relationship which the diagram lacks might be portrayed by using a 3 dimensional instead of 2 dimensional model. The sketch below shows a Moebius strip whose unusual geometrical properties are that it has only one edge and not two as it first appears to have, and (more important) is that it has only one side. It is not two-sided, for if you follow round the 'top side' through the twist you find yourself on the bottom side. Such a model would imply that spirit and matter are two 'sides' of the more comprehensive realm[7] suggested in (vi). In the same way 'qualitative' and 'quantitative' would become complementary and continuous, too.

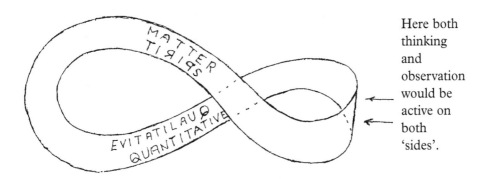

Here both thinking and observation would be active on both 'sides'.

Chapter Notes and References

Preface

1 Henley W.E., *Invictus*.
2 Barfield O., *The Life of the Soul*, containing translation of *vom Seelenleben* by Rudolf Steiner.
3 Steiner R., *The Study of Man*, (translation of his *Allgemeine Menschenkunde*).

Some of the books by other authors inspired by Steiner are listed below:

Evans Dr M. & Rodger I., *Anthroposophical Medicine*, Thorsons, London, 1992.
Edmunds F, *Anthroposophy – a Way of Life*, Crosby Press, Hartfield, East Sussex, 1982.
Heider M. von, *Come Unto These Yellow Sands*.
Koepf H.H., *Biodynamic Agriculture*, Anthroposophic Press, New York, 1976.
Robinswood Press, *Eurythmy an Art of Movement for Our Time*.
Sattler & Wistinghausen, *Biodynamic Farming Practice*, B.D.A.A. publications.
Schaumburg Publications, *Eurythmy – Essays and Anecdotes*, Roselle, Illinois.
Schilthuis W., *Agriculture*, Floris Books, Edinburgh, 1990.
Shepherd A.P., *A Scientist of the Invisible*, Hodder and Stoughton, London, 1975.
Spence M., *Foundations for a Modern World Economy*.
Spence M., *A Context for Renewed Economics*, Association of Waldorf Schools of North America, Fairoaks, CA, 1990.
Thomson J., *Natural Childhood*, Gaia Books, London & Stroud, 1994.
Wilkinson R., *The History of Waldorf Education*.
Wilkinson R., *The Spiritual Basis of Steiner Education*, Rudolf Steiner Press, London, 1996.

4 Steiner R., *The Philosophy of Freedom*, (translated by Wilson M.) Rudolf Steiner Press, London, 1979.

Introduction

1. Others include Porphyrios, Diogenes and Heraklitus.
2. Schuré E., *The Great Initiates,* St. George's Press, New York, 1981.
3. Bindel E., *Pythagoras,* Verlag Freies Geistesleben, Stuttgart, 1962. (Written in German).
4. Verhulst J., *Der Erstgeborene,* Verlag Freies Geistesleben, Stuttgart, 1996.
5. For a comprehensive list of intervals see Grove's Musical Dictionary, in the chapter on 'Just Intonation'.
6. See Jacques' speech 'All the world's a stage...' in *As You Like It.*
7. For further elaboration, see Chapter 4.
8. St John's Gospel, Chapter 21.
9. Bindel E., *Die Geistigen Grundlagen der Mathematik* ('the spiritual bases of mathematics'), Verlag Freies Geistesleben, Stuttgart, 1991.
10. Mosaic in Ravenna, San Apollinaire Nuovo: 'The Calling of St Peter and St Andrew'.
11. Hardy G. and Wright E., *An Introduction to the Theory of Numbers,* Clarendon Press, Oxford, 1988.
12. Gleick, *Chaos,* Abacus, London, 1993.
13. Such traditions had their own validity in the context of their own cultures and stage of world evolution. They were right for their place and time. But simply transposing them onto our own, present form of consciousness, is not helpful for our present needs.
14. A modern spiritual path suited to the Western world goes about developing the chakras in a different way. See F. Lowndes: *Die Belebung des Herzchakra* ('the enlivening of the heart chakra'), Verlag Freies Geistesleben, Stuttgart, 1996.
15. Steiner R., *Knowledge of the Higher Worlds,* Rudolf Steiner Press, Bristol, 1993, or (alternative translation) *How to Know Higher Worlds,* Anthroposophic Press, New York, 1994.
16. Several good sources are to be found in Buddhist literature.
17. Steiner R., *Occult Science – an Outline,* Rudolf Steiner Press, Bristol, 1993.
18. Edwards L., *The Vortex of Life,* Floris Books, Edinburgh, 1993.
19. Stewart I., *Does God Play Dice?* Penguin Books, London, 1990.
20. Who is nevertheless alive in the world of spirit.
21. Cayley A., Inaugural Address to the British Association for the Advancement of Science, 1883.
22. Locher-Ernst L., *Raum und Gegenraum,* Birkhäuser, Basel, 1980. Hawthorn Press, Stroud, may publish a translation of this under the title *Space and Counterspace.*

Chapter 1

1. Kant I., *Critique of Pure Reason*.
1. Steiner R., *Truth and Knowledge*, (Chapter 12), Mercury Press, Spring Valley, New York, 1993.
2. Steiner R., *The Spiritual Ground of Education*, (Lecture 5), Anthroposophical Publishing Co., London, 1947.

Chapter 2

1. M. Winn, *The Plug-in Drug*, Bantam Books, New York, 1978 and Large M. and others, *Who's Bringing Them Up?* Hawthorn Press, Stroud, 1997.
2. Steiner R., *Theosophy*. Rudolf Steiner Press, London, 1989.
3. Steiner R., *Man as Symphony of the Creative Word*, Rudolf Steiner Press, London, 1991.
4. Steiner R., *The Four Temperaments*, (for a modern description of temperaments), Rudolf Steiner Press, 1971.
5. Agrippa von Nettesheim (1486-1535), *On the Might and Power of Numbers*, copies in large museums or libraries. Also consult Andrews W.S., *Magic Squares and Cubes*, Dover Publications, London, 1960.
6. Clausen A. and Riedel M., *Zeichnen Sehen Lernen*, Mellinger Verlag, Stuttgart, 1989.
7. McAllen A., *The Extra Lesson*, Robinswood Press, Gloucester, 1992.
8. Steiner R., *Anthroposophy and Science*, Mercury Press, Spring Valley, New York, 1991.
9. Steiner R., *The Fifth Gospel*, Rudolf Steiner Press, London, 1995.

Chapter 4

1. Steiner R., *Theosophy*, Rudolf Steiner Press, London, 1989.
2. The 'moving stars' are Sun, moon and planets. However, the centred realms indicated refer not to the visible orbs but the earth-centred spheres of variable radius on whose surfaces these 'non-fixed' orbs proceed. This explains why for people living only 500 years ago it was a common conception to denote the 'moving stars' as spheres within which human existence took place rather than as distant optical phenomena.
3. Steiner R., *Man as Symphony of the Creative Word*, Rudolf Steiner Press, London, 1991.

Chapter 5

1. Trades Union leaders please note!
2. Steiner R., *A Modern Art of Education,* Rudolf Steiner Press, London, 1981.
3. A good Californian breakfast might consist of a plate of fried bacon and peaches mounted on a large piece of French toast surrounded by strawberry-topped sausages and the whole covered with a rich sauce of mushroom and apricot.
4. Ball W., *A Short Account of the History of Mathematics,* Macmillan, London, 1947.
5. Old Testament, 1 Moses 46.
6. Carlgren F., *Education towards Freedom,* Lanthorn Press, 1980.

Chapter 6

1. The whole matter of homework will be dealt with in Chapter 10.
2. Steiner R., *World Economy,* Rudolf Steiner Press, London, 1990.
3. Steiner R., *Theory of Knowledge,* Anthoposophic Press, New York, 1978.
4. Exceptions occur when area is taken as one of the three given elements. It is instructive to determine the conditions for this – a task to be undertaken in Class 12, when general metrical geometry (including that of elliptic and hyperbolic spaces) is introduced.
5. Drink a cup of café au lait with the sun or a light shining obliquely above the rim. Before imbibing, observe what the coffee surface presents to the eyes. The enveloped curve made by the lines in the drawing is like the boundary curve between light and dark on the coffee surface. In Class 7 optics you can return to this phenomenon, noticing how angle of incidence OUT is equal to angle of reflection OUV.
6. Students of Steiner's *Occult Science* (rf notes on Introduction chapter) will recall that between 2 planetary conditions of the earth there is a state of pralaya. The old has ended and only the seeds of the new are present. The geometrical situation in this 7th problem is analogous. Whilst such a comparison would be quite unsuitable to voice to a school class, something of its beauty and relevance to future moments in life itself will pass over into the child's soul if the teacher has such a thought.
7. This is a gentle previewing of the subject of graphs.

Chapter 7

1. A favourite expression in Pestalozzi education and fully echoed in Steiner Waldorf education, it can often be heard in Swiss Pestalozzi schools today. Every kind of education designed to nurture the whole human being needs to take account of all three parts of the organism – head, chest and limbs – not merely the extremes of intellect and prowess in sport.
2. For the precise meaning of these three terms, see Steiner R., *The Philosophy of Freedom*, Rudolf Steiner Press, London, 1979.
3. 1 Kings 7, 23 and Chronicles 4, 2.
4. You may not succeed in being quite so accurate.
5. N. Copernicus, inaugurator of heliocentric perspective and author of *De revolutionibus orbium mundi*, only saw its appearance in print on his death bed (A.D. 1543).

The further development of the heliocentric system by Kepler and others gives further good practice with squares and cubes. So Kepler's Third Law – later manipulated by Newton to suggest a law of gravitation – states that (mean distance of a planet from the sun)^3 = (time taken for that planet to go round the sun)^2, when the distance is measured in A.U. (one astronomical unit is the mean distance of earth from sun) and the time is measured in years. Here is a set:

Planet	Distance	D^3	Time	T^2
Mercury	0.387	0.0580	0.241	0.0581
Venus	0.723	0.378	0.615	0.378
Earth	1	1	1	1
Mars	1.524	3.540	1.881	3.538
Jupiter	5.202	140.8	11.86	140.7
Saturn	9.558	873	29.46	868
Uranus	19.30	7190	84.02	7060
Neptune	30.27	27700	164.8	27200
Pluto	39.75	62800	247.7	61400

The brighter pupils in Class 8 could work out these squares and cubes as a project to see how good Kepler's Third Law is. They will already have been introduced to planetary astronomy in a Class 7 main lesson.

On the other hand this could be a simple practice in the use of calculators in Class 9.

Chapter 8

1. Piaget J., *The Child's Conception of Number*, Routledge, London, 1980.
2. Large M., *Who's bringing them up? How to break the TV habit*, Hawthorn Press, Stroud, 1997.
3. Good cartoonists push through our discerning intellect, however, to our sense of humour which certainly lies in the feeling domain of the soul.
4. The area of a semi-circle is an exact decimal part of the area of the square on its diameter (actually $\pi/8$ or 0.3927 to 4 d.p.). Hence the sum of the areas of the two smaller semicircles is equal to the area of the largest semicircle. Now from the *whole* area of the figure subtract the two smaller semicircles and you are left with the triangle. On the other hand, if you subtract the largest semicircle from the whole area, you are left with the two lunes.
5. In a book entitled *The Mathematics of Great Amateurs*, whose author shall be nameless, it is declared that originally only the first four regular solids were known, so they were very conveniently allocated to the four elements which formed the basis of Greek Science. When a fifth solid was discovered, the amateur mathematician Plato, employing the equivalent of the old adage 'The devil take the hindmost' promptly allocated the dodecahedron to a mythical and wholly unsubstantiated 'quintessence'. The author, who formulates many explanations of amateurishness in this manner, and who likes to quote other authors in various foreign languages, might care to contemplate two more. '¡Quien mucho abraza poco aprieta!' 'Plus aloes quam mellis habet'.
6. Cundy H.M. and Rollett A.P., *Mathematical Models*, Clarendon Press, Oxford, 1970, give excellent advice on how to construct plane-faced solids of wide variety. The book contains very good photographs too.
7. Kappraff J., *Connections*, McGraw-Hill, New York, 1991, goes deeply into these relationships. Not only is the book a fine reference book, but it is full of illustrations and shows how the golden ratio was used by Béla Bartók.
8. A set of trees in perspective showing minute detail of leaves can be achieved quickly on a modern computer through the method of fractals. Remarkable coloured plates (showing trees, fern forms, logarithmic shell and inflorescence forms) are exhibited in many books today. Unfortunately the forms are all dead forms, which no living organism would ever produce. The artist can get far closer to living reality than a computer will ever achieve. This does not mean that fractals are useless. The chaos theory which they augment may move strongly towards the overthrow of materialism.

Chapter 9

1. On a graph this would show 60° phase differences on a sine wave.
2. Soesman A., *The Twelve Senses,* Hawthorn Press, Stroud, 1993. On page 6 of Chapter 2 the question is posed 'Why does a man go from A to B every morning?'
3. Steiner R., *First Scientific Lecture Course,* Steiner Schools Fellowship Publications, Forest Row, Sussex, 1977.
4. Cundy H. and Rollett A., *Mathematical Models,* Clarendon Press, Oxford, 1970. Further examples are given there.
   Lockwood's *Book of Curves* also gives a survey of curve forms.

Chapter 10

1. Steiner R., *Three Lectures on the Curriculum,* Steiner Waldorf Schools Fellowship Publications, Forest Row, Sussex, 1998. The essence of them is also given in Steiner R., *Soul Economy and Waldorf Education,* Rudolf Steiner Press, London and Anthroposophic Press, New York, 1986.
2. Stockmeyer K., *Rudolf Steiner's Curriculum for Waldorf Schools,* Steiner Schools Fellowship Publications, Forest Row, Sussex, 1982.
3. Heydebrand C., *Curriculum of the First Waldorf School,* Steiner Schools Fellowship Publications, Forest Row, Sussex, 1982.
4. Jarman R.A., *A Draft Curriculum in Mathematics for Rudolf Steiner (Waldorf) Schools, Classes 1-8, with special emphasis on its relationship to the National Curriculum, 1990.* Pamphlet available from the author.
5. Locher-Ernst L., *Raum und Gegenraum,* Birkhäuser, Basel, 1980.
   Adams G., *Physical and Ethereal Spaces,* Rudolf Steiner Press, London, 1965.
   Adams G. and Whicher O., *The Plant between Sun and Earth,* Rudolf Steiner Press, London, 1980.
   Edwards L., *The Vortex of Life,* Floris Books, Edinburgh, 1993.
6. Stockmeyer E.A.K., (see ref above), Part IV of Section 5 particularly.
7. $8128 \times 1 = 2 \times 4064$
   $ 4 \times 2032$
   $ 8 \times 1016$
   $ 16 \times 508$
   $ 32 \times 254$
   $ 64 \times 127$
   Grand total of factors, including 1 but not 8128 itself = 8128.
   The first 5 perfect numbers are 6, 28, 496, 8128 and 33550336. The next

three have 10, 12 and 19 digits in them. The 23rd perfect number has 6751 digits. Anyone interested in such cosmic aspects of perfection could read a simple and clear account given in:
Beiler A., *Recreations in the Theory of Numbers,* Dover Publications, 1996.

Chapter 11

1. Steiner R., *The Foundations of Human Experience,* Anthroposophic Press, New York, 1996.
2. Steiner R., *The Philosophy of Freedom,* Rudolf Steiner Press, London, 1979.
3. Steiner R., *World Economy,* Rudolf Steiner Press, London, 1990.
4. Unger G., Introduction to Steiner's *Anthroposophy and Science,* Mercury Press, New York, 1922. Dr Unger was for many years the leader of the Mathematical-Astronomical Section of the School for the Science of the Spirit at the Goetheanum, Switzerland.
5. The original German title of this set of lectures, literally translated, is: 'Observation of nature, scientific experiment and the results of acquiring knowledge from the viewpoint of anthroposophy (the science of the spirit).' This gives perhaps a better indication of its contents, but is far too long a title to appear on an English book. In 1917, according to my father, who was a British tank commander at the time, a British look-out in the trenches would exclaim on sighting the enemy: 'Look, a tank!'. His German equivalent, on the other hand, would exclaim: 'Achtung! Man kann da drüben eine mobilgemachte Waffenplatzmaschine beobachten!' In my father's opinion, the disproportionate lengths of the two exclamations was one of the reasons the Germans lost World War 1.
6. Steiner R., *The Relationship of Astronomy to the Diverse Branches of Natural Science* (known as 'The Astronomy Course'), lecture 18. Only available in typescript.
7. Adams G. and Whicher O., *The Plant between Sun and Earth,* Rudolf Steiner Press, London, 1980.
8. Steiner R., 'Astronomy Course', lecture 17. (See above.)
9. Edwards L., *The Vortex of Life,* Floris Books, Edinburgh, 1993.

Appendix

1. Steiner R., *Knowledge of the Higher Worlds*, Rudolf Steiner Press, Bristol, 1993.
2. Steiner R., *The Boundaries of Natural Science*, Anthroposophic Press, New York, 1983. With a foreword by Saul Bellow.
3. Eliot T.S., *Four Quartets*.
4. The words of our language are for the most part adapted to describe material and sense-perceptible phenomena. To put spiritual or noetic experiences directly into words is actually impossible. Only through poetry and other artistic means can one begin to cognize and recognize them.
5. Not to be confused with the ordinary use of the word.
6. In lecture 10 of that volume, now published as *Foundations of Human Experience*, Anthroposophic Press, New York, 1996.
7. I owe this thought to Dr Ray Walder, whose book *Natura Naturans* is soon to be published.

Other books from Hawthorn Press

Between Form and Freedom
A Practical Guide to the Teenage Years
Betty Staley

Betty Staley offers a wealth of insights about teenagers, providing a compassionate, intelligent and intuitive look into the minds of children and adolescents. She explores the nature of adolescence and looks at teenagers' needs in relation to family, friends, schools, love and the arts. Issues concerning stress, depression, drug and alcohol abuse and eating disorders are included.

288pp; 210 x 135mm; illustrations;
1 869 890 08 6; paperback.

Creative Form Drawing 1, 2 & 3
R. Kutzli

These three workbooks form a successful series which aim to encourage people to explore in detail the ways in which forms are created. The exercises provided give a fascinating insight into the relationship between form and content.

Creative Form Drawing 1
152pp; 297 x 210mm; fully illustrated; 0 950 706 28 0; pb.

Creative Form Drawing 2
152pp; 297 x 210mm; fully illustrated; 0 950 706 14 0; pb.

Creative Form Drawing 3
152pp; 297 x 210mm; fully illustrated; 0 950 706 38 8; paperback.

Child's play 1 & 2
Wil van Haren and Rudolf Kischnick

This book follows up *Child's Play 3* as a games book particularly for younger children, suitable for nursery, kindergarten and junior schools. There are 172 games.

192pp; 215 x 145mm; 1 869 890 77 9; paperback.

Child's Play 3
Games for Life for Children and Teenagers
Wil van Haren and Rudolf Kischnick

A tried and tested games book with numerous ideas for running races, duels, wrestling matches, ball games and games of skill and agility. Its clear layout and indexing by age makes this an invaluable and enjoyable resource book for parents, teachers and play leaders.

96pp; 215 x 145mm; 1 869 890 63 9; paperback.

Doctor Knickerbocker and Other Poems
Jane Grell

This book of participative poetry for children is an invaluable tool for inspiring self-expression in the classroom.
Illustrations by Derrick Smith.

48pp; 200 x 200mm; 1 869 890 65 5; paperback.

Drawing and Painting in Rudolf Steiner Schools
Margrit Jünemann and Fritz Weitmann

This comprehensive account of painting and drawing in the Steiner curriculum combines detailed practical advice with clearly defined philosophy on aesthetic education.

206pp; 240 x 170mm; illustrations; 1 869 890 41 8; pb; paperback.

Festivals Together
A Guide to Multicultural Celebration
Sue Fitzjohn, Minda Weston, Judy Large

A resource guide for celebration, based on many cultures from all over the world—Buddhist, Christian, Hindu, Jewish, Muslim and Sikh.

224pp; 250 x 200mm;
1 869 890 46 9; paperback.

Foreign Language Teaching in Steiner Schools
Guidelines for Class Teachers and Language Teachers
Michael Stott

144pp; 216 x 138mm; 1 869 890 70 1; paperback.

Freeing Education
Steps towards Real Choice and Diversity in Schools
Edited by Fiona Carnie, Martin Large and Mary Tasker

Freeing Education addresses the problems in education today—centralised control, a prescriptive National Curriculum and lack of real parental choice. The authors argue strongly for greater choice and diversity within a more equitable state system, and explain how this can be achieved. Here are teachers, parents and leading educationists who make the bold assertion that freedom in education matters.

'The importance of this book is that it mounts a well-informed and many sided challenge to the whole trend of government policy for many years ... the case is very well argued.'

Colin Ward, *Resurgence*, Sept. 1996

192pp; 215 x 138mm; 1 869 890 82 5; paperback.

Games Children Play
How games and sport help children develop
Kim Brooking-Payne

Games Children Play offers an accessible guide to games with children of age 3 upwards. These games are all tried and tested, and are the basis for the author's extensive teacher training work. The book explores children's personal development and how this is expressed in movement, play, songs and games.

Each game is clearly and simply described, with diagrams or drawings, and accompanied by an explanation of why this game is helpful at a particular age. The equipment that may be needed is basic, cheap and easily available. Illustrated by Marije Rowling.

192pp; 297 x 210mm; 1 869 890 78 7; paperback.

Lighting Fires
Deepening Education through Meditation
Jorgen Smit

The author addresses the inner path of the human 'becoming' who lives in every adult and child. Often, the teachers who 'light fires rather than fill buckets' work on deepening their teaching through meditation and personal development.

96pp; 216 x 138mm; 1 869 890 45 0; paperback.

Listening Ear
The Development of Speech as a Creative Influence in Education
Audrey E. McAllen

This book gives teachers an understanding of speech training through specially selected exercises which aim to develop clear speaking in the classroom. The author looks at the links between speech and child development, the speech organs, the effects of artificially produced sounds on speech development, rhythm, metre and the sound groups.

162pp; 210 x 135mm; illustrations; 1 869 890 18 3; paperback.

Looking Forward
Games, Rhymes and Exercises to help Children develop their Learning Abilities
Molly von Heider

This book aims to help teachers with activities that will both benefit children in the early years and lay the foundations for sound learning later on.

160pp; 216 x 138mm; music; 1 869 890 67 1; paperback.

New Eyes for Plants
A Workbook for Observing and Drawing Plants
Margaret Colquhoun and Axel Ewald

Here are fresh ways of seeing and understanding nature with a vivid journey through the seasons. Detailed facts are interwoven with artistic insights, showing how science can be practised as an art, and how art can help science through using the holistic approach of Goethe.

Readers are helped by simple observation exercises, by inspiring illustrations which make a companion guide to plant growth around the year. A wide variety of common plants are beautifully drawn, from seed and bud to flower and fruit.

Dr Margaret Colquhoun researches into plants and landscape. Axel Ewald is a sculptor. The book is the outcome of their teaching and research work.

This book invites us to go on a journey, not simply of the imagination but also of activity and transformation. The invitation is to reconnect with the living forms around us by looking and doing so that our eyes are opened to the nature of plant life. The nature revealed has both the truth of scientific knowledge and the beauty of the creative act so that we experience plants as simultaneously archetypal and forever new. The door opens onto a new way of practising science as an art.

Dr Brian Goodwin, The Open University

208pp; 270 x 210mm; illustrations; 1 869890 85 X; paperback.

Origin and Development of Language
Roy Wilkinson

This wide-ranging survey of the origin and development of language enthusiastically discusses how we can rediscover the truth of how and what we speak. The author, an experienced Waldorf teacher, traces our multi-layered language from its spiritual roots to the almost soulless polyglot that we call language today.

64pp; 216 x 138mm; 1 869 890 35 3; paperback.

Renewing Education
Selected Writings on Steiner Education
Francis Edmunds

This collection of essays is concerned with the spiritual basis of an individual's development from childhood onwards and will be a valuable reference work for all teachers. Francis Edmunds has travelled widely and his talks and writings, emphasising the responsibility of adults and educators towards children, have inspired and educated a world-wide audience.

136pp; 216 x 138mm; 1 869 890 31 0; paperback.

Rudolf Steiner
An Introduction
Rudi Lissau

This portrait of Steiner's life and work aims to point out the relevance of his activities to contemporary social and human concerns.

192pp; 210 x 135mm; 1 869 890 06 8; paperback.

Rudolf Steiner on Education
A Compendium
Roy Wilkinson

Here is an accessible introduction to the educational philosophy of Rudolf Steiner—the pioneer of a comprehensive, co-educational form of education for children from kindergarten to the end of high school.

168pp; 216 x 138mm; 1 869 890 51 5; paperback.

Soulways
Development, Crises and Illnesses of the Soul
Rudolf Treichler

Soulways offers insights into personal growth through the phases and turning points of human life. A profound picture of child and adult development is given, including the developmental needs, potentials and questions of each stage. Drawing on his work as a psychiatrist, Treichler also explores the developmental disorders of soul life—addictions, neuroses, hysteria, anorexia and schizophrenia.

320pp; 210 x 135mm; 1 869 890 13 2; paperback.

Seven Soul Types
Max Stibbe

A description of the seven soul types of man, indicating the most significant inner and outer characteristics of each. Recognition of soul types can be invaluable in communicating with others in social, educational or therapeutic situations.

128pp; 216 x 138mm; 1 869 890 44 2; paperback.

Sing Me the Creation
Paul Matthews

This is an inspirational workbook of creative writing exercises for poets and teachers, and for all who wish to develop the life of the imagination. There are over 300 exercises for improving writing skills. Though intended for group work with adults, teachers will find these exercises easily adaptable to the classroom. Paul Matthews, a poet himself, taught creative writing at Emerson College, Sussex.

224pp; 238 x 135mm; 1 869 890 60 4; paperback.

The Twelve Senses
Albert Soesman

The author provides a lively look at the senses—not merely the normal five senses, but twelve: touch, life, self-movement, balance, smell, taste, vision, temperature, hearing, language, the conceptual and the ego senses.

176pp; 210 x 135mm; 1 869 890 22 1; paperback.

Troll of Tree Hill
Judy Large

Illustrations by Tom Nelson

We have all heard about children who do not believe in fairies or trolls. Here is a story about a troll who does not believe in children. With his age-old hatred of humankind, how will Troll handle the sudden invasion of his woodland home?

72pp; 210 x 297mm; 1 869 890 74 4; paperback.

Utopie
A German language textbook for use by Class Seven
Michael Stott

120pp; 216 x 138mm; 1 869 890 57 4; paperback.

Who's Bringing them Up?
Television and Child Development:
How to Break the T.V. Habit
Martin Large

Updated with recent research, this book describes the effects of television viewing on children's play, senses, thought, imagination, social skills, learning and growth. The author argues that young children need protection from such a powerful medium. Practical ways of giving up the 'T.V. habit' are described so that readers can take positive steps to build a more creative family life.

192pp; 210 x 135mm; illustrations;
1 869 890 24 8; paperback.

For further information or a book catalogue, please contact:
HAWTHORN PRESS, Hawthorn House, 1 Lansdown Lane, Stroud, Gloucestershire GL5 1BJ Tel: (01453) 757040 Fax: (01453) 751138
E-mail: info@hawthornpress.com Website: www.hawthornpress.com

If you have difficulties ordering Hawthorn Press books from a bookshop, you can order direct from:
SCOTTISH BOOK SOURCE, 137 Dundee Street, Edinburgh EH11 1BG
Tel: (0131) 229 6800 Fax: (0131) 229 9070
E-mail: scotbook@globalnet.co.uk
or
ANTHROPOSOPHIC PRESS, PO Box 799, Great Barrington, MA 01230, USA. Tel (413) 528 8233 Fax: (413) 528 8826
E-mail: anthropres@aol.com Website: anthropress.org